Presidents, Professors, and Trustees

*The Evolution of
American Academic Government*

Edited by

Donald T. Williams, Jr.

Presidents, Professors, and Trustees

By

W. H. Cowley

Jossey-Bass Publishers
San Francisco • Washington • London • 1980

PRESIDENTS, PROFESSORS, AND TRUSTEES
The Evolution of American Academic Government
by W. H. Cowley, edited by Donald T. Williams, Jr.

Copyright © 1980 by: Jossey-Bass Inc., Publishers
433 California Street
San Francisco, California 94104
&
Jossey-Bass Limited
28 Banner Street
London EC1Y 8QE

Library of Congress Cataloging in Publication Data

Cowley, William Harold, 1899–1978
 Presidents, professors, and trustees.

 Bibliography: p. 226
 Includes index.
 1. Universities and colleges—United States—
Administration—History. 2. College administrators—
United States—History. I. Williams, Donald T.
II. Title.
LB2341.C83   378.73   79-92461
ISBN 0-87589-448-8

Manufactured in the United States of America

JACKET DESIGN BY WILLI BAUM

FIRST EDITION

Code 8009

The Jossey-Bass
Series in Higher Education

Editor's Preface

For W. H. Cowley, writing this book on academic government became a lifetime occupation. It began when, as student editor of the *Daily Dartmouth,* he goaded President Ernest Martin Hopkins into naming a student committee to study and make recommendations for improving the Dartmouth curriculum. It continued in his graduate work at the University of Chicago with a dissertation on political leadership. At Ohio State University, where he spent nine years of his early academic career, he became friends with Joseph A. Leighton, first chairman of the American Association of University Professors Committee T on the Place and Function of Faculties in University Government and Administration, and with James McKeen Cattell, whose ideas on academic government received much publicity during the early decades of this century. In order to write authentically about academic government, one needs first-hand experience with it; and Cowley gained that experience between 1938 and 1944 as the sometimes controversial president of Hamilton College. From Hamilton, he had the opportunity to move to the presidency of the University of Minnesota, but he chose instead to devote his life to the study of, rather than the practice of, academic government. This decision brought him to Stanford University, where in 1954 he became the first David Jacks Professor of Higher Education, the position he held until his retirement in 1968.

As a full-time professor of higher education, Cowley could turn all of his extraordinary energies to the study of academic government. He sensed that with each flare-up of controversy over facets of the topic, such as loyalty oaths, membership in the Communist Party, or tenure, people from almost every discipline wrote articles and books on the topic but then turned their attention elsewhere. The fires that had been burning for centuries within the precincts of academic government could not be contained, he reasoned, until at least a few scholars devoted their careers to learning more about the fundamental nature and equitable management of academic institutions.

With the aid of his doctoral advisees, a number of whom became college presidents themselves, Cowley began developing the historical and conceptual framework upon which his book could grow. He spent the 1951–52 academic year in England on a Fulbright award to study English precedents and in 1960 served as the George A. Miller Visiting Professor at the University of Illinois, where he gave a series of public lectures on American academic government that formed the first draft of this volume. But he sought more information, greater accuracy, better insight before the manuscript could go to a publisher. During the 1960s and 1970s, while refining and polishing this manuscript, he worked on two others as well: his general history of higher education and his massive taxonomic introduction to the study of higher education. He was still at work, tracking down facts about the early presidencies of Harvard and Dartmouth, when he died in 1978. As the epigraph for one version of his taxonomic introduction, he had quoted the last sentence of chapter thirty-two of Melville's *Moby Dick*: "This whole book is but a draught—nay, but the draught of a draught. Oh, Time, Strength, Cash, and Patience."

What you have before you, therefore, is what Cowley would insist is an incomplete and unrefined part of the whole. Had he found the time, he most likely would have added sections on some current issues affecting academic government, including collective bargaining, litigation, and the growth of middle management. Yet as it stands, the book will be of timeless value in providing a basis for understanding the way American colleges and universities are governed and for dispelling myths about academic government to which academics have clung for many decades. It deserves reading on that basis.

In this book, Cowley, as a professor and former college president, takes as his special target those professors who assume for themselves and their colleagues the dominant role in institutional governance. Such a limited perception of the "republic of scholars" he finds repugnant. Looking into history, he observes few instances where such a limited republic has ever existed. More often, students, the Church, civil government, or college heads have exercised ultimate authority over the faculty. And in those few instances when the faculty has had the final authority, as in the English universities of the nineteenth century, he finds the institutions decaying to the point where members of the faculty had to call out for government intervention to cure their ills.

Cowley thus devotes Chapters One through Three of this book to correcting myths about the republic of scholars and about trustees and presidents. Critics who look upon lay trustees and chief executives as interlopers thrust unwanted and sui generis upon the American academic scene will note that both groups of decision makers have had a long precedent in institutions abroad. Our current trustees, Cowley shows, derive historically from city governments in medieval and Reformation communities where universities were also located, and our college and university presidents derive from the heads of the Oxford and Cambridge colleges.

In Chapter Four, Cowley takes on the myth of faculty as disenfranchised and powerless employees. He shows that for centuries, pace-setting American colleges have operated with formal and actual educational authority vested in the faculty—authority codified for higher education at large in the joint statement on academic governance adopted in 1966 by the American Association of University Professors (AAUP), the American Council on Education (ACE), and the Association of Governing Boards of Universities and Colleges (AGB). The pattern of thinking contained in that document follows nicely from Cowley's history. It gives to the faculty a primary voice in the selection of the curriculum and in the manner of teaching that curriculum, in identifying who will become the permanent members of the teaching faculty, and in determining who will receive the degrees offered by the institution. It gives to presidents the primary leadership role for articulating institutional goals and for representing their institutions before their many publics. And it charges governing boards to define the overall policies and procedures of their institution, to oversee the maintenance of its financial resources, and to mediate between the institution and its environing society. In other words, within the boundaries of the institution—the boundaries of the republic of scholars, if you will—faculty, administrators, and trustees all have their role to play, their set of prerogatives, which other members of the republic should respect (American Association of University Professors, 1966).

Other than supporting a responsible student role in academic government, the 1966 joint statement says little or nothing about other participants in institutional decision making beyond professors, presidents, and trustees. Cowley, however, devotes much of the rest of this book to them. In Chapter Five, he recounts the largely informal but influential role students have played in academic decisions. Increasingly, students have found their way onto formal departmental and institutional committees and boards, and the result has been generally good. Although in no position to dominate decision making in these settings, they are nevertheless assured of having a voice in the process, offering their unique perspective on the academic scene and making valuable improvements in decisions.

In Chapter Six, Cowley chronicles the involvement of alumni in institutional government—through service on both governing boards and advisory councils—their financial contributions, and their accelerating involvement in continuing education. In Chapter Seven, he examines the role of academic associations in influencing institutional decisions, with subject-matter associations having great influence among academics who constitute their membership and with regional accrediting associations having the power to enforce the growth of programs that institutional or external authorities might not otherwise seek. In Chapter Eight, he describes the role of philanthropic foundations in offering incentives for institutions to move in new directions and explore new services. And in Chapter Nine, he demonstrates the long involvement of civil government at state and federal levels in institutional affairs and points out the need to find a proper balance between regulation and laissez faire.

All of these various constituencies have their places within the modern-day republic of scholars, and Cowley's materials show the problems that arise when any one constituent group becomes dominant over the others. Thus he argues in Chapter Ten for amelioration of imbalances rather than reconstruction of present relationships along other models. Maintaining a balance of authority among these constituent groups necessarily involves a constant state of tension among them and calls for constant returning of the balance. But it also requires, as the 1966 joint statement says, "mutual understanding" among these groups; and it is to improved mutual understanding that Cowley devoted his efforts.

In my role as editor, I wondered whether to update Cowley's analysis by referring to events into 1980, but I decided against it. People will read this book because they have been waiting for years for Cowley to finish it. They are interested in his ideas, not mine. As editor, however, I have tried to take into account the recent work of other scholars who share Cowley's interest in the development of academic government. Had he been able, he would have done so himself. Another former Cowley student, E. D. Duryea, has made excellent suggestions for improvements, and he has led me to the writings of Jurgen Herbst and Alan Karp, whose material I have tried to use where appropriate. I am indebted to Duryea, Karp, and Herbst, as well as to Eric Ashby, for kindly reading the manuscript and helping make it as accurate as possible. Where it still lacks accuracy, however, I must take the blame. The continuing research of these and other scholars will in the future expand our understanding of the evolution of academic government beyond what Cowley accomplishes in this general introduction.

In locating some of the sources cited by Cowley, I drew upon the capable assistance of archivists and scholars from several of the nation's leading universities and colleges. I want, therefore, to express my special appreciation to Marie Condon Thornton at the University of California at Berkeley, Paul R. Palmer at Columbia University, Clark A. Elliott at Harvard University, Maynard Brichford at the University of Illinois, Mary Jo Pugh at the University of Michigan, and Cynthia McClelland at Princeton University. Barbara Jones of the Stanford University Archives assisted me time and again in tracking down items from the Cowley collection. I also thank Frederick Rudolph, who helped me find a citation specific to the history of Williams College, and Fred F. Harcleroad, who helped identify sources in Chapter Five.

The number of people who aided Cowley during the decades that he worked on this and his other manuscripts are legion, and I hesitate to mention any for fear of forgetting others. For example, Cowley distributed copies of the latest drafts to students in his courses at Stanford as the basis for his seminar discussions and asked his students to criticize them. They took him at his word, and they deserve recognition here. Four foundations supported his research over the years: The Carnegie Corporation of New York, the William H. Donner Foundation, the Fund for the Advancement of Education of the Ford Foundation, and the Ellis L. Phillips Foundation. They warrant the appreciation of all of Cowley's readers. Betty Risser worked with Cowley for many years as the keeper of his notes and the typist of his many drafts, as did Eleanor Winnek, Heather Bundy, and Kathlene Davenport in more recent years. JB Lon Hefferlin, David Doherty, Russell Y. Garth, and Michael Korff served as his graduate research assistants, as did I. And John Arrillaga contributed funds to Stanford to further this research and underwrite the cataloguing of Cowley's extensive research materials in the Stanford Archives for use by future scholars.

All these friends and more assisted in the production of this book. They encouraged Cowley to finish it, and they kept alive the possibility that someday it would indeed be published. I rejoice with them that this day has come at last.

Seattle, Washington   DONALD T. WILLIAMS, JR.
January 1980

Contents

The Author
and Editor

W. H. (WILLIAM HAROLD) COWLEY (1899–1978), the first David
Jacks Professor of Higher Education at Stanford, was awarded the
B.A. degree from Dartmouth (1924), where he chaired the Undergraduate Committee on Educational Policy. After being awarded
the Ph.D. degree in psychology from the University of Chicago
(1930), he worked in the Bureau of Educational Research at Ohio
State University, helping build a research base for the emerging field
of student personnel services. In 1938 he assumed the presidency of
Hamilton College, and in 1945 he moved to Stanford to establish
the study of higher education as a legitimate field of scholarship. His
extensive library of professional notes, reports, correspondence, and
unpublished manuscripts is presently being organized and will be
open for research use as the W. H. Cowley Papers, Stanford University Archives, Stanford, California.

DONALD T. WILLIAMS, JR., is associate professor of education at the University of Washington. He was awarded the B.A. degree in education from Eastern Washington College of Education (1950), the M.A. degree in counseling from Stanford University (1957), and the Ph.D. degree in higher education from Stanford (1963). He has held administrative positions at Eastern Washington College, Reed College, and Stanford, and has taught at Stanford, the University of Illinois at Urbana, and Pacific Lutheran University.

Presidents, Professors, and Trustees

The Evolution of American Academic Government

INTRODUCTION

Myth and Reality in Academic Government

In whatever it is our duty to act, those matters also it is our duty to study.

Thomas Arnold, 1846

Some years ago Syracuse University professor T. V. Smith, one of the most widely traveled lecturers on college and university campuses during his time, wrote: "In almost every place which I visit, the academic administration is under continuous attack." "Fortunately the worst malcontents," he continued, "do not often get into administration themselves: they only stand at the window and bark . . . I, for one, do not enjoy their raucous yapping" (Smith, 1956, pp. 120–121).

More than forty years as an inhabitant of academia have led me to the conclusion that much of the antagonism of professors toward administrators deplored by Professor Smith results from the persistence of a number of historical myths and of fallacious conceptions of the nature of American academic government. These spurious notions have stunted the relationships of professors, presidents, and trustees, and they continue to retard the flowering of good will needed in dealing with today's perplexities. In this book I seek to explore these myths and fallacies toward the end of helping

1

reduce the problems that arise between the different participants in academic government and thus improving the future health of American higher education.

Consider, for example, the popular myth that lay governing boards and the office of college president are American inventions—and the related fable that wily business tycoons, using the commercial corporation as their model, have foisted lay boards and presidents upon defrauded professors. From among many statements propagating these spurious conceptions, I quote two. Said Professor Anton J. Carlson of the University of Chicago in his valedictory address as president of the American Association of University Professors:

> The legal aspect of the American university is that of a business corporation, a corporation, to be sure, not for profit, but modeled essentially on the corporation for profit in the business world rather than on the traditions of the Old World universities as a free republic of scholars. . . . The president of the university, appointed by the board of trustees, occasionally after consultation with the faculties, is virtually the general manager of this corporation [Carlson, 1938, p. 11].

In the same vein, Professor Max Savelle of the University of Washington wrote as follows in the AAUP *Bulletin:*

> It is a curious anomaly that in the United States, which thinks of itself as the most democratic country in the world, the universities, which should be living laboratories of democracy, are probably the most undemocratic in the world. . . . The university is thought of as a sort of factory; the president is the manager of the factory, and his word is absolute, requiring only the approval of his board of directors (regents). According to this concept the members of the faculty are hired hands. The manager of the faculty may hire or fire at will; the labor force (the faculty) is not organized as a union. The fate of the university is in the hands of one man. All he has to do is convince the regents that they should support him; and, if the regents are businessmen, with the "busi-

nessman's concept" of the university, they usually will [Savelle, 1957, pp. 323–324].

These and similar statements usually emanate from two beliefs: first, that the medieval university constituted, in Professor Carlson's words, "a free republic of scholars," and second, that European universities have continued as such and hence have neither external governing bodies comparable to American boards of trustees nor administrators comparable to American academic presidents. In this book I shall attempt to demonstrate these and other such beliefs to be delusive half-truths.

The Scope of the Book

In no sense do I attempt herein to examine American academic government comprehensively. Not until scores, if not hundreds, of monographic studies have been published can anyone succeed with such an undertaking, and he or she who eventually assays the task requires equipment that I lack. My three purposes are much more modest: first, to puncture the myths that seem to me to interfere with the healthy development of American college and university government; second, to trace the conceptual roots of present practices and trends; and third, to arouse interest in the subject toward the end of stimulating more thorough investigations of academic government than have yet been attempted.

The first two of these objectives require considerable attention to historical backgrounds, and therefore much of the book deals with the roots of present practices. I make no excuse for this because long ago I became convinced that effectively to understand and to deal with a current problem requires a knowledge of its origins and evolution. For some decades, however, a cult of immediacy has dominated the social sciences. Innumerable professors of these subjects declare that they cannot be bothered with the historical backgrounds of the topics they investigate because, they proudly say, they deal with the practical or theoretical problems of the here and now. Most contemporary social questions have long roots, but these Professors of Immediacy appear to be unaware of them and also of the fact that the past has shaped both the problems and the methods employed in studying them. They ignore the fact that, as Abraham Lincoln said, "We cannot escape history."

Other people, such as Professor Savelle, must admit to a different problem. They have studied history and they value highly the lessons it provides. Yet in making their analogies, they draw upon their own, perhaps unhappy, experiences with presidents and board members rather than their knowledge of the broad sweep of history.

Since I have had considerably more formal training in statistics than in historiography, I habitually think of the past-present-future continuum as a graph whereon the present constitutes but a fleeting point in time emerging from the long and direction-pointing past into the ever-arriving future. All previous history has made its markings on the graph, and we add ours to the continuum that the past has created and from which we can deviate only if we have enough power to counteract its inertia. To determine what markings we are able to make requires, first, that we calculate the directions and momentum of the graph we inherit and, second, that we assess the forces at our disposal to swerve it.

Like many other people, I would like to swerve the graph that diagrams the progress and present status of American academic government. To do so requires, at least in part, that I communicate the roots of present practice to my faculty colleagues. Too many of them concentrate their attention on their own professional concerns and those of their departments and hence have insufficient information about the large fundamental questions facing higher education institutions individually and collectively, let alone the history behind those questions. If my faculty colleagues can find the time to share these pages with me, then perhaps we can achieve together the changes that require making.

Kinds of Government

The word *government* has evolved from the Latin verb *gubernare*, "to steer." It denotes any social structure possessing de jure or de facto power to steer or direct, that is, to control the actions of the individuals and groups within its province. Otherwise expressed, a government performs the function of social control.

Governments are formal, informal, and often a mixture of both. I know a family whose foreign-born male parent has posted about the house rules and lists of penalties to which he rigidly holds his four children. That family approaches being a formal government, but most American families constitute informal governments since the controls over their members operate with much less precision. Most crossroads settlements, recreational groups, and some schools function with comparable informality.

Formal governments function, however, under systematized formulas of behavior called rules and regulations, ordinances, statutes, or law. One thinks in this context most readily of civil governments, but a wide range of other types of formal government also operate. Walter J. Shepard, the Ohio State University political scientist who wrote the article on government for the *Encyclopaedia of the Social Sciences*, recognized this range when he wrote, "There is government of the church, of the trade union, of the industrial corporation, of the university. And the definite norms of conduct which are prescribed and enforced by such governments may properly be characterized as law" (1932, pp. 8–9). In a lighter vein, the late Charles E. Merriam, eminent political scientist of the University of Chicago, made the same point: "Obviously there is governance everywhere—government in heaven; government in hell; government and law among the outlaws; government in prison. One of the most interesting documents is the proceedings of the constitutional convention in Sing Sing where the Sing Singers deliberated on the forms of prison government—as far as permitted, of course" (1944, pp. 1–2). Perhaps I do not need to labor the fact that governments other than civil government have vital importance in directing the affairs of society, particularly in pluralistic and nontotalitarian societies such as ours. I do want, however, to expand a little upon the widespread neglect of that fact.

The primary reason for the neglect seems to be the multiplying functions and hence increased visibility of civil government. At the beginning of the century, for example, the typical American had little reason to think more than occasionally about the federal government. To it he paid no income or gasoline taxes; he did not have his food and drugs inspected and standardized by government employees; he did not live in a house covered by a federal mortgage loan or deposit his savings in a government-insured bank; he collected no social security pension or federally sponsored unemployment insurance; and he did not have to fill out the multifarious forms required not only by the national but also by the state, county, and local bureaucracies. In sum, in scores of new ways, public agencies touch the lives of Americans; and this fact explains in part, I suggest, why people, by and large, limit their understanding of the word *government* to civil government.

My interests focus, however, on academic government, and I shall close this introduction by clarifying the concepts relating to that expression. I have already defined a government—any government—as a structure that performs the function of social control. It follows from this definition that structurally an academic government consists of those entities that control an academic institution. Functionally, academic government denotes this control. These definitions include several terms that need elucidation, namely, *academic*, *institution*, and *control*.

The word *academic* commemorates the name of the first enduring higher educational institution of the Western World—the Academy founded by Plato in 387 B.C. and continuing in operation for 916 years until A.D. 529, when Justinian destroyed it in an early academic freedom controversy: Its faculty refused to become Christians. Beginning during the Renaissance, the name *academy* came to denominate societies of learned men devoted to the study of the literatures of Greece and Rome or of experimental science, both of which the universities of the period disdained. This meaning continues in such names as the *Académie française*, the American Academy of Arts and Letters, and the National Academy of Science. (Since members of these academies are called academicians, I shall refer to the personnel of colleges and universities as academics.)

Today the word *academic* has several conflicting meanings other than that just cited. To laymen it often implies talky-talky speculation. For many educators, it designates courses and institutions concerned only with nonvocational subjects. It also refers to colleges and universities in general as distinguished from elementary and secondary schools. I employ the last of these meanings in this book and thus deal only with the control of higher educational institutions.

These institutions, like all social organizations, have scores of characteristics, but four relating to their control need present identification. First, every social institution operates in an environment inhabited by other organizations, some of which have varying degrees of authority or influence over it. Moreover, the influence of these other organizations will vary according to the times. Thus state legislatures, in keeping with the times, will regulate state universities through appropriations and through their occasional exercise of the state's police power, and the rulings of the courts and of other governmental units affect the activities of private colleges and universities as well as public. Accrediting bodies, learned societies, and pressure groups also act upon colleges and universities, and to this extent need to be considered as participants in academic government. In this book I discuss what seem to me the most important of them: academic associations, philanthropic foundations, and state and federal government.

Second, every social institution constitutes a mechanism for the transformation of social energy and the accomplishment of specified goals. Legislatures and private donors contribute money that boards of trustees, faculty bodies, and administrators convert into buildings and equipment, professors' salaries, books, and the like, for the purposes of research and teaching. This energy transformation requires a formal organization; and even in small institutions it results in a hierarchy of power, each level of which has a measure of influence over the others and over the determination and achievement of these purposes. These levels of control reach from the regulation of the work of the two janitors, for example, who clean the building in which I teach at Stanford, to the board of trustees of Stanford, which determines ultimate policies. A number of intermediate control levels separate these two extremes of Stanford's organizational hierarchy, but all of them derive from the board of trustees, which alone has status in public law.

Third, parallel to its formal structure or hierarchy of power, every institution has an informal power pattern which often has very considerable impact upon its counterpart. For example, perceptive professors know that the secretaries of top-level administrative officers must be reckoned with since they can promote or hinder the interests of professors. These and other personal interactions go a long way toward explaining the ways institutions operate. Scores of social scientists investigate the informal power structures of social institutions including colleges and universities; and their work is of huge importance in understanding academic government. This book seeks to describe both the formal and the informal power structure of academic institutions.

Turning to the concept of *control*, in any social institution one can identify kinds as well as levels of control. Two kinds of control seem to be overriding in every social structure: (1) the determination of policy, including the resolution of conflicts (called the legislative and judicial functions in the terminology of political scientists), and (2) the control of the day-to-day operations of the enterprise (variously called the executive function, management, or administration). Those concerned with the study of different varieties of social institutions employ divergent terms for these two kinds of control, but in discussing academic government I have come, after much struggle with these conflicting terminologies, to prefer the terms *policy control* and *operational control*. Both, I would emphasize, constitute components of academic government, and both are the subject of this book. Indeed, many of the major controversies over academic government concern the role of various participants in one or the other of them. The more complex an institution becomes, the more numerous and diverse grow the bodies and the individuals who, with the approval of the board, have surveillance over portions of the domain for which it has final responsibility. These subordinate entities include faculty governing bodies, which generally today hold all but final policy control over educational and research activities. They also include administrative officers who have wide powers in operational control. In short, the control structure of a present-day academic institution is an enormously complex mechanism comparable to, say, the human nervous system: It orchestrates the vast network of institutional activities.

This very complexity accounts, in some measure, for the confusion and misunderstanding connected with academic government. From that confusion and misunderstanding come the problems to which I now turn.

ONE

The "Free Republic of Scholars"

In this subject as in others the best method of investigation is to study things in the process of development from the beginning.

Aristotle

Perhaps one of the most persistent myths prevailing in American higher education insists that a golden age once existed wherein professors operated their own institutions in some sort of "free republic of scholars." Those who so believe assert that European universities of an earlier time permitted professors to manage their own affairs unchecked by external authorities. Just when the so-called golden age may have occurred is not clear, but those who harken back to it most likely refer to the universities of western Europe, especially during medieval times, or to the German universities of the nineteenth century. On the surface, the academics at these institutions may appear to have enjoyed a certain autonomy, but a closer reading of the history of those periods reveals genuine limitations on that autonomy.

Stimulated during the eleventh and twelfth centuries by such circumstances as the phenomenal expansion of trade attendant upon the Crusades, the importation from Cordova and Constantinople

9

of the writings of Aristotle, and the example of the Muslim institutions of higher learning in Spain, the scholarly interests of a host of individuals throughout western Europe quickened (d'Irsay, 1934). Students from all over Europe gathered in Salerno to hear the medical lectures of Constantine the African, in Bologna to listen to the legal discourses of Irnerius, and in Paris to sit at the feet of Abelard as he flayed his theological and philosophical opponents. Others continued the work of these fabulous teachers and their associates, and to protect and promote their interests they organized themselves into societies or guilds. So also did the students.

These groups arose spontaneously and, following the example of numerous other societies, called themselves *universitas*. The term derived from Latin *unus* + *verter*, "to turn as a unit or whole." The word meant *guild* and had no academic connotations. It designated organized groups from bakers and butchers to merchants and professional men. Many town governments considered themselves universities, and some called themselves such (Pollock and Maitland [1899] 1968). Not until the fifteenth century would the term be generally limited to institutions concerned with higher education. Meanwhile, such structures typically went by the name of *studia generalia,* each of which embraced guilds of masters and guilds of students. These two kinds of guilds related to one another in different ways depending on whether they followed the model of the great *studium* at Bologna or that of the towering *studium* at Paris. Thus there developed two chief patterns of medieval academic government: the student-dominated Bolognese and the faculty-dominated Parisian.

The Bolognese Pattern

What eventually came to be known as the University of Bologna began as a school of arts but took form primarily because of the stature of the law teachers who resided there. Law had been a preeminent study throughout the domain of imperial Rome; and, though enfeebled after Constantinople became the capital of the Empire, it had been kept alive by private teachers living chiefly in northern Italy. Prominent among these teachers was Irnerius, who died about 1130. He, his associates, and their successors made Bologna in particular famous throughout Europe for the study of both civil and canon law.

Like almost all medieval teachers, Bolognese teachers derived their incomes chiefly, if not entirely, from the fees paid directly to them or to their agents, called *famuli*. In short, they were private entrepreneurs in the business of merchandising their specialized, newly valued knowledge. They therefore organized societies comparable to the guilds which other kinds of merchants had earlier found essential for collaboration and security. The same reasons impelled their students to launch brotherhoods closely resembling the craftsman (worker) guilds. In the ensuing exchanges over prerogatives between the students and their teachers, the student groups rapidly and unmistakably took command.

The students gained the upper hand, to begin with, because in the heyday of the Italian universities most of their students were mature men, many of whom held or would soon hold important positions. Animated by the flowering of legal learning, they had headed for Bologna and other Italian cities in continuously growing numbers to study civil law, canon law, or both. Revitalized by the robust saltation in commerce, politicians and high-ranking bureaucrats came from other cities. Commercial families sent their sons and agents, principalities of the Holy Roman Empire sent the heirs and mentors of rulers, and the Church sent ecclesiastics already holding or designated for hierarchical preferment.

At the outset, only local students had civil rights. This put the great majority of their fellows at the mercy both of profiteering landlords and merchants and of short-changing lecturers. Worse, they had no legal recourse when municipal authorities rightly or wrongly accused them of crimes. To remedy their disadvantaged position, the students sent representatives to the Diet of Roncaglia convened in 1158 near Milan by Frederick Barbarossa, recently crowned Holy Roman Emperor. Probably because the Bologna jurists favored the Empire in its embittered feud with the Papacy, Barbarossa looked kindly upon the student petitioners. In any case, his professorial advisors assenting, he granted the immunities and privileges that wily student politicians soon used to subjugate not only town authorities but also their innocently cooperative professors. Thus emerged the student-controlled universities of Italy and southern France.

The imperial charter—endorsed later by papal bulls and municipal ordinances—authorized students to adopt self-governing statutes which included the right to elect their own officers, to administer methods of instruction and fee collection, to try accused students in their own tribunals, and—most important of all—to migrate to another city if they judged themselves unfairly treated. Two facts suffice to illustrate the resulting high level of student power. First, before the end of the fourteenth century, Bolognese students migrated more than a dozen times—in 1321, for example, to Siena, 85 miles away, where they remained more than a year. Second, they subjected their professors to "inconceivable servitude." According to an English historian: "The professor may not leave the city without depositing a sum of money as security for his return. He is fined for unpunctuality at lecture; on the other hand, when the bell rings for tierce [9 A.M.] not only is he bound to cease, but his pupils are bound under pain of fine to rise and leave him. The doctor is fined if he skips a chapter; the textbooks are now formally marked off into roughly equal divisions, each of which the lecturer is bound to have finished by a specified date. He deposits caution-money with a banker, who may return it at the year's end only to the rector, who may in turn deduct a certain sum for every day the professor is behind his time" (Coulton, 1913, p. 653).

Vestiges of these practices continued in Italy and southern France until Napoleon's armies swept across Europe, but by then student authority had slowly been eviscerated by faculties and civil authorities. On their part, professors in the fourteenth century threw off their fetters by signing contracts with municipal governments, thereby blunting the economic weapon of the organized students. In turn, city councils set up committees of citizens to administer the contracts and, in the process, to bring under their superintendence the several student universities and the corresponding professorial colleges which the students had manacled. By these methods, they eventually brought under unified management the competing groups of the universities styled after Bologna.

The resemblance of these municipal committees—called boards of curators, governors, or managers—to the governing boards of American colleges and universities will be discussed further in later chapters. Meanwhile, one conclusion concerning the universities such as Bologna is clear: Those who write or talk about medieval universities as "free republics" of professors obviously cannot be referring to Bologna and the universities modeled after it.

The Parisian Pattern

The University of Paris and its progeny followed a quite different pattern. In northern Europe, for instance, theology rather than law reigned supreme. Like their counterparts in Bologna, brilliant teachers attracted students to Paris, where Abelard baited the established powers with his theories and his morals. He and less famous teachers dug the foundations of what became the University of Paris, but he had been dead more than half a century before the King of France officially recognized the burgeoning institution and its corporate form took shape.

The recognition resulted from the collision of two antithetical traditions. The first put the control of teaching in the hands of the Church. Thus when secular priests and laymen began, in the eleventh century, to replace monks as teachers in the cathedral schools that antedated the universities, church officials selected and licensed them. These and related educational functions were assigned to a member of the episcopal staff called archdeacon, scholasticus, or—as in Paris—chancellor. The other tradition required an apprentice to be accredited by the man under whom he had studied in order to attain the title of master (originally equivalent to doctor and professor, the titles favored in Italy and later adopted in northern Europe).

The increasing influx of students attracted by the pyramiding reputation of Parisian teachers brought the two traditions into conflict. The masters precipitated it by organizing a guild that outlawed the upstart teachers spawned by the ceaseless increase of students. They accomplished this by deciding who could study for the mastership, who could be licensed later as teachers, and—most important of all—whom they would admit to their guild. To promote these objectives they sent to Rome for papal support.

One of the first of these delegations had the good fortune to find a former Parisian student and teacher on the papal throne—Innocent III. That history-making accident helped the nascent University of Paris become a corporation and, as such, escape from under the antagonistic thumbs of neighboring ecclesiastical authorities.

About 1210, for example, Innocent gave written statutes to the University of Paris; in 1215, his legate, Cardinal Curzon, extended and strengthened them; and the next two popes issued bulls permanently invalidating the weapon of wholesale excommunication which the Bishop and Chancellor of Paris had wielded against the embattled Parisian teachers. Not until 1246, however, could the University display a seal, a symbol of corporate status. A confrontation had undoubtedly prepared the way. It involved "an attack by a mob of masters and scholars armed with swords and sticks upon the legate's house: the doors had already been broken down when the cardinal was preserved from further outrage by the arrival of the soldiers of the king" (Rashdall [1895] 1936a, p. 317).

As in Bologna, the teachers of Paris and its offspring organized self-serving guilds. These soon federated into holistic institutions that differed profoundly, however, from those in Italy and southern France in that neither students nor laymen participated in their government. Furthermore, one of the teachers' guilds acquired primacy in the general assembly (legislature) of the unified university.

At Paris as elsewhere, four groups of teachers (faculties) represented medieval higher learning in full bloom—the "inferior faculty of the arts" and the "superior faculties of law, medicine, and theology." The inferiority of the arts faculty consisted in the fact that it prepared adolescent scholars for admission to the superior faculties. Governmentally, however, the presumptive underdog soon achieved superiority. This resulted from the interweaving of the arts faculty and the four Parisian "nations." These nations were academic adaptations of the "confederations of aliens on foreign soil"—chiefly traders and their retainers—which in ancient times, and again since the revival of commerce, had been organized for camaraderie and socio-political cooperation.

More than thirty nations had been organized in Bologna during its early years, but before long they had coalesced within the student universities. A quite different situation developed, however, in Paris, where four nations—French, English-German, Norman, and Picard—became corporate entities with statutes, seals, and the other appurtenances of incorporation. The four nations, further, constituted the faculty of arts which, under the system of block voting, gave it four votes in the general assembly. The superior faculties, in contrast, had a total of only three votes. Thus, possessing a majority of the votes in the University's governing body, the "inferior faculty of the arts" acquired and firmly retained control of the University.

The fame of its theologians primarily accounted for the eminence of the University of Paris; but its faculty of theology had only one of seven votes in the general assembly. Furthermore, the teachers of theology, like those of the superior faculties of law and medicine, could not even attend the meetings of the nations although each faculty retained nominal membership in one of them. Many circumstances led to this lopsided situation, including the fact that between two thirds and three quarters of those attending the University of Paris were wards of the faculty of arts.

The word *wards* in the last sentence has been chosen advertently. Freshmen (commonly called "yellowbeaks") ordinarily arrived at the age of twelve or thirteen. Since the University of Paris—like Oxford and Cambridge to this day—did not require newcomers to matriculate at a central office, each "scholar" put himself under the *in loco parentis* tutelage of a member of the arts faculty. The latter would almost certainly be in his early twenties and remain a master only long enough to satisfy the requirement that he teach for two to five years prior to satisfying the obligations of his degree. Once graduated, he was virtually assured a position of leadership in church or state.

In short, the Parisian "free republic of scholars" so frequently and enthusiastically lauded by professorial and other proponents of unrestrained faculty power was, in fact, an inverted oligarchy: Its governors were not seasoned professors but, *mirabile dictu,* a fluctuating, fast-changing body of youths who, though titled "masters," were typically no older than the younger graduate students of present-day American universities, usually younger than the student governors of the University of Bologna and, moreover, generally more violent. Here, from the pen of a preeminent medievalist, is one of the many vivid descriptions of the beardless undergraduates of medieval Paris egged on and led by their young master of arts mentors: "Theirs was a rough and violent age, and what with the *prévôt's* men and the townsmen, the monks of St. Germain and the friars, there was no lack of opportunity for a brawl. . . . Many of them go about the streets armed, attacking the citizens, breaking into houses, and abusing women. They quarrel among themselves over dogs, women, or whatnot, slashing off one another's fingers with their swords, or, with only knives in their hands and nothing to protect their tonsured pates, rush into conflicts from which armed knights would hold back" (Haskins, 1929, p. 60).

To quell the relentless turbulence in the University of Paris, the King of France became increasingly involved in its affairs. Then in the latter part of the fifteenth century, having lost patience with the institution which his predecessors had so long and so tolerantly favored, Louis XI ordered "the extinction of the last relics of the old independence and influence of the university as of so many of its ancient liberties. . . . For some two centuries the university had behaved as if it owed its rights and privileges to some *ius divinum* underived from any earthly authority, civil or ecclesiastical. It was now to be rudely reminded that privileges which the King gave, the King could take away" (Rashdall [1895] 1936a, p. 430).

Several elements thus came together to limit the "free republic of scholars" at the University of Paris. First, the University derived its authority from Rome and therefore was subject to the popes. As Rashdall ([1895] 1936a, p. 307) expresses it: "By every appeal to the Roman Court [the University of Paris] . . . naturally lost to a great extent its own autonomy. It entered into the ecclesiastical system . . . and became as completely subject to ecclesiastical regulation as the monasteries or the [cathedral] chapters." The "republic," in truth, became what one might call a church-related college. Secondly, the authority within the "republic" resided within the youthful and itinerant masters of arts faculty, a group even younger than the "students" who controlled Bologna. Finally, as the authority of the monarchy arose in France and as the university failed to keep stride with these changes, the "republic" fell increasingly under the control of civil government.

The English Pattern

The government of American higher education evolved from models brought to this country not primarily from continental universities such as Paris and Bologna but from the colleges of Oxford and Cambridge, from adaptations of Dutch, Scottish, and Irish practices evolving within the Calvinist sector of the Protestant Reformation, and from advanced secondary schools on the continent and in England. As relates to the myth of the "free republic of scholars," the model provided by Oxbridge requires special attention.

Like the United States of America, Oxford and Cambridge are federations, each being composed of about a score of colleges. These English academic federations, however, differ basically from the American federation of states. The American federal government has extensive and expanding powers, but in Oxford and Cambridge the principle of state (or college) rights has had, through most of their history, such undisputed ascendancy that, until the decade of the 1960s, university central governments were entirely subordinate to their colleges. Consider these facts: First, the presiding officer of Oxford, the Vice Chancellor, has a term of only four years and his or her opposite number in Cambridge a term of only two years; second, both are chosen from among the heads of the colleges; third, the combined endowments of Oxford and Cambridge's colleges until the 1960s exceeded those of the universities of which they are a part; and fourth, the colleges themselves operate their own admissions offices.

Like Paris, from which they sprang, both English universities began with the four faculties typically found in medieval universities: law, medicine, theology, and arts. The first two of these, however, early disappeared: The Inns of Court took over instruction in secular law, the study of canon law declining and finally ending with the Reformation, and the hospital schools of London and other cities largely expropriated the teaching of medicine. This left Oxford and Cambridge with theology and the remnants of the lower faculty of arts derived from Paris. Thus each of the two English universities (the only ones existing until the nineteenth century) in effect unified its teachers within single groups or faculties (Smith, 1869).

In England, as elsewhere, the Church insisted upon its educational prerogatives, but no conflict developed between the University of Oxford and the bishop of its diocese primarily because the City of Oxford belonged in the diocese, not of a nearby bishop (London, Salisbury, Winchester, for example) but of the Bishop of Lincoln, who resided 120 miles away. Thus geography gave the rising university an uncharacteristic degree of freedom from ecclesiastical interference. Another happenstance had a similar result—the Lincoln See lacked a consecrated incumbent for more than a third of the time between 1167 (when Henry II forbade Englishmen to study in Paris, thereby encouraging Oxford's growth as a center of learning) and the first recorded mention of an Oxford chancellor nearly half a century later.

Nominally the Bishop of Lincoln ruled Oxford through its chancellor, but feisty politicians among the youthful masters of arts soon exploited the battening power of their faculty to annul his prerogatives. First they successfully negotiated the privilege of nominating one of their members for the chancellorship. Then by "barefaced assertion and bold usurpation," (Rashdall, [1895] 1936b, p. 119) they succeeded in substantiating their demand for suffrage as well as for nominating powers. These maneuvers not only deprived the distant bishop of his canonical authority over the university but also gradually converted the chancellorship into the secular, honorific position that it started becoming late in the sixteenth century.

Primarily examining and degree-granting bodies, Oxford and Cambridge gave over their instructional duties to teaching fellows. These were originally young men studying for advanced degrees with financial assistance in the form of fellowships established for that purpose. The colleges and not the universities, however, controlled the fellowships, a fact of focal importance to be expanded upon directly.

Few of the teaching fellows intended to make careers of

college teaching but, instead, planned, as did John Locke and Adam Smith, to be tutors of noblemen's sons or else take a benefice in the gift of a college. Being temporary teachers, they did badly. According to Rashdall (1913, p. 588): "The average standard was low. The complaint that he had been fined twopence for not attending a lecture which was not worth a penny, was Samuel Johnson's testimony to his tutor's incompetency; and his experience was not exceptional." The standard did not improve as more and more teaching fellows stayed on permanently. The donors of the funds that supported them had intended their recipients (like American graduate students) to leave for other positions upon the completion of their studies, but the less able and the lazy chose to remain. They had no trouble arranging this because of two convenient facts: First, the holders of fellowships were the trustees of the funds supporting them, and second, they had the legal right under the statutes of the colleges to reelect themselves. Thus a kind of senatorial courtesy developed which made Oxford and Cambridge colleges into clubs for lackluster and lazy academic remittance men. "Fellows now," writes Rashdall (1913, p. 587), "lived in separate rooms, and 'commonrooms' were built in which Fellows talked and boozed away most of the time after dinner." This farcical and scandalous situation resulted from the system of English college government which must now be sketched.

The colleges had begun as facilities provided by benefactors moved by concern or religious conviction to make them available for poor students, and, with the establishment of Merton College at Oxford in the middle of the thirteenth century, they had become self-governing units. Rashdall (1913, p. 581) reviews this history as follows: "The 'rule of Merton,' a body of Statutes given the College in 1263 and amended in 1270, was imitated by later founders [of colleges] and permanently fixed the type of English college. The leading note of the College . . . was its complete autonomy. The only external authority which could meddle with its affairs was the Visitor—in the case of Merton, the Archbishop of Canterbury. The scholars [later generally called fellows] elected their own Warden and other officers, filled up their own ranks, and controlled the management of their own property."

Four points in this quotation must be highlighted. First,

when college fellows "filled up their own ranks," they could reelect themselves if they chose. Second, they elected their own administrative officers. Third, they "controlled the management of their own property" and thus served as their own trustees. And fourth, only an external officer known as the Visitor could "meddle" with their complete autonomy. In other words, the fellows of Oxford and Cambridge colleges came as close as anyone to forming free republics of scholars. As their own boards of trustees, they controlled both appointments to fellowships and college property. But even they acted under the direction of the college administrator, who, although elected by them, possessed life tenure in the headship, and also under the general supervision of an external officer known as the Visitor. In Chapter Three, I shall describe the massive and all but irrevocable prerogatives that these college heads accumulated despite their republican election. For present purposes, however, the consequences of the fellows' republican autonomy must be examined, for this autonomy contained within it the flaw that led, in the nineteenth century, to external intervention and imposed reform.

That many if not most professors are dedicated people, few even of their critics will deny. It does not follow, however, that dedicated people ipso facto conduct their group affairs with the general welfare consistently in mind. Most social groups begin with lofty conceptions of their obligations; but, when uncurbed by adequate community restraints and hence insensitive to the purifying currents of external criticism, their ideals shrivel. Many self-interest groups become so irresponsibly unresponsive to the rights of others that they incite public condemnation and retribution. They must therefore be reformed or regulated. Certainly this was true of the Roman Catholic clergy during the Middle Ages, of the Aristotelians who delayed the progress of experimental science during and after the Renaissance, and of the French and Russian ruling classes before revolutions destroyed them. It is currently true of unregenerate sections of American business, medicine, and organized labor. And, despite their dedication, it has been true of academics, as witness the history of Oxford and Cambridge from the mid seventeenth century to the mid nineteenth. During this period college fellows at both universities ran their "republics of scholars" almost entirely free of public interference. The results led Adam Smith, Edward Gibbon, Matthew Arnold, Benjamin Jowett, Mark Pattison, and numerous other Britons to grieve publicly over their scandalous torpor and degradation. Further, the sad state of the two universities made it necessary for the British government to send royal commissions into each of them in 1850 and again in 1871 to reform them dramatically.

An Oxonian who became a famous Scottish philosopher, Sir William Hamilton, started the agitation that led to the appointment of those commissions and also of others to examine the Scottish universities. I quote from his writings on the question of whether or not professors should be exempt, because of their dedication to learning, from public controls:

> The history of Universities—in truth, of all human institutions, lay or clerical, proves, by a melancholy experience, that seminaries founded for the common weal, in the furtherance of sound knowledge, are, if left to themselves . . . regularly deflected from the great end for which they were created, and perverted to the private advantages of those through whom that end, it was confidently hoped, would be best accomplished. And this melancholy experience is, though in different forms, almost equally afforded in all our older British Universities; for all of these the State has founded and privileged, but over none has it ever organized adequate controlling power. And what is the consequence? What is their condition? What ought they to be, and what are they? Corrupt all;—all clamant for reform. But unless reform come from without, we need not, in any University, have any expectation of a reform from within [Hamilton, 1866, pp. 731–732].

Left uncontrolled by external agencies, even academics tend to lose sight of the obligations held for them in the environing society. Perhaps this explains why every English university established during the past two centuries has followed a governance pattern different from that of Oxford and Cambridge. As Van de Graaff

(1978, p. 86) has commented, these later British universities "have been open to lay influence, to an extent surpassed only in U.S. institutions."

The German Pattern

In contrast to Oxford and Cambridge, the German universities during the nineteenth century became the cynosure of forward-looking academics the world over. From every advanced nation of all the continents they swarmed to Berlin, Göttingen, Leipzig, and their sister institutions to sit at the feet of world-famous, pioneering professors. Between 1815 and 1914 their numbers included some ten thousand Americans (Thwing, 1928, p. 40), the majority of whom returned home to professorships. According to one college president at the turn of the century, "No young man looking forward to securing a professorship in any department of our American colleges would deem his preparation finished until he had taken a degree from a German University" (Chamberlain, 1898, p. 41).

Not unnaturally, some German-trained Americans concluded that the superiority of the German universities resulted, in large measure, from their system of government. Advocates of the "free republic of scholars" will often propose the reconstruction of the American pattern after their conception of the German. I say "their conception" because, as I shall show, it differs from the original.

Universities did not appear in German-speaking territories until late in the fourteenth century, Heidelberg (1385) being the oldest within the boundaries of modern Germany. The fourteen established before the Reformation followed the Parisian rather than the Bolognese scheme of academic government, but the upheavals of the sixteenth and seventeenth centuries changed them profoundly. All German universities from Heidelberg on functioned under close supervision by civil governments, and the Reformation converted them, along with the twenty-one subsequently organized before the Napoleonic invasions, into severely restricted agencies of state policy. Friedrich Paulsen, professor of philosophy at the University of Berlin, has described their subservience during this period:

"Each individual government endeavored to secure its own university in order, in the first place, to make sure of . . . instruction in harmony with the confessional standards of its established church; in the second place, to retain the training of its secular officials in its own hands; and, finally, to render attendance at the foreign [including other German] universities unnecessary on the part of its subjects, and to keep the money in the country" (Paulsen, 1906, p. 36).

The much-praised self-governing rights and academic freedom of German professors could not exist in such starkly provincial institutions; and, although Halle (1694), Göttingen (1737), and Jena (1558) began to break away from the limitations that Paulsen has summarized, the big change did not come until after the opening of the University of Berlin in 1810. That is to say, the German system of academic government, so much admired by many American professors until the Hitler regime, did not develop until the nineteenth century.

The designers of the University of Berlin planned an institution in which "the search for truth" would be unfettered, and toward that end they turned over academic matters to the professoriate. This soon became standard practice in the other German universities, each of which established a governing board made up of the full professors, who elected a rector each year from their own number to administer academic affairs. In turn, each faculty annually elected its dean from among the full professors. Thus academics controlled the internal affairs of German universities, a circumstance impelling Professor Adolph Harnack to introduce President Benjamin Ide Wheeler of the University of California to the Kaiser, upon his becoming Roosevelt Professor at the University of Berlin for 1909–10, with the observation that "he comes from a monarchy within a republic to a republic within a monarchy" (Heller, 1927). Many Americans similarly judged the German universities to be ideally governed, as witness the following statement from a Carnegie Foundation bulletin of 1908: "No intermediate nonacademic board is interposed between the ultimate authority of the crown and the plenary academic authority of the professors, and the rector . . . has powers analogous to those of the presiding officer of a legislative body; while the powers of an American college president resemble those of the president of a railroad" (Carnegie Foundation for the Advancement of Teaching, 1908, p. 65).

Many Americans admired the German universities not only because of the governing prerogatives of the professoriate but also because of their adherence to the concept of *Lehrfreiheit,* "freedom of teaching." During the forty years following the opening of the University of Berlin in 1810, authoritarian rulers throughout Germany not infrequently circumvented *Lehrfreiheit* by dismissing professors who refused to knuckle under to them, but the situation changed remarkably for the better after the middle of the century. Alarmed by the Revolution of 1848, Prussia two years later adopted a new constitution which endorsed academic freedom and established the principle that a professor should not be removed from office. From Prussia the concept spread to all the German universities and became a characteristic of which German professors ceaselessly boasted and which many of their American counterparts apparently considered ideal.

The government of German universities, however, had a side which the Americans who applauded it bypassed entirely or mentioned only briefly and uncritically, namely, the powers of the ministry of education in each of the German states. Two of these powers kept the really important governing rights in the hands of the state: the control of finances, including the preparation and approval of budgets and the management of endowments and buildings, and the appointment of all holders of salaried academic posts. Further, the ministry after 1819 stationed an official at each university with continuing tenure, usually called the curator (Paulsen, 1906). Since both rectors and deans changed each year, in contrast with the curator who continued in office at the pleasure of the minister, the curator virtually operated the institution except for the curriculum. In turn, except for the curriculum, the minister made institutional policy. "Professors and other salaried staff were," in the words of Van de Graaff (1978, p. 16), "civil servants."

As observed, most Americans overlooked the focal and essentially ultimate power of the minister and his representative at each university, and so also did most Germans. Some of the latter, however, understood the situation clearly. After President David Starr Jordan of Stanford University praised the German system in an

address, for example, a member of the audience reported the lauda-
tion to Professor Rudolph Virchow, the famous University of Berlin
biologist, who commented: "You tell Dr. Jordan that I think he is
mistaken. No greater autocracy exists in education anywhere than
in the Prussian universities. But arbitrary power is vested in the
Minister of Public Instruction, not in the Rector, who is mainly an
honorary figure. Each professor is regarded as an agent of the government" (Jordan, 1922a, p. 86).

Unrestricted by endowment stipulations and trustee authority, the German minister had an almost free hand. German universities had never had significant endowments—in 1864, for instance,
the income of the University of Berlin from capital funds amounted
to less than .08 percent of its budget (Arnold, 1868, p. 224) and
that for all the Prussian universities in 1931 to 1.1 percent (Swift,
1939, p. 645). But the ministry managed even these small endowments and, unchecked by governing boards comparable to those in
this country, had the continuing and unquestioned power of the
purse. The adoption of the German system by the United States
would have meant that not only state universities but also all private
institutions would be under the financial domination of state com-
missioners or superintendents of education. American Germanophiles
neglected this gravid fact.

They also overlooked the supremacy of civil government in
the appointment of professors. Early in this century, Paulsen (1906,
p. 83) described German appointment practices as follows:

> In Prussia the sovereign himself appoints the
> ordinary [full] professors and the minister of education
> the extraordinary [associate] ones. The faculty, however,
> has the right, based upon tradition and also, for the most
> part, upon statutory regulations, to cooperate in the
> appointment, in the following manner. When a vacancy
> occurs in a chair, the faculty suggests, as a rule, the
> names of three men who, in its judgment, are suitable
> for the position. But the government is not bound to
> confine its choice to those names, and, as a matter of fact,
> they are not infrequently disregarded in that neither the
> faculty's first choice, nor, indeed, any one of the men
> suggested receives the appointment. And for the first ap-

pointment to a newly created chair the faculty's right to make nominations is, generally, not recognized at all.

Paulsen supports this statement by detailing statistics showing that, in the Prussian universities, almost a quarter (23.77 percent) of the appointments to the faculties of law, medicine, and theology from 1817 to 1900 had been made without or contrary to faculty recommendation. These statistics make it clear that the vaunted academic freedom of Germany applied only after the government sifted out the "safe men" from among those recommended by the professoriate. Now and then, groups of professors protested a government selection, but they could not change it or even get it reviewed judicially. Incidentally, Paulsen, a preeminent member of the University of Berlin faculty, although critical of some of the actions of the Prussian minister of education, approved of the minister's appointive prerogatives. Thus in his autobiography, Paulsen (1938, pp. 367–368) wrote: "I am prepared to state it as my opinion that to make the faculties the sole arbiters in the appointment of professors would be the quickest way to ruin the German universities. The very fact that the proposals of the faculty are subject to revision by a higher authority keeps arbitrariness within bounds."

The two most frequent criticisms of American academic government made by Americans who praised the German system were, in the words of one of them, the "one-man power" of the president and the "interference of governing boards with purely academic matters" (Thilly, 1906, p. vii). Naively exhibiting what psychologists call selective perception, they took little notice of the infinitely greater authority of the German minister of education, who combined the "one-man power" of the American president and the functions of boards of trustees.

German professors controlled the curriculum and, once appointed, had permanent tenure (including their base salaries until death); but they had little voice in the assignment of funds and much less influence in the selection of their colleagues than many of them and their American partisans believed. Thus the control of "academic matters" and even their boasted *Lehrfreiheit* were but icing on the cake of their thralldom, through the minister of education, to an authoritarian state.

Those who consider "thralldom" too harsh a characterization should recall three historic events. When, in 1870, Bismarck "edited" the Ems Telegram, thereby misrepresenting the French position and making war between Prussia and France all but inevitable, Heinrich von Treitschke, the professor of history at Heidelberg, applauded Bismarck's "clever" duplicity (Lilge, 1948, pp. 34–35); and no German professor took either the Iron Chancellor or his academic apologist to task. Then in 1914, when Germany invaded Belgium to precipitate the First World War, the "Manifesto of the Ninety-Three Intellectuals," many of them professors, again supported German militarism (Jordan, 1922b). Third, when Hitler took over in January 1933, university people did not protest; and he had no difficulty in immediately adapting the universities to his destructive purposes (Lilge, 1948). Hundreds of Jewish professors migrated to the United States and other countries, but relatively few "Aryan" academics followed their example or took issue with the Nazi regime until some years later. Then, as previously, they were, in Virchow's words, "agents of the government" and as such had neither the means nor the traditions of controverting its actions.

The refusal of the minister of education to allow German professors to migrate to the United States—or even to visit it for extended periods—also illustrates the thralldom of German academics. In 1888, President G. Stanley Hall went abroad to seek faculty members for the newly organized Clark University, and in Germany he negotiated with the eminent mathematician Felix Klein and the brilliant chemist Victor Meyer. Concerning his invitation to Klein, he later wrote: "The salary was agreed upon and he consented to come for a term of three years, when to his and my surprise difficulties were placed in his way which were never overcome. . . . When I broached this matter to the minister of education he replied that the government would be somewhat reluctant to permit its good men to leave and that there were many precedents for refusing this permission, unless, indeed, it be for a short time and for professors whose departments were not intimately connected with the industrial development of the country" (Hall, 1923, p. 273). Hall encountered the same difficulties with his invitation to Professor Meyer. "The Kultur minister," he wrote, "positively forbade him to leave the country, for Germany could not jeopardize her supremacy in the chemical industry which employed so many experts and which led the world" (Hall, 1923, p. 274).

The First World War and the Hitler years disillusioned most American professors about German academic government, but the myth that Germany's academics operated within a "free republic of scholars" has not died easily. German professors did indeed have a major voice in curricular matters and their senior members possessed lifetime tenure, but the influence of the ministry of education remained dominant.

It would appear, therefore, that Germany's pattern of academic government, like those in Bologna, Paris, and Oxbridge, also had its flaws. The medieval universities, at various times in their history, found themselves beholden either to their students, the Church, or the monarchy. Professors in English universities, when they finally did manage to attain autonomy, found that it led to a deterioration of their institutions so serious as to warrant government intervention. German professors owed their appointments to the ministry of education and thus remained limited in their autonomy from that source. In short, "the free republic of scholars" has seldom existed; and when it has, as in England before 1850, it has needed the help of outside forces to counteract the deterioration that ensued.

TWO

Trustee Responsibility

When I first discovered that the American board of trustees could not lay claim to having sprung Minerva-like from the forehead of our own ancestors, I must admit to a certain pleasure.

James B. Conant, 1938

Many American academics decry the existence of the lay governing board as the improper imposition of practices common to the business world on the American college and university. Yet lay people have a voice in the affairs of institutions of higher education throughout most of the world. Indeed, the control of several European institutions of higher education had fallen to lay boards of trustees long before the emergence of the first colleges along the east coast of colonial America. Such a pattern of control developed throughout Europe—in Bologna, Basel, Geneva, Leyden, Edinburgh, and Dublin. It also developed in a number of advanced secondary schools in Britain and on the continent during the decades prior to the founding of Harvard (Herbst, 1974). Such practices put asunder the myth that American academics suffer under a unique system forced on them by the business community.

Lay boards of academic control appeared in Italy, for example, when the professors joined hands with city officials to free themselves from the domination of the student guilds. For city

29

officials and the professors alike, the students had become a common enemy, and they set forth in the fourteenth century to gain the upper hand. Following precedents of the Hellenistic and Roman eras, city authorities began appointing public professors, and, as such, they paid salaries to the teachers from the city treasury. By the end of the fourteenth century, twenty-three Bolognese professors of law had achieved such status, and thereafter their numbers in all subjects increased rapidly, private teachers slowly disappearing (Coulton, 1913). Paying the professors required that the treasury budget funds for this purpose, and this led to the appointment of groups of officials and citizens to administer the grants and later also to supervise their recipients. They went by various names, two of which, slightly modified in translation, continue in use today in American colleges and universities: boards of curators and boards of governors (Eells, 1961). Rashdall ([1895] 1936a, p. 212) has described their appearance and effect: "In the course of the fourteenth and fifteenth centuries such a body . . . was established by the city government or Prince in all Italian universities, and the real control of the university more and more passed to this body of external governors, which by the sixteenth or seventeenth century succeeded in destroying the student autonomy or reducing it to a shadow."

Thus, some 200 years before the founding of the first American college and at least half a century before Columbus set sail to discover the Americas, the primary progenitors of American boards of trustees had begun to take command of Italian higher education. These boards arose in Italy over a concern for trusteeship over the public funds made available to the professors. Trusteeship and visitation constitute two of the major functions performed by lay boards today. Following is a description of the medieval origins of these two functions.

Trusteeship and Visitation

The medieval universities began without endowments and, until well along in their development, they owned no buildings. Their curators, therefore, resembled the original board members of municipal colleges and universities rather than the boards of trustees of institutions like Harvard and Yale, which acquired trust funds during their first years.

A trust is a legal arrangement under which a person or institution administers property for the benefit of another or others. The ownership rests in the hands of a trustee or trustees who perform their duties as defined by law. Under the concept of trusteeship, religious bodies have developed charitable trusts for a wide variety of purposes, and educational institutions—especially in English-speaking countries—have benefited from them abundantly. When, for example, the "College at Newtowne" received the legacy of about 400 pounds left it by John Harvard, its governors accepted the bequest for administration in the same way that the colleges of Oxford and Cambridge had for centuries been accepting similar bequests. The legal instruments founding Harvard in 1636 did not mention the word *trustee*; but the 1693 charter of William and Mary did, and so also did the Yale charter of 1745. The concept of trusteeship, in brief, had been transported from England to its American colonies. So too with visitation.

Long before Gratian codified canon law in the twelfth century, bishops exercised the unquestioned right to visit the churches of their dioceses and thus to supervise their affairs. Only by laying of episcopal hands could the ritual of confirmation be performed; and when a bishop visited a church to admit new members, he also reviewed its spiritual and temporal well-being. Between visits he continued his superintendence. Archbishops had similar visitorial authority over bishops, vicar generals and other such officers of the religious orders over monasteries and abbeys, and—beginning with Gregory VII in the late eleventh century—the pope over the entire Church.

Since the Church considered the universities its daughters, a bishop in whose diocese a university existed could "visit" it whenever he saw fit. In time, however, papal injunctions limited this right to the church officials appointed or approved by the pope. Thus Cardinal Curzon, the legate sent by Innocent III to Paris in 1215, "imposed upon" the University its first "permanent Code of Statutes" (Rashdall [1895] 1936a, p. 309). Indeed, Paris did not become a university until Curzon's statutes made it such (Post, 1934). Later in the thirteenth century, the pope sent two bishops and the dean of a cathedral to visit Paris, and soon thereafter he set up a "Court of

Conservation" (Rashdall [1895] 1936a, p. 342) to conserve the rights granted by papal bulls. In short, the visitors became a permanent body. Visitors also became fixtures of the numerous residential colleges associated with Paris, Oxford, and Cambridge. Meanwhile, the civil authorities also exerted the right of visitation. In England it became embodied in common law, and in time it crossed the Atlantic to help shape the government of the American colonial colleges and their successors.

Reformational Influences

Although American colleges embraced the medieval concepts of trusteeship and visitation early in their history, that history was also strongly influenced by changes brought forth during the Reformation. The Reformation, in fact, constitutes one of the principal pivots in the history of European and hence of American education. In some measure, it has modified every component of all educational levels and has been decisive in both European and American academic government.

At the outset, it must be observed that the Calvinistic sector of the Reformation need alone be discussed. The Lutherans organized about a dozen universities in Germany during the sixteenth and seventeenth centuries, but they had no significant influence upon the American colonial colleges. Only Calvinist patterns of thought and action, therefore, will be considered, commencing with the fountainhead at Geneva.

Geneva. When, upon the invitation of the town authorities of Geneva, Calvin took up permanent residence there in 1541, he found a well-established government. Through it, he immediately put into effect the strongly held theocratic ideas he had catalogued in his prodigious *Institutes of the Christian Religion* published five years earlier. These included essentially Augustinian theological concepts, insistence upon a simplified and austere liturgy, emphasis upon the necessity of an unbending supervision of morals and opinions, and an underlining of the urgent need for solidly educated and well-disciplined ministers and citizens. In this context, only the last of these requires elaboration.

From the beginning, Calvin "saw that a Protestant ministry

could never hold its ground without solid learning," (Coulton, 1957, p. 38) and hence, soon after he took command of Geneva in 1541, he lectured regularly on theology. His educational plans matured most fully, however, with the opening in 1559 of the *Académie de Genève*. Calvin's new establishment followed the pattern of John Sturm's Strassburg *gymnasium* (Herbst, 1974), which Calvin had visited before coming to Geneva. It consisted of a primary school, the *schola privata*, which served the youth of Geneva, and the Academy or advanced school, the *schola publica*, which drew its students from "all parts of Christendom" and offered instruction in "the liberal arts, Greek, Hebrew, philosophy, and theology" (Herbst, 1974, p. 32). Calvin succeeded in bringing outstanding teachers to the Academy, and they in turn attracted good students, despite the Academy's failure to award a degree (Monter, 1967).

Geneva's government consisted of both civil and ecclesiastical branches, and both had a voice in the affairs of the Academy. On the ecclesiastical side stood the Venerable Company of Pastors, one of whose subunits consisted of a college of ministers and professors. This "college," whose faculty members were required to be clergymen only if teaching theology, selected from among its members all instructors and administrators at the Academy. The civil branch of Geneva's government, however, dominated the affairs of the city; and it also dominated the affairs of the Academy. As Karp (1979) has concluded: "The civil government founded the Geneva Academy and from the very beginning served as its financial patron and controlled academic appointments." This control it exercised through its executive body, known as the Small Council. All appointments to the Academy made by the Venerable Body of Pastors, for instance, required the approval of the Small Council.

The internal governance of the Academy fell to the chief academic officer, called the rector, and the faculty. The rector stood at the head of the faculty, regardless of their rank. Although not necessarily a clergyman, he had responsibility for both the religious and scholarly character of the Academy. Elected by the college of ministers and confirmed by the Small Council, the rector served a two-year term. A second term could, and sometimes did, follow. To the rector fell control over financial management, superintendence of the library, governance of the faculty, and adjudication

of disputes between the faculty and students. The faculty met weekly
to discuss such matters as student discipline and graduation requirements (Karp, 1979).

Because they essentially controlled the Academy, the four
syndics of the Small Council paralleled the external curators of the
Italian universities described earlier. They differed in that Geneva's
civil government itself both organized and operated the Academy,
whereas its counterparts in the Italian cities turned over the control
of the universities to legal entities that they established. As will be
seen, the College of Edinburgh followed the Geneva plan and the
University of Leyden the Italian plan. The important point here,
however, is that under both of these European arrangements laymen
had the decisive voice.

Leyden. Sixteen years after the founding of the Geneva
Academy, the University of Leyden opened, the second Calvinistic
institution of higher learning. During the next several decades, three
others would follow: Franeker, Groningen, and Utrecht. All
adopted the Leyden pattern of academic government.

In his classic, *The Rise of the Dutch Republic*, Motley
(1855) reports the enthusiasm of the citizenry for the creation of
the University of Leyden: They chose it in lieu of ten years of
freedom from taxation as the symbol of their throwing off the
Spanish yoke. He also describes the brilliant ceremonies with which
the institution opened on February 5, 1575, and the handsome
revenues it derived from the endowment provided by the city from
expropriated Roman Catholic religious property.

From the beginning, Leyden stood as a "bulwark of Calvinistic theology" (*University of Leyden,* 1928, p. 3). It followed
the Italian plan of government by setting up a board of curators
who, along with the mayor of Leyden, constituted a lay governing
board for the new institution. The curators, in turn, appointed a
senatus academicus, which controlled the internal government of the
University (Herbst, 1974). Ian van der Does, a young citizen who
had distinguished himself as soldier, statesman, and scholar, served
as the first chairman of the board of curators until his death twenty-
nine years later. As such, he both designed the University and
directed its administration.

The plan adopted at Leyden in 1575 has continued in

operation, with but minor changes, ever since. Those who dog-
matically declare that only American colleges and universities have
lay boards of trustees may, therefore, find interesting the following
portion of a letter I received in 1961 from the President Curator
of the University of Leyden:

> The board of curators is in fact the link between
> the government and the university. All correspondence
> with the government goes through their hands. They
> promote in a general way the interests of the university
> and they are responsible for the application of the law
> governing university matters; they take care of the hous-
> ing of the university institutes; they administrate all
> financial matters; manage the university properties;
> appoint the staff, except the professors who are appointed
> by the Crown on their proposition; and, last but not
> least, prepare the annual budget and present it to the
> Minister of Education. They number five to seven mem-
> bers and remain in office for four years but are reeligible
> up to the age of seventy years.
>
> Up till recently the curators were as a rule chosen
> from the higher official ranks, renowned lawyers, or mem-
> bers of parliament. I, for example, combined during nine
> years the functions of President of the Board of Curators
> with those of Governor of the Province of Noordholland.
> The presidents of the Universities of Utrecht and Gron-
> ingen are also governors of their provinces.
>
> The members of the board do not get any remun-
> eration, nor does their chairman. But the new law
> [January 1, 1961] provides the possibility of an allow-
> ance. The board has a full-time secretary, nominated by
> the Crown, who of course has a rather extensive clerical
> staff [van Steenwijk, 1961].

This letter and other documents from universities such as Leyden
should be pondered by those who assert that American college and
university government has been modeled on that of the modern
commercial corporation.

Edinburgh and Aberdeen. The world has long known the
institution in Edinburgh as the University of Edinburgh, but it

began in 1583 as the College of Edinburgh. The Town Council founded it under a charter granted by Scotland's first Protestant monarch, James VI, son of the imprisoned Mary, Queen of Scots. Its chief sponsors had drunk deep of Reformation doctrines at Geneva. "The precedent and model," writes a historian of the institution, "was Geneva—Geneva, to which the Scottish Kirk looked as the fountainhead of its doctrine and discipline—Geneva, which had been the asylum for refugee Scottish Reformers from 1554 till 1560" (Grant, 1884, p. 126).

The Edinburgh authorities did not, however, faithfully follow the Geneva model of academic government. To begin with, they did not give the ministers of the city the power of their compeers in Geneva. A quarter of a century after the initiation of the College, the Council agreed to consult with the Session of the Kirk about faculty appointments, but it kept final decisions in its own hands. Further, it immediately gave the College the right to issue degrees, a step that the Geneva authorities had not taken, apparently because of doubts about the political powers of the city.

At Geneva, the four syndics of the Small Council had assumed the overall direction of the Academy, and a similar arrangement went into operation at Edinburgh: The Town Council asssigned responsibility for the College to a committee of its members. Most of its members, however, had quite inadequate capacities for the management of an institution of higher education, and later many informed Scotsmen—especially Sir William Hamilton (Hamilton, 1834)—severely criticized the Town Council's control. It continued, however, until 1858 when the Universities Act for Scotland established the method of government still in effect.

In a thorough appraisal of Scottish influences upon American academic government, attention would need to be given to the three other universities that had been established in Scotland before the founding of Edinburgh: Aberdeen, Glasgow, and St. Andrews. Only Aberdeen, however, needs briefly to be cited here. Like Edinburgh, it supplied one of the original administrative heads of the nine colleges in colonial America. (William and Mary's James Blair came from Edinburgh; William Smith from Aberdeen became the first provost of what today is the University of Pennsylvania.) It also influenced American practices in two other ways: Both of its colleges (King's and Marischal, independent of each other until

1858) had *boards* of visitors; and both, like Edinburgh, granted degrees.

The Scottish universities had extensive influence on the American colleges; but the organizers of the first two (Harvard and William and Mary) did not adopt their governmental methods. Rather, their methods look more like those of Leyden or of Trinity College, Dublin.

Dublin. Anglo-Irish, English, and Scottish Puritans who did not separate from the Church of England acquired a charter from Queen Elizabeth in 1591 for the establishment of the University of Dublin; and in 1593 they launched Trinity College (Maxwell, 1946). They hoped that other colleges comparable to those of Oxford and Cambridge would later arise around it, but circumstances prevented that development. Trinity College and the University of Dublin long continued, therefore, as substantially one and the same.

The founders of Trinity broke from the historic English practice of appointing a single Visitor and adopted the *board* of visitors plan already developed at Aberdeen and inherent in the governmental structure of Calvin's Academy at Geneva. Visitors in England had almost always been bishops or archbishops, but the Irish did not give them power over their institutions. The Trinity charter, instead, assigned the function of visitation to a board of seven, all nonacademics and none a bishop or archbishop.

Trinity did look to England, however, rather than to Geneva or to Scotland for part of its plan. Its charter provided for two governing boards: not only the Board of Visitors but also a Board of Fellows. To the latter, composed of the "head" and members of the faculty of the College, it assigned the trusteeship or ownership function and also internal administration. In short, academics "owned" and managed Trinity just as did their counterparts in the colleges of Oxford and Cambridge, but Reformation conceptions of polity required that an external board of nonacademics have surveillance over this internal board.

American Adaptations

Of the nine colleges that opened during the colonial period of what became the United States, three—Harvard, William and Mary, and Brown—adopted the two-board or bicameral structure just described at Trinity College, Dublin. The other six developed a unicameral system which became the predominant American model.

The General Court of the Massachusetts Bay Colony founded Harvard College on October 28, 1636. The Court had originally been what would in the United States today be called the board of directors of the commercial company that settled the colony. Its Puritan organizers, however, had forehandedly brought to New England the charter that Charles I had issued them. With it and themselves out of reach of the Crown, they converted their enterprise into a full-fledged civil government (Miller, 1933). Had it not been for the Puritan Revolution, this hazardous plan would probably have failed; but the success of the Puritan uprising authenticated it until the government of James II abrogated the charter in 1684 (Haskins, 1960). A de facto civil government, therefore, created Harvard and empowered the infant institution to grant degrees.

Harvard. Harvard opened in the summer of 1638, took its permanent name the following March, and graduated its first class of nine bachelors of arts in 1642. During its first five years, the College functioned under the direction of a committee of the Court consisting of the governor, deputy governor, treasurer of the colony, three magistrates, and six clergymen (Herbst, 1974). By legislative act in 1642, this committee became the governing board of the College and took the name of the Board of Overseers. In its new form it grew to twenty-one members, eleven of them public officials, nine Congregational ministers, and the College president. Then, in 1650, the Court granted the College a charter which established a second governing board known then and ever since as The Harvard Corporation but legally as the President and Fellows of Harvard College.

During the short initial period that Harvard had only one board, it consciously or unconsciously adopted a number of governmental characteristics of the Dutch universities. No Harvard historian whose writings I have read asserts this; but the ablest of them by far, Samuel Eliot Morison, has supplied much of the data which seem to me to make this conclusion reasonable. He has cited, for example, the strong influence of the University of Franeker upon early Harvard, an influence attributable chiefly to William Ames, the Puritan divine who served as professor of theology at Franeker for a decade just before the founding of Harvard. Ames' thinking significantly affected that of many if not most of the New England ministers. He also trained Harvard's first head—Nathaniel Eaton. Morison has written that had he not died in 1633, Ames "would have been offered the Harvard presidency" (Morison, 1935, p. 143).

When, in 1650, the dual-board plan went into effect, however, Harvard shifted toward the Dublin model. Witness these facts: First, it did not adopt the governmental method of Oxford and Cambridge colleges; second, as described earlier, Trinity College, Dublin, had two comparable governing boards; and, third, both the General Court and the Harvard Board of Overseers knew about the Dublin design because one of the most important members of both bodies—John Winthrop, Jr., son of the leading figure in the colony, Governor John Winthrop—had been a student there.

William and Mary. The second colonial college, William and Mary, also had two boards. Early in 1693, the joint English sovereigns whose names it took issued its charter and also granted generous financial support. The prolix provisions of the charter relating to the government of the College were summarized as follows by the eminent American political historian, Herbert B. Adams of Johns Hopkins University:

> The power to establish and to organize a certain place of universal study, or perpetual college, for Divinity, Philosophy, Languages, and other good Arts and Sciences, consisting of one President, six masters or professors, and a hundred scholars, more or less, graduates and nongraduates, was intrusted by the charter . . . to a self-perpetuating board of eighteen trustees, resident in the colony. They were to have the appointing power, and were to form the board of governors or visitors. . . . The charter provided that the president and professors should constitute a body corporate, and that to it ultimately the trustees should transfer their entire endowment as soon as the institution should be fairly established. This was actually done [in 1729]; so that, in after time, the trustees remained simply as the board of annual visitors, with general superintendence and the appointing power [Adams, 1887, pp. 18–19].

In brief, William and Mary, like Harvard, opened with a single governing board; but, under the provisions of its charter (again like Harvard), it organized a second board after the College had been firmly organized. The president and the professors (to a maximum of six) constituted the corporation or "owning" board. Eighteen Virginia laymen sat on the senior board and served, in the words of the charter, as "Visitors or Governors." After 1729, this latter board had no control of college funds, but it did have final authority in all other matters—an authority it chose frequently to exert. This division of power contributed to the controversies that ensued between the two boards. The controversies ended, however, with the close of the American Revolution, after which the powers of the faculty "board" diminished severely.

Brown. Four one-board colleges got under way before the founding of the third two-board institution in 1764, namely, Rhode Island College, which forty years later took the name of Brown University. Its original and continuing governmental structure, however, in no way resembles those of Harvard and William and Mary. In fact, the charter, issued by the Governor and General Assembly of the colony, did not actually provide for two boards but, instead, for two branches of the same board. That is to say, the charter created a corporation made up of thirty-six members called trustees and twelve members called fellows. This body of forty-eight (now fifty-four, the number of trustees having been increased to forty-two) possesses the property of the institution and generally oversees its affairs. President Henry M. Wriston some years ago described how the plan works:

> The governmental structure of Brown University is unique, different from any other in all the world. . . . The Corporation is bicameral, being composed of a Board of Trustees and a Board of Fellows. Its meetings are extraordinary, absolutely without parallel. The two bodies assemble separately in the same room at the same time, the Trustees under the chairmanship of the chancellor, the Fellows with the president as chairman. They follow the same agenda and have a joint secretary. Each body votes separately, but every motion requires concurrent action. . . . The Board of Fellows, however,

possesses separate and distinctive powers in addition to those shared with the Trustees. The Charter specifically delegated to the Fellows . . . control of "the instruction and immediate government of the College." They, therefore, can and do meet separately when discharging their functions of approving curricula, establishing degree requirements, and voting degrees.

I confess that after my first meeting with the Corporation I did not understand how a body so organized could ever reach a responsible decision upon a matter of great difficulty. Experience has shown that it can [Wriston, 1946, pp. 7–10].

The majority of American colleges and universities, of course, have not followed the lead of Harvard, William and Mary, or Brown. They have instead relied on a single board. Such a pattern began at Yale early in the eighteenth century.

Yale. The dual board system followed by Harvard and William and Mary had combined two historical precedents: first, the medieval practice (in effect in the colleges of Oxford and Cambridge) of allowing the beneficiaries of endowments to serve as their trustees, and second, the concept (originating in the Italian universities during the fourteenth century and vigorously espoused by European Calvinists) of giving nonacademics a large if not the decisive voice in conducting the affairs of colleges and universities. The unicameral system, however, went further: It gave nonacademics complete governing power. Why?

The search for an answer to this question must obviously begin with Yale, established only eight years after the issuance of the William and Mary charter. Its ten ministerial "undertakers" probably knew little about the Virginia college, but they knew a good deal about Harvard. Nine of them were its alumni. In seeking approval for their college, however, they did not propose to the General Court of Connecticut that the governmental plan of their alma mater be copied. They had their reasons, which primarily had been propounded by Increase Mather, the chieftain of the conservative Calvinists and president of Harvard.

The story begins in 1684 when the government of James II revoked the Massachusetts Bay Colony charter signed by his father. This action disbanded the General Court, voided the Harvard charter of 1650, and greatly discomfited the cherished procedures of the colony. Among other things, it placed Harvard for some years more directly under the control of the royal governor and his personally selected council. Because the governor, Joseph Dudley, was a native son and Harvard alumnus, things for a time went reasonably well; but the new governing body had trouble finding a head to replace President John Rogers, who had died some months before its organization. Reluctantly, Increase Mather, pastor of the wealthy and influential Old North Church of Boston and "the most eminent man in the colony" (Murdock, 1925, p. 43) accepted the post. He held it for sixteen years, throughout which he continued his Boston ministry. His persistent refusal to give all his time to the College (he also spent part of his years as Harvard president in Europe), together with the general uncertainty of the colony's status and his frequent differences with the royal governor, created oppressive tensions for the College. These would not be resolved until the restoration of the charter of 1650, which finally occurred in 1707. Six years earlier, however, Mather had been forced to resign.

Meanwhile, Harvard's legal status oscillated banefully, several charters being proposed and two of them, plus an informal arrangement of 1700, being temporarily in force. This grievous situation undoubtedly colored Mather's thinking about academic government, but even more potent was his growing concern over the weakening position of Calvinistic Protestantism in Europe and the inroads being made in New England by Episcopalians, Baptists, and latitudinarian Congregationalists. He strove to check these trends, and he also counseled the founders of Yale to make plans consonant with his. Sharing his views, they did.

Mather knew the European situation well. He had spent four years after his 1656 graduation from Harvard in England, Ireland, and Guernsey; and he had returned home because the reinstatement of the Stuart dynasty in the person of Charles II brought an end to the Puritan hegemony in England and made life miserable, if not perilous, for Congregationalists. Two years later, the Act of Uniformity closed Oxford, Cambridge, and Trinity College, Dublin, to nonconformists. This made Harvard the only

English-speaking Calvinistic institution of higher learning outside of Scotland.

Protestantism had also encountered alarming difficulties in France, where the toleration granted in 1598 by the Edict of Nantes had led Huguenots to organize thirty-two colleges and universities (Foster, 1911). The persistent persecutions of Cardinal Richelieu, the chief minister of Louis XIII, however, had circumvented the provisions of the edict; and Louis XIV made the destruction of French Protestantism a major item of his policy. His activities culminated in his 1685 abrogation of the Edict of Nantes, which closed the few remaining Protestant colleges and forced all but a small number of the surviving Huguenots to flee France.

Events in New England also troubled Mather. He had endorsed James II's proclamation of religious liberty and had helped negotiate the new Massachusetts charter which terminated religious tests for voting, but the rapid spread of Episcopalianism among leading citizens of his own Boston and even among Harvard graduates struck him as ominous. So also did the increasing acceptance by New England Congregationalists of liberal theological ideas. He set his face stubbornly against the continuation of these attritions and hence, immediately after his return from England in 1692, he succeeded in getting temporary acceptance of a charter which one of his biographers has summarized as follows: "Its essential feature was that it put all authority in the hands of a corporation of ten, which was to be self-perpetuating, and subject to no supervision by 'visitors' or 'overseers.' Plainly, Mather felt that the only way to ensure Harvard's continuing a nursery, not only of learning but of piety, was to put it into the hands of men who felt as he did, and to allow them to choose their successors. Without outside supervision, they could then continue the traditions of the college under no necessity of conforming to any changes which might come in the views of its alumni or the community" (Murdock, 1925, p. 340).

The authorities of Whitehall, however, did not accept Mather's ideas about eliminating external controls. Nonetheless, he persisted and submitted another and similar proposal. It met the same fate. Harvard operated from 1700 to 1707, therefore, under

a plan approved temporarily by the reconstructed Board of Overseers. It provided for a single board of seventeen members, thirteen
of them ministers.

During these unstable Harvard years, the long-delayed plans
for a Connecticut college matured. They came to a head in 1701,
that is, during the period that Harvard had a governing board
stacked with ministers. Small wonder that the ten orthodox ministers who projected the new college should follow the lead of the
alma mater of all but one of them. Small wonder, either, that they
sought orthodox counsel about how to proceed. Thus, in the early
summer of 1701, they wrote for help to Increase Mather, to his
prodigious son Cotton, and to a pair of the strictest Calvinists among
Massachusetts laymen: Judge Samuel Sewall and Richard Adding-
ton, Secretary of the province (Quincy, 1840a).

All four recommended a single governing board, the two
ministers urging that all of its members be sound-in-the-faith ministers. Increase Mather, for example, suggested a membership of
seven which could, he wrote, govern adequately "especially if these
be pastors of the next neighboring churches" (Dexter, 1916, p.
4). His son proposed that a synod be organized by right-minded
pastors and that twelve of them become the governing board of
the College. "Let none be allowed to act as Inspectors [trustees],"
he cautioned, "until they subscribe to certain Articles, relating to
the *Purity of Religion* (Dexter, 1916, p. 17). The two laymen felt
more tolerant of lay trustees and advised that the board be composed of ministers and soundly indoctrinated "gentlemen." The
Mather opinion prevailed, however, and the founders decided to
exclude nonclergymen. Despite the hazards pointed out by Connecticut lawyers as well as the two from Massachusetts, moreover,
they made no provision for visitation by civil authorities.

The Connecticut General Court, nonetheless, accepted the
plan that the ministers submitted to them. Whether or not they
knew it, they thereby created an entirely new pattern of academic
government, a pattern which completely and probably willfully
disregarded English common law and deeply embedded Calvinistic
tenets. Religious fears essentially explain the point of view of the
ministers, but how did they manage to push such a precedent-

breaking and legally questionable scheme through the Connecticut legislature?

The political skill of academics is well documented, and similar observations can be made about many clerics. In any case, the ministers drew upon the early arrangements of Harvard and William and Mary, which fit closely the trustee relationships of private secondary schools of Europe (Herbst, 1974), and thus made no mention of a college in their application. Their bill called instead for "An Act of Liberty to Erect a Collegiate School"—a school, be it noted, not a college. Such wording would have guarded against a negative response from the government in England to the more ambitious founding of a college. Nevertheless, the Yale founders specified that the "school" should have the one characteristic that above all others distinguishes institutions of higher education from schools, namely, the power to grant degrees (Dexter, 1916). The facts collected by Yale historians suggest that on the question of degrees the ministers decided to take a gamble.

The extraordinary speed with which their bill went through to passage probably accounts, in large part, for their success. Ten days after the two Massachusetts lawyers posted their draft of the bill to the leader of the ministerial group, it became law, even though the document had to be conveyed from Boston to New Haven and be twice revised after its arrival. Despite the fact that the common law of England under which the colonies operated, never mind well-established academic and Calvinistic precedents, required visitation and limited the right to confer degrees to higher educational institutions, the bill passed without amendment. Patently, either the ministers had the support of like-minded members of the legislature or managed to get it passed without careful scrutiny.

In any event, the ministers got what they wanted: a college over which "right-minded" clergy would hold full visitorial and trustee authority. Later in the century, Connecticut authorities forced the institution (it became Yale College in 1718 and acquired a charter in 1745) to add public officials to its governing board, but never, in those times, did the faculty gain the semblance of authority implied by the dual board arrangements at Harvard and William and Mary. As Herbst (1976b) has written in the context of Yale's controversial midcentury president Thomas Clap, those in authority just simply did not trust the faculty.

Princeton. The faculty fared no better at the institution known today as Princeton University. The twelve ministers among the twenty-three charter trustees of the College included six graduates of Yale, three of Harvard, and three of the Log College, a private training school whose evangelical activities helped precipitate Princeton's founding. These trustees preferred the single-board arrangement fostered at Yale.

The just-mentioned Log College operated some twenty miles from Philadelphia under the direction of William Tennent, a graduate of the University of Edinburgh and father of the ebullient Gilbert Tennent. He gave his students solid grounding in the classics and theology, and most of them became eloquent if not explosive revivalists. Following his example, several of his former students set up similar schools; but in 1738, the Presbyterian Synod of Philadelphia, stronghold of the Old Lights group which opposed the revivalists, refused to ordain the products of the Log College and its satellites. It would admit to the ministry only those who held degrees from Harvard, Yale, or one of the Protestant institutions of Europe (Wertenbaker, 1946).

This action impelled a group of revivalist (New Lights) ministers and three parishioners of one of them to project a college and to negotiate with the New Jersey authorities for a charter. Six were Yale graduates; the seventh, one of the ministers, had been educated at Harvard. The lawyer among the group stood at the top of his profession in the middle colonies and drafted the charter submitted to the Governor of New Jersey. Unlike the 1701 Act creating Yale and also in 1745 Yale charter, it provided for participation of both laymen and ministers in the government of the proposed college. It envisioned, however, New Lights control and, further, made no provision for any representatives of civil government. In rapid succession, therefore, two Episcopalian governors turned it down.

At this juncture, the Crown appointed a new governor in the person of Jonathan Belcher, a former governor of Massachusetts, graduate of Harvard, long-time member of the Harvard Board of

Overseers, and an ardent Congregationalist. Belcher enthusiastically supported the idea of a New Jersey college but he insisted upon a broader governmental base for it than the "seven founders" had proposed. He wanted not only civil government representation but also the inclusion of a larger number of trustees (Wertenbaker, 1946). The negotiations that followed led to a compromise—the still-operative Princeton charter which Belcher signed in 1748 in the name of George II. It created the College and placed it under the control of a board of twenty-three members, twelve of them ministers who served as individuals and not as denominational agents. The eleven laymen included the governor as the sole ex officio representative of civil government, but four members of the colonial council also served as citizen members of the original board. A member of the Baptist church, an Episcopalian, and two Quakers kept the body from being composed entirely of Presbyterians (Savage, 1961). Besides the governor, only the president had ex officio status. Vacancies among the other twenty-one board members would, the charter stipulated, be filled by co-optation, that is, by board election.

Later colleges. None of the colleges established later during the colonial period exactly copied the Princeton model, but all except Brown followed the unicameral plan. The University of Pennsylvania was organized, for instance, by leading citizens of Philadelphia in 1755 as the Academy and College of Philadelphia upon foundations going back to 1740. As at all the other unicameral colonial colleges except Yale, nonacademics have always predominated in its governing board. Its original board, in fact, consisted of twenty-four laymen: eight merchants, four physicians, and twelve others, including Benjamin Franklin (Herbst, 1976b). Like the College of Edinburgh, the Philadelphia institution had no clergymen on its first board. In 1754, ministers and laymen of several denominations organized and chartered King's College (renamed Columbia College after the Revolution, and Columbia University in 1912). Episcopalians had the ascendancy, and the charter required that the president be of that communion. Church officials and colonial authorities dominated its board and administration during the pre-Revolutionary period (Herbst, 1976b). Founded by royal charter in 1766 as Queen's College, Rutgers took the name of a benefactor in 1825. The Dutch Reformed Church dominated it, but from the beginning members of other denominations and New Jersey public officers sat on its essentially nonministerial board. As the second college chartered in New Jersey, Queens broke the pattern of "provincial" colleges followed in the colonies to that time and started the move, so prevalent in the nineteenth century, toward more strictly private institutions (Herbst, 1976b). George III chartered Dartmouth College in 1769 primarily to educate Indians, the chief purpose of the Congregational minister who organized it and served as its first president. Its original board included Congregationalists, Presbyterians, and Episcopalians, some of them New Hampshire officials.

Quite obviously, the facts do not support the notion that American lay boards of trustees have been foisted upon defrauded academics by the business community. To be certain, the bicameral arrangements at Harvard and William and Mary gave the promise of faculty involvement in institutional policy control, but that promise soon faded in the face of domination by outside officials. Those outside officials—clergymen and government officials in Calvinist-dominated earlier times and, more recently, lawyers and businessmen—have permitted the faculty voice to grow in volume and authority. But the trustees have not relinquished—nor can they do so under terms of the charters by which they operate—their place at the top hierarchical rank in all academic government.

THREE

Presidential Leadership

In the academic jungle the president is my black beast.
James McKeen Cattell, 1913b

Another of the myths concerning academic government in the United States holds that the academic presidency germinated in this country and, additionally, that it has never developed elsewhere. The first half of this misconception stems from a failure to realize that American colleges, until about a hundred years ago, modeled themselves administratively on the colleges of Oxford and Cambridge and not on the universities which they inhabit. Mark the word *inhabit*. I use it deliberately because each Oxford and Cambridge college is an autonomous corporation with an administrative organization completely independent of university authority. The American academic presidency had its genesis in the headship of these colleges and, therefore, its origins lie in the thirteenth century.

Consider some of the evidence supporting this statement. First, there is the matter of tenure of administrative heads. During the Middle Ages, the tenure of major administrative officers of a *university* never exceeded a year and often lasted only three months. This practice continues currently in a number of countries and also, in modified form, in Oxford and Cambridge universities, where the vice-chancellors (the presiding officers) serve for four and two years respectively. Like American presidents, however, the heads of their *colleges* have, although elected by the fellows, always had indefinite tenure. Until a few decades ago, this meant, for better or worse, that they administered their colleges until they died.

Consider next the titles involved. The college heads at Oxford and Cambridge may make use of one or another of seven appellations: *dean, master, president, principal, provost, rector,* and *warden.* All but the first and the last of these have denominated the administrative heads of American colleges. Harvard styled its first head *master* and its eighth, during part of his term, *rector.* Yale applied this latter title to its first five executives. Pennsylvania used the designation of *provost* for a century and a quarter, that is, until 1930, when the Wall Street banker who then assumed the office persuaded its board of trustees to adopt the title of *president.* During their early history, half a dozen other Pennsylvania institutions entitled their heads *principals.* But William and Mary, Princeton, and the vast majority of institutions have always called their chief administrators *presidents* and in doing so have followed the example of four Oxford colleges (Corpus Christi, Magdalen, St. Johns, and Trinity), and of Queens College, Cambridge.

The error of the second half of the assertion under present review—namely, that no administrators comparable to American university presidents have developed in other countries—can be disposed of with dispatch by merely naming those countries besides England whose institutions of higher education have such officers. First there is Holland where, since the establishment of the University of Leyden in 1575, the head of the board of curators of each of its universities has powers similar to those of American university presidents. Note these comments by James Bryant Conant, made during his presidency of Harvard: "I was shocked to find that the pioneer college president had also been anticipated by the Dutch in the sixteenth century. I had always imagined that Gilman at Johns Hopkins, or Stanley Hall at Clark, or Harper almost singlehandedly building the University of Chicago, were prodigies who could arise only in this new land of enterprise. I had supposed that never before had one man had the power to build a faculty *de novo.* The account of the founding of the University of Leyden in 1575, however, proves that Gilman had a predecessor. . . . A board of three curators was appointed and the thirty-year-old Ian van der Does was chosen chairman. . . . His was the responsibility for the formulation of the plans of the new university" (Conant, 1938, pp. 7–8). Second there is Scotland, whose university heads—called principals and vice-chancellors—have had indefinite tenure and wide-ranging authority since the sixteenth century and whose administrative model has been followed by all the English universities other than Oxford, Cambridge, and London. Third is Australia, whose universities have also followed the Scottish tradition. And fourth is Canada, whose universities have long been organized administratively much like those of this country. This list, may I say, is not complete, but it suffices to fracture the fable that the management of American universities is unique or the result of American business management and therefore reprehensible.

Importation of the College Presidency

At Cape Henry, Virginia, on the evening of April 26, 1607, the first group of English colonists to land on American shores introduced the office of president into American life. A year earlier, James I had chartered The Virginia Company as a joint-stock enterprise to colonize the New World. Before sailing up Chesapeake Bay to disembark at Jamestown, those of the stockholders who had made the journey elected Edward Maria Wingfield "President of Virginia." A third of a century later, on August 27, 1640, the term *president* entered American academic life when ten magistrates and sixteen elders meeting in Boston elected Henry Dunster, a thirty-year-old Master of Arts of Cambridge, president of Harvard College.

The majority of the university men who migrated to New England during its early history had been educated at Cambridge, where all but two of the colleges called their heads *master*. Quite naturally, therefore, Dunster's predecessor and first head of Harvard, Nathaniel Eaton, took that title. He so besmirched it, however, that it disappeared with him. A savage beating he administered to his assistant, the low quality of his wife's cooking, and his fraudulent financial dealings led to his indictment, his dismissal from office, and his eviction from Massachusetts (Morison, 1935). Another colonial college head—Provost William Smith of Pennsylvania—

spent some months in jail, and a few more recent presidents have had even more serious encounters with the law; but Nathaniel Eaton holds the all-time record for corruption. Happily, he held his position for less than two years, and Harvard historians usually hurry over his brief tenure to describe the career of his successor.

Dunster's assumption of the title of *president* seems to me to be explicable only in terms of Eaton's flagrant behavior. The Harvard authorities undoubtedly wanted to extinguish the memory of Eaton's scandalous administration, and hence it seems reasonable to conclude that they decided to give his successor a quite different designation. Why they chose *president* instead of *warden, principal, provost,* or one of the other Oxford and Cambridge titles, no one knows. Styles in naming can seldom be explained. In any case, its vogue began with Dunster and has continued ever since.

Conditions in the early colonial years had much to do with the role of the college presidency. Other than the president, the only members of the instructional staff were the tutors, few of whom remained in their positions for long. Under such conditions the president assumed an authority over internal affairs which few, if any, would have questioned.

Prior to the Civil War, American higher education had two striking characteristics that affected the presidency: All institutions were small, and only a handful of them included units concerned with professional education. Otherwise expressed, no universities worthy of the name existed, and the colleges primarily concentrated on the liberal or general education of very small student bodies. For example, John Adams' Harvard graduating class of 1755 had only twenty-four members, Ralph Waldo Emerson's of 1821 had fifty-nine, and Charles W. Eliot's of 1853 eighty-nine. Yale, which during most of the nineteenth century enrolled more students than any other college, graduated its first class of more than a hundred in 1826, a number unequaled by Harvard until its class of 1860. The state universities did not begin their fabulous growth until the 1880s, Harvard continuing to be the country's largest institution of higher education until about 1910 when the University of Michigan passed it with a registration of 5,383 compared to Harvard's 4,123.

Professional schools did not begin to appear until the second half of the eighteenth century, the medical school of the University of Pennsylvania, established in 1765, being the first of them. Until late in the nineteenth century, they operated quite independently of the colleges whose name they bore, and until about the same time the majority of their students entered directly from secondary schools. Practitioners with the title of *dean* managed them in their spare time, and they functioned with few if any checks from presidents. Typically, presidents focused their ministration on the historic colleges and generally were the colleges' only administrative officer. As jacks-of-all-trades, they not only dealt with their boards of trustees, professors, and tutors but also raised money, conducted the college correspondence, taught heavy schedules, presided over most of the twice-daily sessions of compulsory chapel, preached on Sunday, recruited new students, and handled the ever-present problems of discipline. Faculty members helped them with their chores, but responsibility rested with the president. Francis Wayland of Brown spoke for most of his presidential colleagues when he wrote his sister: "I am a perfect drayhorse. I am in harness from morning to night, and from one year to another. I am never turned out for recreation" (Murray, 1891, p. 79). Some decades earlier, Ezra Stiles of Yale wrote in the same vein: "At best the Diadem of a President is a Crown of Thorns" (Stiles [1777] 1901, p. 209).

The great majority of presidents prior to the Civil War wore their prickly crowns dutifully as ministers of the gospel, but some laymen—most of them distinguished—were also persuaded to wear it. Harvard, for example, had three nonclerical presidents: John Leverett, a lawyer and judge who took office in 1707; Josiah Quincy, an astute businessman who served five terms as mayor of Boston a bit over a century later; and Edward Everett, who early left the Unitarian ministry for a political career as a congressman, governor, United States senator, minister to England, and secretary of state in the cabinet of President Fillmore. Columbia has all but specialized in lay presidents: During its entire history, it has had only three ministers in the position. The others during the period before the Civil War included a United States senator, a judge, and the editor of a New York newspaper. United States senators also became presidents of Rutgers and the University of South Carolina, a state senator became president of Hampden-Sydney, a governor of the University of North Carolina, and a congressman of Amherst (Schmidt, 1930, pp. 184–185). Few professors attained the office until after the Civil War. With rare exceptions, boards of trustees chose "outsiders" who seldom considered themselves to be scholars. Nor were any presidents administrative specialists. The concepts of scholar-presidents and specialists-in-administration did not incubate until later.

A few American institutions, it should be noted, have sought to operate without presidents. One of them—the University of Virginia—did so from its opening in 1825 until early in this century. Thomas Jefferson, its founder, wanted William Wirt, the United States attorney general, as its president; Wirt declined, and soon after the University opened, Jefferson died (Martin, 1905). Meanwhile, a committee of professors administered the institution, and they and their successors maintained that Jefferson had opposed the establishment of the post. My examination of the relevant literature leads me to believe that they misinterpreted Jefferson's position; in any case, after a long and acrimonious controversy, the Board of Visitors created the office in 1904 and elected as its first incumbent Edwin A. Alderman, then president of Tulane. In Michigan, the 1837 legislation that created the present University of Michigan made no provisions for a president, and the institution operated under a "president of the faculty" annually elected by his fellows in the Literary Department. The system led to such troublesome bickerings, however, that the 1850 State Constitution required that the office of president be established. Two years later, Henry Philip Tappan became its first incumbent. The California Institute of Technology followed a committee plan during most of its history until Lee A. DuBridge became its first president in 1946. And similarly, the New School for Social Research opened just after the First World War under the direction of a group of professors who agreed about the undesirability of college presidents and who tried to handle its work through their own committees. They quarreled so often that within two years they decided to recommend the appointment of an administrative head, now called *president*. Like most other organizations, these institutions found it efficient to vest control over operations and the execution of policy in the hands of continuing administrative specialists.

The protracted debate at Virginia about its method of operational control reflected a widespread difference of opinion concerning the nature of the presidency. Points of view clustered about two general positions: one that the office should be "weak," the other that is should be "strong." During the early years of all institutions and also during times of peril, presidents almost inevitably have to be vigorous if not dominant personalities; but with the achievement of security and also with the growth of faculties, some boards of trustees and professors have preferred less forceful presidents. Harvard and Yale during the period before 1870 illustrate these conflicting views.

Throughout its early history, Harvard adhered to the concept of a weak presidency, with its chief executives acquiring their power from their personal strength and from their chairmanship of the Corporation (Quincy, 1840b). In the faculty (then called "the Immediate Government"), the president "always stood in the relation of *primus inter pares,* without other authority than that of a double vote, in case of an equivocate" (Quincy, 1840b). Early in the nineteenth century, however, the Corporation and the Board of Overseers decided that President John Kirkland, elected in 1810, should have added powers and responsibilities. "One of the most remarkable presidents that Harvard has ever had, and the best beloved" (Morison 1936c, p. 196), Kirkland exercised his augmented authority with extraordinary wisdom and graciousness; but the ensuing controversy about the right of faculty members to seats on the Corporation led a leading professor, Andrews Norton, to protest against the revised statutes that would expand the president's administrative scope. A passage from the pamphlet Norton published sharply stated a thesis that would later be expressed in scores of other institutions: "The provision made in the plan under consideration, to secure the faithful performance of the duties of the other officers, by the oversight, or as it is called, the 'complete visitatorial power of the President,' seems to imply that he alone can be interested in the prosperity of the institution; and that they are to be regarded as a set of idle day-laborers, who will not do their work faithfully without an overseer. Why is it presumed that the President will have this peculiar interest in the good of the College, not felt by the other officers? Suppose he is deficient in this respect; who is to be the overseer of the President? Or if that be effectually provided for, who are to oversee his overseers?" (Norton, 1824, p. 6). The statutes under discussion went into effect regardless of Professor Norton's protest, and the Harvard presidency has been of the "strong" variety ever since.

Yale meanwhile followed a course almost exactly opposite to Harvard's. The governing board allowed its first several heads little leeway; but when Thomas Clap succeeded to the office in 1740, he took command of a situation that clearly required firm and concentrated leadership. Almost single-handedly he beat off the attacks upon the College; but he made so many enemies both without and within the institution that he resigned in 1766. From 1778 to 1817, during the strong administrations of Ezra Stiles and Timothy Dwight the Elder, Yale so prospered that it surpassed Harvard in size and, to a degree, in general esteem. Under Jeremiah Day (1817–1846), however, there developed what one of his successors called "the Yale idea" of administration, involving the concept of a weak presidency, and Yale began to lose leadership to Harvard. "Too cautious, and too slow in his movements," Day characteristically deferred to his professorial associates in making decisions and "never used his official position and dignity in the way of interference with their individual duties or prerogatives" (Dwight, 1903, pp. 44–45). Thus the focus of Yale's operational control passed to its faculty, where it has remained ever since.

A "weak" presidency did not always or even usually mean, however, that power passed to professors. Often boards of trustees, groups of trustees, or individual board members acquired it by meddling in administration. Cheyney (1940) has described the deleterious effects of such trustee interference during the early history of the University of Pennsylvania; Schmidt (1930) has reported clashes at Columbia, Dickinson, Kenyon, and Virginia; and Becker (1944) has cited the resulting conflicts at Hamilton, Michigan, Wisconsin, and Union. Among these, the most protracted and influential conflict seems to have occurred at Hamilton. It continued during the fifteen-year administration of President Henry Davis (1817–1832), who had declined the presidency of Yale, his alma mater, to accept that of the new and promising college in central New York. Davis found an unruly student body, and when he disciplined its leaders, some of the trustees sided with them against him and the faculty. Later student disorders produced even worse interference, and the introduction of other issues into the quarrel cut the size of the student body from 110 to 9 and almost closed the college.

The pamphlet that Davis wrote about the vendetta (Davis, 1833) had wide circulation and influenced developments at Oberlin College in particular, the college in which trustee meddling in administration has been notably absent, at least since 1851. In that year, its governing board invited Professor Charles G. Finney to become president. As an alumnus of the academy that anteceded Hamilton and as a resident in the neighborhood of Hamilton during the Davis regime, Finney accepted the Oberlin invitation only on condition that he and the faculty would be free from trustee intrusion in the internal regulation of the College. "Not always, however," writes Schmidt (1930, p. 74), "were trustees so complaisant." Until the twentieth century, the majority of boards of trustees did not accept the concept that operational control should be the responsibility of administrators and their staffs, and some seem not to have accepted it even now.

That many old-time college presidents conceived of themselves as more than *primus inter pares,* there can be no doubt. Eleazar Wheelock, the first president of Dartmouth, has been described as follows by a Dartmouth historian: "His conception of an effective form of government for his undertakings was an autocracy, with himself in the role of a kindly but absolute despot. He regarded his subordinates as properly subject to his unquestioned authority. When opposed by them, even in matters of relative unimportance, his feelings rose almost to the point of vindictiveness. With entire honesty, he regarded those who opposed him as guilty of a dereliction of the moral law. He had so convinced himself of the righteousness of his projects that he came to regard opposition to himself as opposition to the cause of Christ" (Richardson, 1932a, p. 191). A sizable proportion of clerical presidents appear to have had ideas similar to Wheelock's, and even today one hears tales of comparable tyranny.

Such autocracy had its progenitors abroad. Just as American college presidents cannot match the record for longevity of English college heads, they have not surpassed them in one-man rule. Indeed, longevity and despostism seem not unrelated. America's record-holder for presidential tenure, Eliphalet Nott, who died in office in 1866 after directing the affairs of Union College for sixty-two years, failed to equal what seems to be the record sixty-three-year tenure of Joseph Martin Routh as president of Magdalen College, Oxford, beginning in 1791. Edward Hawkins, provost of Oriel College, Oxford, remained in office fifty-four years (1828–1882) until he reached ninety-five. Clare College, Cambridge, had only two masters between the Battle of Waterloo and the First World War, both serving into their nineties. And Francis Barnes earned the following reputation as master of Peterhouse, Cambridge: "In this capacity the college suffered under him for fifty years. He died on May 1, 1838, having attained the patriarchal age of ninety-five; and on the day of his death a Fellow of Peterhouse, not given, we are told, to extravagance in language, recorded in writing that 'the experience of fifty years has too lamentably demonstrated to the college how little he was qualified for the discharge of any duty which required the exercise of high notions of morality and a careful regard to what is just, decent, and venerable' " (Winstanley, 1935, p. 294).

This criticism cannot be dismissed as the judgment of a bitter faculty member. Comparable statements abound decrying the flagrant authoritarianism of the English college heads. Consider, for example, Richard Bentley, Master of Trinity College, Cambridge, from 1700 to 1742:

> For forty years . . . he kept not only the College but the University simmering and exploding with angry broils, punctuated by rival pamphlets and involving a ceaseless succession of lawsuits, an element which he enjoyed as a fish the water, or rather as a salamander the fire. His ability was consummate. Usually in the wrong, he usually had the best of it, and even when defeated for a while he rose again triumphant.
>
> Bentley's genuine desire for the progress of learning was largely stultified by another motive in his College policy. He was avaricious, autocratic, and self-interested . . . and regarded the Mastership as a means of obtain-

ing money and power for himself, often in unstatutable
and even dishonest ways. In most of these designs he
succeeded, although the Fellows managed to save their
beloved Bowling Green. His greed and love of rule so far
swallowed up his zeal as a reformer that he caused his
son to be elected a Fellow at the age of fifteen [Treve-
lyan, 1943, pp. 52, 55].

Twice the fellows of the College cited Bentley to the Visitor, but
twice he escaped penalty. The first time, he protracted the proceed-
ing so long that the Visitor died before he could read his prepared
statement vacating the office. The second time, the Visitor did de-
prive Bentley of his mastership, but, taking refuge in a legal tech-
nicality, "the old badger lay snug in his earth undrawn" and "spent
the last four years of his life unassailed" (Trevelyan, 1943, p. 64).

Barnes and Bentley may be extreme examples of bad college
heads, but even the best of them managed the affairs of their colleges
autocratically. Nicholas Murray Butler, for instance, has told a story
about Benjamin Jowett, the much-honored head of Balliol College,
Oxford, who died in 1893:

A few years ago he was one of those who extended
an invitation to the extension students to meet at Oxford.
Desiring to find lodgings for some of them at Balliol College, he suggested to the dons that it would be a graceful
thing for them to vacate their rooms for a fortnight, and
allow him to assign rooms thus set free to the visitors.
The dons demurred, looking upon such a proposition as
an invasion of their ancient and honorable privileges. The
Master, however, had other weapons at his disposal besides persuasion. He had sole control of the chapel services and of the buttery. The former he lengthened very
considerably, and the resources of the latter were reduced
to the lowest ebb by his connivance. This policy had the
desired effect, and the dons began to leave town for a
holiday [Butler, 1894].

Jowett is credited with embracing the administrative principle,
"Never retract. Never explain. Get the thing done and let them
howl" (Tollemache, 1895, p. 117). The point of view thus ex-

pressed represented that of not a few heads of Oxford and Cambridge colleges through the nineteenth century. Until quite recently, they had much more power than professors would tolerate in American college and university presidents.

The Age of Titans: 1870–1910

Autocrats such as Jowett coerced people into following them; leaders have the ability to persuade others to follow them. Prior to the Civil War, perceptive American college presidents—especially Francis Wayland of Brown—foresaw the coming of the industrial age, but their efforts to lead their institutions and others in preparing for it failed. After the Civil War, others had more success, in part because of the Land Grant College Act of 1862. Cornell University, the land-grant institution of New York State, opened in 1868 with Andrew Dickson White as cofounder, educational architect, and first president. White was committed to educational concepts that would be followed in other states and that would, moreover, influence all private as well as public higher education throughout the country.

White had taught history at the University of Michigan during Henry Philip Tappan's troubled years there, and he considered Michigan the first American university worthy of the name and Tappan the first broad-gauged administrator. White, however, surpassed Tappan, and his presidential colleagues at other institutions surpassed White. These included: Tappan's successor once removed, James Burrill Angell, who became president at Michigan in 1871 and who, during his thirty-eight years in office, led it to acknowledged primacy among the fast-growing state universities; Charles W. Eliot, who took the helm at Harvard in 1869 and who transformed it from a small, backward-looking college into a comprehensive university; Daniel Coit Gilman, who became president of the University of California in 1872 (after having been passed over, to its loss, by Yale, his alma mater) and who moved four years later to Baltimore to design and for twenty-five years to head the Johns Hopkins University, the initial pacemaker of the era of research; and—to abbreviate a formidable list—William Rainey Harper, who opened the University of Chicago in 1892 by at first bewitching and later goading John D. Rockefeller into pyramiding his original benefaction of $600,000 into a score of millions for financing actions undreamed of even by Harper's remarkable group of just-named colleagues.

Of the many characteristics of this brand of presidents only a few can be touched upon. All five just named, to begin with, were nonclerics. Princeton, Yale, most of the small colleges, and some of the state universities continued for several decades to select ministers as presidents; but even in institutions tightly controlled by churches other than the Roman Catholic, the office gradually became secularized. All except Harper and White gave whole-time attention to administration. The old-line presidents usually did considerable teaching, but the demands upon the energies of the avant garde presidents of this period made teaching impossible for most of them. White taught an occasional course in history, but Harper, a veritable dynamo, carried a heavier teaching load than most of his professorial colleagues. His successors at the University of Chicago have not usually taught, although for a period Robert Maynard Hutchins and pansophic Mortimer Adler conducted a joint Great Books seminar. President Conant also participated in a science seminar at Harvard during the 1940s. In general, however, the period 1870–1910 activated the changeover to whole-time administrators.

The towering presidents of the period were much more, however, than administrators. To a man, they studied higher educational history, observed European practices first hand, and proposed plans for meeting the rapidly changing educational requirements of the nation. In the best sense, they became social prophets; and by skillful public speaking, lucid writing, and adroit statesmanship, they persuaded their associates and the general public to share and to finance their visions. These encompassed a wide range of topics, but all radiated about the same axis, namely, the resolute aspiration to build not just colleges but, rather, great universities equal to those of Europe and especially of front-running Germany.

Despite Jefferson's hopes for the University of Virginia and Tappan's efforts at Michigan, the United States had no university worthy of the name until the opening of Johns Hopkins in 1876. For decades, discerning laymen and educators had been urging their establishment but to no avail. Hence all but small numbers of

American professional men got their training through the outmoded apprenticeship system; and those desiring advanced training in academic specialties went abroad to study, chiefly in German universities. National pride and national needs made this situation intolerable, but changing it required masterful statesmen-executives. Happily, the times produced a number of them, and after prolonged experimentation their efforts created a uniquely American type of capstone institution—the comprehensive university, combining the historic college with a graduate school and professional schools at the graduate and undergraduate levels in a single institution unmatched by the universities of other nations and of eariler historic eras. Conceiving, building, and learning how to manage this new structure constituted the basic task of administrators during the period from 1870 to 1910.

What has generally come to be called the nonacademic staff multiplied phenomenally in both variety and quantity during this era, and the academic staff began to proliferate hardly less extensively. Methods of operational control, however, did not start to change commensurately until later. The leading university presidents of the period possessed superlative administrative abilities and initiated significant operational procedures, but their pioneering ideas did not flower or spread widely until after they passed from the scene. By the close of 1909, all had died or retired. With them ended what seems to have been the most creative chapter to date of American college and university history.

Administrative Rationalization Since 1910

Present-day concepts of the presidency did not begin to take form in any social institutions until technological advance set in motion the structural leviathans of today. To operate them required experts who in industry—and now increasingly in higher education —have come to be called management. Frederick W. Taylor, one of the first exponents of the principles that the new genus adopted, began about 1878 making time-and-motion studies in simple mechanical processes related to the manufacture of steel. His successes led him to move on to more complex plant operations, then to office procedures, and finally to overall management problems. In 1911 appeared his history-making *Principles of Scientific Management.*

Taylor trained a cadre of disciples, and not long after the chartering of the Carnegie Foundation, its head, Henry S. Pritchett, former president of the Massachusetts Institute of Technology, invited one of them, Morris L. Cooke, to examine the operations of the physics departments of six universities and two small colleges. The Foundation published Cooke's findings and recommendations in 1910 under the title *Academic and Industrial Efficiency.*

Three fundamental ideas permeated Cooke's study, as they did also what came to be called the Taylor Movement and later management engineering: functional organization, efficiency, and operational research. The first of these concepts, functional organization, had been understood by military men of the ancient world and during the nineteenth century would be elaborated by the Prussian generals Karl von Clausewitz and Helmuth von Moltke. John Locke and Montesquieu had meanwhile advocated it for civil governments, and the United States Constitution adopted its major tenets in distinguishing among the executive, judicial, and legislative branches of the federal government. Among educational administrators, White had applied it at Cornell's opening by appointing a vice president and several other administrative associates, and so had Eliot just a few months after his inauguration at Harvard by creating the nation's first undergraduate deanship (Cowley, 1937). Management engineering did not strongly influence most administrators, however, until the 1930s; and at many institutions, it has still to pass beyond the elementary stage. Cooke's 1910 volume, however, can be said to have created the first academic awareness of the concept of functional organization.

The second basic Taylor concept, efficiency, derived from his demonstrations of the fact that most routine operations involved very considerable waste that could be eliminated by analysis and rationalization. The success of these activities in industry led other social institutions, including education, to become self-conscious about waste. The attitude germinated late in the century, as witness the fact that in 1899 William Rainey Harper and John Dewey each published a paper entitled "Waste in Education." The ideal of efficiency propagated slowly, however, and has not seriously affected higher education even yet. Its mere mention, moreover, has made some professors see red.

Interest in the third Taylor concept, operational research, also began before 1910. Eliot at Harvard and Harper at Chicago, in particular, filled their reports to their governing boards and to alumni with profuse statistical tables, and both attacked new problems by the research route. A few of their colleagues followed their example, but only since the 1960s has operational research (usually called institutional research) begun to be widely recognized as an essential ingredient of sound academic administration. It has by now advanced beyond the primitive state and seems certain to widen in scope and significance.

These management concepts resulted in a redefinition of the presidency beyond that of jack-of-all-trades or administrative titan. The duties of the college president have been variously categorized by management specialists, but the arrangement that appeals most to me identifies four areas of responsibility: superintendence, facilitation, development, and leadership in policy making. I discuss each of these functions in turn.

Superintendence. The statutes of every college and univesity name superintendence as the first duty of the chief administrative officer. Consider, for example, the statutes of Harvard, which read that the duty of the president is "to exercise general superintendence over all its concerns." This and similar statements in the ordinances of all colleges and universities mean that the president carries the ultimate responsibility for the work of the institution. College presidents do only a small fraction of this work themselves, but the trustees and the general public hold them responsible for everything done by everyone within the institution.

The chief executives of all enterprises have this same responsibility, but the college president's task of superintendence can hardly be matched for complexity and difficulty because he or she administers an institution with two extraordinary characteristics: Its chief product—education—defies measurement, and its major staff members—professors—defy regulation. On cannot easily supervise the work of people who believe supervision unnecessary and who, to boot, hate one's very existence, as do professors like the distinguished scientist on the faculty of the University of Chicago who, forty years ago, is reported to have walked by President Judson's home "each evening so that he could spit on that gentleman's sidewalk." One of Judson's successors observed that "academic communities, whatever their protestations to the contrary, really prefer anarchy to any form of government" (Hutchins, 1946, p. 400).

The great majority of professors today have a much better understanding of the importance and necessity of the superintendence function of administrators than did predecessors of earlier decades; but the day will never come when they will be as amenable to supervision as people in business, military, governmental, and most other organizations. They will continue to be individualists and they will never submit to taking orders. This means that in performing their superintendence function, college presidents must depend upon the arts of persuasion and not upon the power to command. The fact is that college presidents cannot command. If they tried to, they would immediately be engulfed in large quantities of scalding rhetoric. They must reason, negotiate, persuade—and these are time-consuming activities. To superintend effectively, a college president must give more time to the function than the chief executive of almost any other kind of institution.

Facilitation. In 1919, a group of professors established in New York City a new higher educational institution called the New School for Social Research, which, they announced, would exemplify sound educational and administrative ideas. Among other things, they eliminated the office of president and handled its work through committees of professors. The plan did not work, and after two years they abandoned it, just as other institutions have done, because they discovered that they needed someone to give continuous and undisturbed attention to what used to be called the ministerial function and what now more commonly goes by the name of facilitation. They saw that unless someone relieves professors of concern for the myriads of house-keeping minutiae involved in keeping a college in operation, they cannot perform their essential duties. In short, they needed a president if only as a facilitator to minister to their needs.

In large institutions, presidents have many assistants to help them with their facilitation responsibilities; but in most small colleges, presidents are so badly staffed that they must, unfortunately, give most of their time to ministerial activities. The presidents of such colleges and, indeed, of many large universities are so bogged down in housekeeping duties that they have little if any time left for the major presidential functions of development and of leadership in policy making. They are unable to be educators because many professors and some trustees conceive of them chiefly as "educaterers."

The catering obligations of the presidential office, even in a small college, should be handled by second-line administrators and not by the president. The facilitation activities of presidents should not extend beyond the development and establishment of a well-coordinated administrative structure. They should facilitate facilitation, but otherwise do nothing that can be done by some other member of the staff. Most of the time, they ought, figuratively if not literally, to have nothing on their desks but their feet and nothing on their minds but the basic problems of the enterprise and plans for resolving them.

I resigned my college presidency when I discovered that no one in my institution had any such conception of the presidency. Everyone expected me to be involved in the details of the institution, to see them whenever they wanted to be seen, to attend innumerable committee meetings, to introduce every visiting speaker, to greet every returning alumnus, and, to boot, to entertain all faculty members and their spouses at lunch or dinner at least once a year. Most college presidents continue to live this kind of a harried, hurried, routine-full life with the result that they are always weary, always short of time to do the crucial business that they alone can do, that is, to organize, to coordinate, and to carry forward the institution to new intellectual and social fronts.

Fortunately, some presidents have been able to persuade their boards and their faculties that they should have personal assistants of high competence, administrative or executive vice-presidents, and a full complement of administrative officers to handle routines. These chief executives—and as yet their numbers are few—are able to handle their positions properly and to put their energies where they ought to be put, that is, to development and policy making.

Development. Trustee and faculty committees seeking help

in finding college presidents usually emphasize the developmental function more than any other. Those from private colleges and universities want presidents who can develop new sources of income; those from state institutions want presidents who can develop more profitable relationships with legislatures. The discovery of new financial fountains and the improvement of existing ones is clearly a paramount kind of development whose crucial importance no sane person would deny, but the president's developmental function includes a good deal more than raising funds. Everyone but psychopathic misers knows that money is only a means and that preoccupation with finding and exploiting means to the neglect of the ends for which they are to be spent constitutes veritable folly. No college president with even a vague understanding of the office would think of limiting his or her developmental activities to money raising, and the best presidents engage in the enterprise with specific ideas about operations that need improving and about new programs that need initiating.

The president of a college is the only person who has a total view of its work. Professors see primarily their own specialties and have glimpses of those of their friends; department heads concentrate upon their departments and deans upon their colleges; and the trustees primarily give their attention to financial and material matters. No one but the president sees the whole, and hence he or she has the best opportunity and the most insistent obligation to plan for the future. To be equal to this opportunity and to this obligation the president must be a student of social and educational trends and apply his or her scholarship to the development of the institution at large.

The day has passed when college presidents can continue to be scholars in the academic disciplines of their teaching years. Today they must be students of higher education and of American society. In his *Autobiography,* William Lyon Phelps (1939) described the difference between the old-time college president and his modern successor. When he went as a young man to the office of President Noah Porter of Yale, Phelps usually found him reading Kant. When he later went to see Porter's successor, Timothy Dwight, he almost always found him reading the balance sheet. Today, however, professors ought to find presidents reading fundamental books and reports about the huge problems that American higher education faces: how and what to provide for the diversity of students in attendance, how to assure up-to-date instruction, how to raise salaries and also professorial efficiency, how to mesh more effectively the teaching and research duties of professors, how to serve society in the score of new directions called for by perceptive educators and laymen. These and associated problems will be solved by rule of thumb unless college presidents in particular conceive of their developmental responsibilities as much more extensive and even much more insistent than money raising.

Currently, American education changes with greater rapidity than ever in history, and its future depends upon the developmental planning of many kinds of people. Presidents will, of course, be prominent in such planning but they will be equal to the challenge before them only if they have the leisure to be careful and, indeed, profound students of higher education and of its place in American life. American higher education came of age during the last quarter of the nineteenth century when the five university presidents I mentioned earlier—White, Angell, Eliot, Gilman, and Harper—and their associates had the leisure, the vision, and the ability to meet the problems of their day. They faced less complex problems than those that today demand solutions. It will be catastrophic if presidents who today have the potential to be the seers and builders of our era are snowed under by administrative minutiae and the responsibilities of fund raising. They must be given the opportunity to give increasingly larger portions of their time to comprehensive developmental thinking.

Leadership in Policy Making. Developmental planning leads to the fourth function of college presidents—leadership in policy making. In the American system of academic government, trustees have the final word in determining policy, but most boards have learned from experience that they cannot legislate wisely without the active help of coordinate legislative bodies made up of faculty members, alumni, and students. Of these bodies, the faculty has the most knowledge and hence the most importance. Indeed, in the best-governed colleges and universities throughout America, faculties propose almost all academic policy to boards of trustees, but they largely depend upon the leadership of their presidents. Traditionally and usually legally, presidents have the right to propose policy, and they are expected to exercise it. All groups associated with colleges and universities look to them for such leadership, and no one respects those who do not exert it or whose proposals fall short of obvious needs.

Unfortunately, too few of the college presidents of today seem to be leaders. Too many are *headmen*. Earlier I defined a leader as an individual who has the ability to persuade others to follow him, and an autocrat as an individual who coerces people into following him. A headman either is satisfied with the status quo or cannot persuade people to go where he wants to go.

Educational autocrats are much less numerous than they used to be, and so I need not enlarge upon their nefarious ways. Headmen, however, abound and thus deserve considerable attention. Like Gilbert and Sullivan's description of the House of Lords, they "do nothing in particular and do it very well." They are the amiable but aimless fellows who never take risks, who abound in caution, who keep things going with reasonable smoothness but who have no developmental plans or programs. In a word, they are the stand-patters who hum to themselves "God's in his heaven, all's right with the world" or who just do not know how to organize people to change the things that they see are not well with the world.

Great colleges and universities have become great under the direction of brilliant leaders, whereas other institutions with comparable and sometimes greater potential have lagged or languished because of headmen. In 1869, Harvard shot forward to eminence in competition with Columbia, Pennsylvania, Yale, and other Eastern universities because of Eliot. Within ten years, Johns Hopkins threatened Harvard's leadership because of Gilman. Within twenty more, Chicago staggered the academic world because of Harper. The University of Michigan had become the greatest of the state universities by this time, clearly because of the impressive leadership of James Burrill Angell; and the University of California and the University of Minnesota challenged it when Benjamin Ide Wheeler and L. D. Coffman became their presidents. Beyond these large universities, consider such small colleges as Antioch, Bowdoin, Reed, and Swarthmore. Arthur E. Morgan at Antioch, William

DeWitt Hyde at Bowdoin, William T. Foster at Reed, and Frank Aydelotte at Swarthmore towered above their fellows; and their colleges zoomed to eminence under their leadership and primarily because of their leadership.

In sum, name a great American college or university, and you will find in its history a commanding leader or leaders who held its presidency. Name an institution with a brilliant but now-withered past, however, and you will probably have little difficulty in identifying the weak headmen presidents who have blocked its progress. Our American social system, as well as our political system, thrives or falters depending upon the quality of its leadership. Colleges and universities, focal institutions in the life of the nation, need especially strong leaders. By this I do not mean that presidents should autocratically make policy themselves. Instead, they should see that policy gets made—and made wisely—by faculty and trustees and that it then gets carried out.

Some professors and trustees mistakenly think that in order to govern an institution, they must administer it. But administration means getting the work of an institution done, and they can establish policy and hold administrators accountable for implementing policy without themselves doing any administrative work. Andrew Sloan Draper president of the University of Illinois from 1894 to 1904 and New York commissioner of education from 1904 to 1913, had an epigram that seems to me to apply here: "Groups legislate; individuals execute." Otherwise expressed, boards of trustees and faculty senates, as well as any institutional commissions or committees, have a role in policy making but not in policy execution. For the execution of policy as well as for leadership in recommending policy, they must hold the president responsible.

FOUR

Faculty Authority

*For determining the educational policy of a seat of learning
the faculties are the most important bodies.*

Charles William Eliot, 1908

Among the fallacies and half-truths surrounding American academic
government is that which insists that professors labor under undemocratic conditions. According to this line of thinking, faculty members,
whose work is basic to the institution, operate under the improper
authority of others—most notably trustees and presidents. Today,
however, the great majority of faculties have primary authority for
determining the educational and research policies of American colleges and universities. The history of faculty authority since the
Harvard and William and Mary bicameral charters of 1650 and
1693 shows the remarkable strides faculty members have made in
gaining this focal role in institutional government.

Faculty Participation at Harvard and
William and Mary

In 1650, Harvard initiated a hybrid scheme of academic
government. The Reformational concept from church polity that
laymen should oversee the operation of all social institutions, stem-
ming from Geneva, Leyden, and Edinburgh, had led to the earlier

71

creation of Harvard's Board of Overseers; but the idea that the "owning" corporation should be composed of academics had come from the medieval era via the colleges of Oxford, Cambridge, and Dublin. In drafting the 1650 charter, President Henry Dunster coupled the two concepts. "Dunster hoped," writes Morison (1936a, pp. 14–15), "to establish a self-perpetuating corporation of President, Treasurer, and five teaching or research fellows, who would hold their positions during good behavior; but this worthy ambition was thwarted by lack of funds." The smallness of the College and the deeply-embedded belief in the system of external visitors also hampered Dunster's plan. Hence his ardent desire to import the English system of trustees never took hold. Two vigorous efforts would later be made, however, to consummate Dunster's design. Both failed.

The first such effort occurred in 1721 when two members of the teaching staff claimed places on the Corporation. They achieved their objective chiefly because of the bitter politico-theological conflicts of the day, but they did not succeed in establishing the principle that, besides the president and treasurer, *only* faculty members should constitute the Corporation. Thus both teachers and ministers of neighboring towns served. This arrangement continued until 1779 when, as President A. Lawrence Lowell has written, "a notable change began." According to Lowell (1921a, p. 22): "The convulsions of the Revolution, the growth of the University, and the financial difficulties caused by the war, indicated to the Corporation, in the words of Quincy, 'the wisdom of selecting men of experience in business, and practically acquainted with public affairs.' The first man of the new type was James Bowdoin, elected in 1779; and since that time almost every choice was of this kind, the occasional clergymen elected being chosen not because [they were] incumbents of the neighboring parishes but for their personal value as counsellors."

Peace prevailed for almost half a century after Bowdoin's election, but in 1824—apparently to parry the "bothersome inquiries and reforms" concerning educational procedures initiated by the Corporation and the Board of Overseers (Morison, 1936c, p. 233)—the second effort began. The nine members of the instructional staff protested the virtual exclusion of faculty members from the Corporation. A war of pamphlets followed, one of the most strategic being written by Professor George Ticknor in opposition to the protest of his colleagues. Ticknor's opinions carried extraordinary weight because of his four years of study in Europe, his preeminence in Boston society, and the dramatic legal and statistical data he gathered to support his arguments (Ticknor, 1825). The controversy waxed hot but it subsided after the Overseers voted unanimously as follows in 1825:

> Resolved, first, That it does not appear to this board, that the resident instructors of Harvard University have any exclusive right to be chosen members of the Corporation.
> Resolved, secondly, That it does not appear to this board, that the members of the Corporation forfeit their offices by not residing in the College.
> Resolved, thirdly, That, in the opinion of this board, it is not expedient to express any opinion on the subject of future elections [Quincy, 1840b, p. 342].

Thus ended the dispute, and the problem of faculty membership on the Harvard Corporation has never again been seriously revived. It should be noted, however, that the resolutions did not prohibit faculty representation on the Corporation. Instead, the third signified in effect that future memberships would be determined pragmatically, that is, the best qualified individuals—in the judgment of the Corporation—would be co-opted. This judgment has led to the election of only one faculty member since the 1825 settlement, namely, a professor of history and dean who served from 1884 to 1886. The gradual but decisive abandonment of Dunster's plan to give the ultimate power in the government of Harvard to academics does not mean, it must be emphasized, that faculty members there do not participate in making its high policy. They do, but avenues other than Corporation control and membership have supplied the means.

I have earlier described how under the College charter of William and Mary its "Visitors and Governors" turned over the funds of the College to a corporation composed of the president and six professors. Beginning in 1729, as required in the charter, the faculty controlled the College funds; but the Board of Visitors had charter authority to write and revise the statutes at their pleasure, to select and elect the president, to choose the professors, to discipline both professors and students, to petition the General Assembly of Virginia for funds, and generally to manage the affairs of the College in all matters other than the control of the endowment. Under such an unrealistic plan of government, confusions and conflicts inevitably developed. These led the president and professors to address the Visitors in a 1768 document entitled "Memorial for the Better Government of the College." It did little to improve the situation because, by this time, an infinitely more disturbing cause of contention had arisen and taken precedence—the collision of colonial and British interests.

The president and professors, all clergymen of the Church of England and as such committed to continuing its tax-supported privileges as the established church of Virginia, found the leading visitors opposed to them on this count even more than on questions of academic government. This, for example, was the position taken by Jefferson, who considered his bill for separating church and state in Virginia one of his greatest achievements. Patrick Henry also served on the Board of Visitors during this period; and because of his hatred of British rule in Virginia and of supporting Church of England clergymen with public funds, he opposed the professors less on the issue of the financial control of the College than on the issue of its religious control. It was as an attorney in a suit brought by the professors and their clerical associates against the General Assembly of Virginia that, in 1765, he projected himself into eminence as a spokesman for the colonial cause by shouting his celebrated oratorical anticlimax: "Caesar had his Brutus; Charles the First his Cromwell; and George the Third may profit by their example" (Henry, 1891, p. 86).

After the Revolution, William and Mary encountered severe financial difficulties. The sovereigns whose names it bears had richly endowed it, but the war destroyed or canceled out most of these sources of revenue as well as the substantial properties bequeathed it by the famous English scientist, Robert Boyle. As governor of Virginia and hence member of the Board of Visitors, Thomas Jefferson, an alumnus, cooperated with the postwar president in revising the curriculum of the College, thereby setting it in the forefront of higher educational progress. However, the economic circumstances of the state, together with the removal of the capital to Richmond, prevented these pioneering efforts from thriving. The College prospered for a brief period just before the Civil War, but that calamity not only closed it but also devastated most of the beautiful buildings that Sir Christopher Wren had designed for it.

College work resumed in 1865; but low registrations, persistent economic troubles, and repeated agitations about moving the institution to Richmond undermined its stability. In 1881, therefore, it closed again. It reopened seven years later after the Commonwealth of Virginia agreed to assist temporarily. Finally, in 1906, it became a state institution. During the century and a quarter that elapsed between the end of the Revolution and 1906, the bicameral system remained in force. The president and professors (often the president alone) controlled the drastically diminished funds of the College; and, although it did not meet for long periods, the Board of Visitors continued to have legal status. A unicameral board, however, took over in 1906.

Early Faculty Governing Boards

The efforts of two Harvard tutors, beginning in 1721, to establish their right to ex officio Corporation membership did not succeed, but as early as 1692 the resident staff of the College had become a legislative and executive body. By 1720, it had acquired the name of "the Immediate Government" (Morison, 1936b, p. 538). A century or so later, President Quincy described its scope as follows: "The general superintendence of the seminary, the distribution of its studies, the appointment of Tutors in case of any sudden vacancy, and in short of all the executive powers relative to discipline and instruction, when not exercised by the Corporation itself, were carried into effect by the President, Professors, and Tutors, constituting a board denominated 'the Immediate Government'" (Quincy, 1840b, pp. 335–336).

Another Harvard historian has written that "the recognition of the College Faculty was formally made in 1725" and that "thus the Faculty came to be recognized as a distinct body, whose records date from September, 1725" (Thayer, 1898, p. 60). This quotation includes the term "the College Faculty"; but that name did not supersede "the Immediate Government" until 1825, the year in which ended the century-old debate over the right of the resident staff to seats on the Corporation. In the extensive reorganization that occurred that year, the Corporation and the Overseers promulgated a new edition of Harvard's "Statutes and Laws" which assigned the Faculty, under the direction of the President, responsibility for administering the admission of students, their discipline, their residential arrangements, and their instruction (*Statutes,* 1826). In all these matters, the Corporation and the Overseers, designated in the statutes as "the Government of the University," retained final authority. The following article, however, gave the faculty extensive powers in proposing changes in educational policy: "It being the design of the Government to have the Faculty invested with ample power to administer the instruction and discipline of the University, they are expected and desired to propose at all times to the Government, any laws or measures, which they may find requisite or useful for the effectual exercise of their functions" (*Statutes,* 1826, p. 7).

This and related statutes did no more than confirm practices long in effect, but others made two significant changes. First, Article Nineteen exempted the president "from such duties as are merely ministerial" so that he could devote his energies to the "wants of the whole Institution; to study its growth, the increase of its resources, the extension of instruction, and the better adaptation of it to the state of science and of society" (*Statutes,* 1826, pp. 7–8). This article committed Harvard to the principle of a "strong" presidency but it did not make the president an autocrat. Rather, it made him, in President Charles W. Eliot's words in 1869, "a constitutional" executive (Eliot, 1961, p. 22), checked on the one hand by the two legal entities (Corporation and Overseers) and on the other by the Faculties.

The second significant change related to internal structuring. Article Fifty-Eight established nine departments within the College and stipulated that they, like the already organized professional schools of medicine, law, and divinity (then called departments) would each be governed by a board of its full professors, and that such boards would have virtual control of the curricular and instructional affairs of their units. This article led to the appointment of professional school deans and of department heads, but both the president and the faculty members circumscribed their powers. Otherwise expressed, they too functioned as constitutional executives.

During his long administration of forty years (1869–1909), President Eliot steered Harvard through a minor reorganization in 1870 and a major one in 1890 (Wert, 1952), but these in no way impaired faculty governing prerogatives. Because of Eliot's forceful and austere personality, a faculty member now and then alluded to him as a tyrant, but the majority approved the concept of a strong presidency checked by well-defined faculty powers. Thus when, two years after Eliot's retirement, Cattell investigated faculty criticisms of American academic government, he received little support from the twenty-six Harvard professors who commented on his questionnaire (Cattell, 1913b).

Faculty participation in governing both Harvard and William and Mary began early because of their bicameral structuring. At the unicameral colleges (the great majority), it progressed at a slower pace because their charters gave legal entities (composed of nonacademics) complete authority and also because, until well into the nineteenth century, their smallness made the formal organization of faculties unnecessary. When, however, the number of professors increased beyond the two or three who had, along with a handful of tutors, made up the typical college faculty, some presidents began to share their responsibilities and their authority with their colleagues. This happened, for example, at Yale during the administration of President Jeremiah Day (1817–1846). The faculty then acquired "the dominant share in management" (Pierson, 1952, p. 129) that it has retained ever since. How this came about has been described by the son of one of Day's close professorial associates:

> It was [President Day's] opinion that the administration of the affairs of the institution would proceed more harmoniously if all questions connected with the policy to be pursued were discussed and decided in a

full meeting of all its officers. The action of the united
Faculty would carry more weight with the community
of students. The officers themselves, also, would feel more
thoroughly committed to assist in carrying out measures
that they had helped to shape, and which had been
voted upon and adopted after a discussion in which an
opportunity had been given them of expressing their
opinion. In this way . . . that method of college government came into distinct form known as "the government
of the Faculty." Henceforth it was understood that no
important action of any kind was to be taken, even by
the corporation, without the recommendation or assent
of the corps of instructors; in particular that no professor
or other officer was to be appointed without the consent
of those who were devoting their lives to the daily instruction and government of the institution, and with
whom any new office would be associated. This type of
government was at first, in great measure, peculiar to the
college; but its advantages have been seen to be so great
that it has been adopted in other institutions [Kingsley,
1879a, pp. 126–127].

Day's conception of academic government spread over the
country for the reason that, until the twentieth century, Yale appears to have produced a larger proportion of college presidents
than any other institution. Not all Yalemen who became presidents
went as far as Day, but the generalization can safely be made that,
as a group, they carried from their alma mater the doctrine that
faculty members should be active partners in the control of colleges
and universities. Most of them seem to have organized or supported
existing faculty governing bodies. Many of them met—as did the
Yale faculty—with great frequency. Thus at Hamilton, which
during the nineteenth century had five Yale alumni as presidents,
a leading faculty member registered his annoyance at the time they
took by proposing that his epitaph read "Died of Faculty Meetings"
(North, 1905, p. 60).

Because most of the writers of institutional histories have
neglected or touched lightly upon the topic, I have not been able
to discover when faculty governing structures originated in most of

them. The next several paragraphs, however, report some of the facts that I have been able to glean about the older ones.

The 1755 "Rules and Statutes" of the college that developed into the University of Pennsylvania opened with two sections devoted to the executive and legislative powers of the faculty. They gave it virtual control of the educational program of the institution under the leadership of the provost and subject to the endorsement of its "Ordinances and Regulations" by the board of trustees. They also required the faculty to meet at least once a fortnight or oftener if "any two members" demanded. Incidentally, these statutes introduced the term *faculty* into the nomenclature of American higher education. Harvard did not adopt the term until seventy years later (Montgomery, 1900).

Princeton operated for forty years without a faculty organization, but in 1788 the trustees "resolved and ordered, that the president and professors form the faculty, and that the government of the College be vested in the said faculty, whose authority shall extend to every part of the discipline, except the final expulsion of a student" (Kirkpatrick, 1931, p. 78). The bicentennial historian of Princeton has commented, however, that for a period (he gives no dates) the trustees assigned the faculty "no more authority than was absolutely necessary, and that grudgingly." He continues: "Their writings were scanned anxiously for any signs of unorthodox opinion; their unpublished lecture notes were examined; their power of discipline was limited to admonitions and suspension, the right of expulsion being reserved for the board; their minutes were subjected to close scrutiny; one committee of the trustees pried into instruction in the college, another into discipline" (Wertenbaker, 1946, p. 121).

The Columbia faculty, not long after the termination in 1787 of the New York State dispute concerning the status of the College, organized as the Senate Academicus, a name with Scottish and Dutch antecedents. No Columbia historian whom I have read traces the course of this early governing body, but apparently it languished, probably being replaced by another structure. In any case, during the last years of the administration (1864–1889) of President F.A.P. Barnard, a Yale alumnus, Columbia gradually changed from a small college into a university. The growing pains associated with the conversion led in 1889 to a proposal that a university senate be organized to coordinate the activities of the bodies earlier formed for governing the various instructional units of the institution. As one of his first acts, therefore, Barnard's successor, Seth Low, brought together all members of the several faculties in a series of meetings to discuss the idea and related topics. From these 1890 sessions came the University Council, an advisory body to the president and board of trustees (Burgess, 1913). It proved unsatisfactory, and hence two years later, in 1892, the Board amended its statutes giving the Council "definite legislative and administrative powers which are substantially those still in full force and effect" (Special Trustee Committee, 1957, pp. 38–39).

Observe the dates cited—1890 and 1892. The period of three years which they encircle has strategic importance in the history of American academic government. Harvard went through a basic reorganization in 1890, and later I shall be describing a significant change made at Cornell in 1891 which had immediate repercussions at Stanford and the next year at the University of Chicago. Before expanding upon these developments, however, the evolution of faculty governing bodies in two or three other old-line colleges must be considered.

As already mentioned, Eleazar Wheelock, the founder and first president of Dartmouth, ruled it autocratically. During his regime, however, the College had only one professor who, with the president and two or three tutors, constituted the teaching staff. Sometime during the administration of John Wheelock (1779–1817), Eleazar's son and successor, the addition of several professorships led to the formal organization of the faculty, and by trustee resolution in 1811 it acquired "parity with the president" in controlling the internal operations of the College (Richardson, 1932b, p. 820). Like most faculties of the period, it should be observed, it gave most of its attention to problems of discipline. Thus student pranks and general hell-raising constituted the chief business of the fifty-one meetings held during the year 1828–29 and of the sixty-eight held four years later (Richardson, 1932a, p. 461).

Union College, established in Schenectady, New York, in 1795, early organized a faculty governing body, but Eliphalet Nott, who served as its president for sixty-two years beginning in 1804, scuttled it. When asked late in his career about faculty meetings, Nott replied: "I remember having one once, some thirty-six years ago, but I never wish to have another" (Dwight, 1903, p. 110). Union stood high among American colleges during Nott's regime, but it declined rapidly thereafter. "Because he centered all authority in himself," writes one of his biographers, "his faculty and his trustees were unable to produce the leadership needed to fit Union College into the industrial America which grew up following the Civil War" (*Union Worthies*, 1954, p. 13). Other institutions, it should be remarked, have had much the same experience not only because of autocratic presidents but also because of power-hogging board chairmen, deans, and department heads, or trustee and faculty oligarchies.

I might enlarge here upon faculty government at Oberlin, Amherst, the University of Virginia, and elsewhere, but perhaps the examples just given suffice to establish the fact that faculty participation in American academic government has a venerable history. At some of the older colleges, it did not have smooth sailing, a generalization that also applies to institutions established later.

Later Structures

By 1867, Thomas Wentworth Higginson, a prominent literary figure and Harvard alumnus, declared: "What we need is a university." "Whether this," he continued, "is to be a new creation, or something laid at Cambridge, or New Haven, or Ann Arbor, is unimportant. Until we have it somewhere, our means of culture are still provincial" (Higginson, 1867). For almost a century, a number of colleges had been calling themselves universities, but few knowledgeable persons took the designation seriously. Some had organized loosely affiliated, low-level professional schools, but none provided significant graduate instruction or sponsored research as an essential function. Thus when Higginson wrote the statement quoted above, he expressed an opinion with which no one disagreed. Nor did anyone argue when the following year Mark Pattison, a leading Oxford figure, asserted that the United States "has no universities" (Pattison, 1868, p. 150).

Hardly before the ink had dried on these assertions, however, universities began to come to life in all parts of the country. Cornell, the first of a series of newly created private universities, opened in 1868, to be followed by Johns Hopkins in 1876, Catholic University and Clark in 1889, Stanford in 1891, and Chicago in 1892. Concurrently, a number of long-established colleges located in or near large cities began to transform themselves into top-rank institutions: Harvard upon the accession of Charles W. Eliot to its presidency in 1869, Yale upon resolution of its legal entity in 1872 that the College had attained the form of a University, Pennsylvania under the leadership of Provost William Pepper who took office in 1880, Columbia that same year upon the establishment of its Graduate Faculty of Political Science, and—to abbreviate a sizable list—Princeton during the administration of James McCosh which began in 1868. Concurrently, the state universities, directly or indirectly affected by the Land Grant College Act of 1862, commenced the spectacular growth that has continued ever since. California, Michigan, and Wisconsin rose to eminence first, but soon a score of others emulated their size and quality. In sum, American universities came of age during the last third of the nineteenth century.

All the new institutions among the three groups just identified immediately or soon after their opening organized faculty governing bodies. Herewith I describe some of them, beginning with Cornell.

Andrew Dickson White, Cornell's first president, had graduated from Yale and hence knew about the prominence there of the faculty in its government. As a wide-ranging student of higher education, moreover, he knew of the situation at Harvard and at other institutions. From the beginning, therefore, he worked closely with the faculty and deferred to its judgment when it disagreed with him (White, 1907). Not until several years after White's retirement from the presidency, however, did faculty participation in governing Cornell become formalized (Becker, 1944). This occurred in 1891 when the Board of Trustees issued new statutes codifying recommendations made by a trustee committee. A historian of Cornell has described the spirit of the committee report and of the resulting statutory provisions:

The relation which the faculty should sustain in the administration of the university was so conceived as to give great dignity and importance to their deliberations. That system of college government was criticized in which the president appropriates the main functions of administration, originates action, and is responsible alone for whatever he may do, while the faculty have no share, or only a limited one, in determining the courses of study and the character of the work that shall be done in the university. The faculty "are not merely advisors, but legislators," they should have stated meetings for the purpose of conducting the general administration of the institution and memorializing the trustees, discussing general questions of educational policy, and presenting papers upon special subjects [Hewett, 1905, pp. 143–144].

The new Cornell statutes provided for an academic senate as the general faculty legislative body, and its establishment directly influenced the plan of faculty government adopted at the University of Chicago, which opened the following autumn. William Rainey Harper, Chicago's fabulous first president and designer of its precedent-shattering program, had planned a policy-making council made up of a handful of professors of his own choosing, but two of the distinguished professors he attracted to Chicago from Cornell objected and proposed a senate like that just created in Ithaca. Harper promptly remade his plan and organized both a senate and a council. The former, to be chaired by the president and to consist almost entirely of "head professors" or department heads, would handle educational policy. The latter, also chaired by the president and composed of deans and other administrative officers, was to handle housekeeping problems "subject to review and reversal by the Senate, until the Board of Trustees decides otherwise" (Goodspeed, 1916, p. 140). The plan also provided for a series of administrative boards with immediate jurisdiction over the more important specialized functions of the institution.

Harper ran into widely publicized difficulties in the Bemis case in 1895 (Hofstadter and Metzger, 1955) and in the resignation of John Dewey in 1904 (McCaul, 1961), but it seems clear that he did not deserve the epithets of "czar," "tyrant," and "autocrat" leveled at him by both academics and the press (Mayer, 1941). A Yale Ph.D. and formerly a professor there, he believed firmly that faculty members should share in institutional management, but his vast plans for the new university and his titanic dynamism sometimes conflicted with his latent aversion to controversy (Goodspeed, 1928) and with what John D. Rockefeller called his "exquisite personal charm" (Rockefeller 1909, p. 202). "A born diplomat" (Goodspeed, 1916, p. 202), he did not always say no clearly to faculty proposals with which he did not agree, and some professors incorrectly interpreted his comments as approval. The resulting confusions probably provoked the following paragraph in a paper he wrote not long before his death in 1906 at forty-nine:

> The college presidency is a profession in which a large percentage of one's time and energy is occupied in saying no. Real risk is taken when, for the sake of variation, even in a small proportion of these cases a kindly interest is shown. To be brutal may not be so good a policy at the time, but in the long run it probably pays. One of the most distinguished university presidents now living [undoubtedly President Eliot of Harvard] was noted during a large portion of his career for his extreme brutality. It is altogether probable that the high success which he has achieved is due in no small measure to this fact. He is said to have become greatly softened in his later years. One can afford to practice a policy in later years which would spell ruin in the early career [Harper 1938, p. 180].

The paper from which this passage has been taken did not get into print until more than thirty years after Harper's death, but ever since first reading it in 1938, I have thought it one of the most fertile discussions of the American academic presidency yet published. Among other topics, it discusses faculty participation in academic government, and therein Harper recorded the principle he followed at Chicago: "In educational policy he [the president] must be in accord with his colleagues. . . . He cannot secure forward movement except with the cooperation of those with whom he is associated" (p. 182).

I have digressed a bit to discuss Harper's ideas and his application of them not only because of their inherent significance but also to relate his career with that of another man in a crucial presidency influenced by Cornell: David Starr Jordan of Stanford.

Jordan, a Cornell alumnus, greatly admired Andrew Dickson White and desired to model the government of Stanford after that of his alma mater. He undoubtedly knew about the organization of the Cornell Senate in 1891, the year the new university founded by Senator and Mrs. Leland Stanford opened. He therefore immediately organized a University Council made up of himself and all professors and associate professors, and he also established a dozen or so faculty committees. The stipulations of the founding grant, however, assigned to the Stanfords during their lives all the powers of trusteeship and hence of control (*Register*, 1891–92). Senator Stanford died twenty months after the opening of the University, but Mrs. Stanford survived him by almost twelve years. For a decade of the intervening period she literally, but not always wisely, ruled the institution through Jordan (Elliott, 1937).

Jordan, a gifted biologist and publicist, did not compare as an administrator or as a leader with the towering university presidents of the period. He did, however, believe in faculty governing rights, even though his failure to prevent Mrs. Stanford from dismissing Professor Edward A. Ross in 1900 (Hofstadter and Metzger, 1955) earned him the reputation among professors over the country "as having horns and a tail" (Zinsser, 1940, p. 191). Not until Mrs. Stanford's retirement from her sole trusteeship in 1903 could his early hopes mature. Faculty participation then began in earnest when, early the next year, the nonoperative board of trustees adopted "Articles of Organization of the Faculty." The document created an academic council, faculty members of all ranks having suffrage therein. This body the board "vested with all the powers and duties usually vested in the faculties of similar institutions" including "all University regulations, statutes, and rules within the provinces of the Faculty." Only "requirements of admission, the course of study," and "the conditions of graduation" would be subject to Board approval" (Stanford University, 1920, p. 9).

Before moving on to the situations in two or three state universities, something needs to be said about the governance pol-

icies of Daniel Coit Gilman, the second president of the University
of California and later the architect of the history-making program
at Johns Hopkins University. Recommended to the Johns Hopkins
board of trustees by the presidents of Cornell, Harvard, Michigan,
and Yale independently of one another, Gilman moved to Baltimore
to organize the first American institution to emphasize graduate
instruction and research as core university functions. During the two
years before the opening of the new and richly endowed institution,
Gilman hunted out the best academic brains available in Europe
and the United States. Some of those to whom he proffered positions
turned him down, but The Hopkins, as it immediately came to be
called, opened in 1876 with a distinguished faculty of six full professors and a dozen others called associates. Meanwhile, during a
European hunt for staff, Gilman drew up a plan in 1875 for the
organization of the University which included the following delinea-
tion of faculty powers: "The Faculty shall determine the courses of
instruction to be established; the conditions of admission, promotion,
and graduation; the rooms to be assigned to the different instructors;
and the regulations requisite for the promotion of order and morality among the students and for the encouragement of study" (Corson, 1951). Because of the smallness of the faculty, Gilman worked
with it informally over the first several years, but in 1880 the board
of trustees created the Academic Council, which Gilman had also
proposed in his 1875 organizational plan. It assumed "the chief
responsibilty for guiding the internal affairs of the University"
(Hawkins, 1960, p. 213) but its membership included only Gilman
and the professors, later continuing to be six in number until 1883
and not increasing beyond nine until the nineties (Hawkins, 1960,
p. 126). The voicelessness of the younger men caused some friction
and seems to have helped to create the circumstances that induced
eighteen members of the Hopkins faculty in 1913 to trigger the
series of events that led to the organization of the American Association of University Professors (AAUP).

Because of its unprecedented and successful emphasis upon
graduate teaching and research, Johns Hopkins almost immediately
came to be called the nation's "first real university" (Hawkins, 1960,
p. 308). Meanwhile, however, "the real beginnings" of the American system of state universities had been made at the University of

Michigan (White, 1907, p. 292). As recorded earlier, a number of states had established institutions that became state-supported universities, but until after the Civil War they typically operated without regular legislative grants and generally under partial church control. For a time, the University of Michigan struggled under these limitations but it surmounted them earlier than its sister institutions. For about a half a century, therefore, it stood out as the chief exemplar of "the state university idea." The definitive change-over occurred in 1852 when Henry Philip Tappan, an erstwhile Congregational minister who had taught briefly at what later developed into New York University, became the first president of the struggling institution.

The roots of the University of Michigan reach back to the Catholepistemiad or University of Michigania chartered by the Territorial Legislature in 1817. But that bizarre scheme had never taken effect, and twenty years later the legislature superseded it by passing "the organic act" which created the present university. The 1837 charter identified three substructures, called departments (Literature, Science, and the Arts; Law; and Medicine), all three of which were to admit students directly from the still-primitive secondary schools of the state. The "immediate government" of these units the Act "entrusted to their respective faculties" under the regulatory direction of the Board of Regents. Despite these arrangements, only the Literary Department opened by 1842, followed in 1850 by the Medical Department and in 1859 by the Law Department.

One of the most influential failures in the history of American higher education, Tappan had been invited to Ann Arbor by the Regents because of the monumental program that he had described in his recently published book, *University Education* (1851). Had he succeeded in making the University of Michigan what he envisioned, American education would almost certainly have followed a course of development quite different from that adopted. Because of his ineptness in public relations, however, and also because of deeply entrenched contrary forces, his focal plan of killing off the historic four-year colleges and of pushing back general education into the secondary schools aroused intense opposition. The Regents therefore dismissed him in 1863, but during his eleven years in office he staunchly supported the concept of faculty participation in the government of the University.

Although the 1837 charter entrusted the immediate government of the University to the three separate faculties it created, Tappan brought all professors together for joint meetings. This led the Board of Regents in 1859 to take the position that, in order "to represent the University in general as one institution, the professors of the several Faculties shall constitute a University Senate" (Hopkins, 1942, p. 231). Because of the increasing size of the institution, an executive committee called the Senate Council took over most of these functions in 1906, but the full senate retained the right to review and to revise the council's actions (Hopkins, 1942). Such evolutionary facts, however, are not important in this context. The point to be stressed is that the Michigan professoriate has been involved in governing the University throughout its history.

The observation just made also applies to the University of Wisconsin. Organized in 1848, soon after the admission of the state to the Union, it admitted its first students the next year under legislation implementing the stipulation in the state constitution that "a state university" be established. On the topic of faculty governing powers, the statutes copied the Michigan Act of 1837 almost verbatim: "The immediate government of the several colleges shall be entrusted to their respective [four] faculties," and so forth (Boell, 1961). Because of the smallness of the institution, unit faculties did not take form until the late nineties, but in 1851 the full faculty of the University organized formally and held weekly meetings "for a great many years" (Curti and Carstensen, 1949a, p. 173). The complex developments thereafter need not here be detailed, but the circumstances leading to a historic 1894 action of the Board of Regents must be recounted.

In 1892, Wisconsin attracted from Johns Hopkins the brilliant young economist Richard T. Ely, a supporter of the German historical school of economics (Gabriel, 1940). Soon his writings bestirred a member of the Board of Regents to accuse him in the press of "utopian, impractical, or pernicious doctrines" and, in particular, of encouraging strikes and boycotts (Curti and Carstensen, 1949a, p. 509). The charges fell upon fertile ground because of the panic of 1893, the unrest and series of strikes that followed in its wake, and the federal injunction issued two weeks previously against the railroad strikers in Chicago. Ely contemplated a libel suit, but the Regents took the situation in hand and appointed a committee to investigate the charges. It not only completely exonerated him but, no less important, also submitted a report that included the following affirmation of academic freedom:

> We could not for a moment think of recommending the dismissal or even criticism of a teacher even though some of his opinions should, in some quarters, be regarded as visionary. Such a course would be equivalent to saying that no professor should teach anything which is not accepted by everybody as true. . . . We cannot for a moment believe that knowledge has reached its final goal, or that the present condition of society is perfect. We must therefore welcome from our teachers such discussions as shall suggest the means and prepare the way by which knowledge may be extended, present evils . . . removed and others prevented.
>
> We feel that we would be unworthy [of] the position we hold if we did not believe in progress in all departments of knowledge. In all lines of academic investigation it is of the utmost importance that the investigator be absolutely free to follow the indications of truth wherever they may lead [Curti and Carstensen, 1949a, p. 525].

The Board of Regents adopted its committee's report and, to boot, passed a resolution censuring its member who had caused the furor. Like all other colleges and universities, the University of Wisconsin has had governmental problems, but the position of its Board of Regents in the Ely case has been a beacon that has helped to light the road to their relatively smooth resolution. Thus only four of the thirteen Wisconsin professors who responded to Cattell's questionnaire of 1911 endorsed his revisionist proposals (Cattell, 1913b). The setting up two years earlier of a Regents-Faculty conference committee at the suggestion of President Charles R. Van Hise also undoubtedly contributed to this result (Curti and Carstensen, 1949b).

Among the great present-day state universities of the Middle West, only Michigan and Wisconsin had become well enough established to be invited, along with twelve other institutions, to be charter members of the Association of American Universities upon its organization in 1900. After slow starts, however, a number of institutions moved ahead rapidly on all fronts, including faculty participation in the government. On the latter score, developments at one of them, the University of Illinois, illustrate their progress.

Because Jonathan Baldwin Turner of Illinois had been a prime mover in getting Congress to pass the Land Grant College Act of 1862, and because he campaigned for the higher education of "the industrial classes," the Illinois legislature adopted his suggestion and called the land-grant institution that it created in 1867 "The Illinois Industrial University." Further, fearing that its executive head "would lust after the conventional studies of metaphysics and the classics" (Nevins, 1917, p. 42), the board of trustees gave him the title of Regent rather than that of President. This title continued in use until 1894, nine years after the legislature—chiefly because of alumni pressure—changed the name of the institution to the University of Illinois (Nevins, 1917). Meanwhile, faculty participation in government had been solidly established by regulations adopted by the board of trustees early in 1869. These included the following provisions:

1. The government of the Illinois Industrial University shall be and is hereby committed to the Regents and Faculty, who shall, as soon as possible, prepare a system of rules for the proper government of the students, and maintenance of order in the University, and, from time to time, such additional rules as may be found necessary, and such rules shall be in force on the authority of the Faculty until they can be approved by the Trustees.

2. The Faculty shall meet statedly at such times as they shall appoint for the transaction of business pertaining to the management of the internal affairs of the University; and all questions coming before such meetings shall be determined by the votes of a majority

of the members, with the concurrence of the Regent
[Board of Trustees of the Illinois Industrial University,
1869, pp. 90–91].

Illinois remained small until the arrival in 1894 of Andrew
Sloan Draper, its first administrative head to be called *president*.
During his ten years in office, the number of students grew from
810 to 3,593 and the number of colleges from four to ten, three
of the new ones being located in Chicago. Concurrently, the biennial
legislative appropriation increased from just below $300,000 to
almost $1.25 million (University of Illinois, 1929). In internal gov-
ernment, the University made equally significant advances. A year
after Draper took office, the board adopted a "Plan of Government
of the Instructional Force of the University of Illinois" (Board of
Trustees of the University of Illinois, 1896), which he prepared for
its Committee on Instruction. It confirmed the traditional rights of
the general faculty to "exercise general legislative functions touching
the education policy of the University or any particular matter
incidental thereto." It similarly endorsed the work of the unit faculties, codifying their power to "exercise legislative functions touching
any matter appertaining exclusively to the internal work of that
College and the progress of students therein." Thus the Illinois
professoriate achieved prerogatives in academic government comparable to those of other leading institutions over the country.

Faculty Powers

Thus far this chapter has primarily been concerned with the
beginnings of faculty governing structures in a dozen or so front-
running institutions. This final section canvasses the evolving powers
of such structures. Almost every statement made in what follows
can, I know, be challenged with contrary examples; but I believe
that I faithfully report developments in the better-governed institutions. From these efforts came practices that generally, if also slowly,
have been copied over the country.

Consider, first, student discipline. Most of the documents
quoted earlier refer to this topic for the reason that, before the rise

of athletics and other present-day diversions, sporadic deviltry provided students with almost the only available relief from the oppressive monotony of a dehydrated curriculum and of stark concepts of teaching and college life. Pranks like stealing the clapper of the college bell, setting fire to privies, and rolling heated cannon balls down dormitory corridors were commonplace; but every few years outbreaks of more serious import rived the air of most colleges. Between 1766 and 1841, for example, Harvard experienced nine such upheavals. Some resulted from the poor food provided in commons. These included the "Great Butter Rebellion" of 1766 which "took more than a month to quell" (Quincy, 1840b, p. 99), the "Bread and Butter Rebellion" of 1805, and the "Rotten Cabbage Rebellion" of 1807. Student dissatisfaction with the prevailing methods of disciplining and teaching sparked others, and one of these—the "Great Rebellion" of 1823—helped bring about the Harvard reorganization of 1825 cited earlier.

Until well into the nineteenth century, the legal entities of most institutions projected themselves into the disciplinary actions made necessary by these explosions, but in the course of time it became apparent to the more perceptive of their members that they had better let "the immediate government" deal with the miscreants. Some boards, like that at Hamilton, learned the wisdom of that judgment the hard way; and a few backward boards still, on occasion, meddle with student discipline. By and large, however, trustees keep their hands off even under pressure. An incident at Dartmouth and another at Harvard illustrate the change.

For a long period, Dartmouth students chastened their unpopular teachers by means of a technique called "horning," namely, relays of students blowing tin horns continuously day and night outside the homes of the victims until they cried for mercy or packed up and departed. The horning that occurred in 1896 led the president and the faculty to decide that such barbarism would have to stop. Their investigation identified seven leaders whom they forthwith dismissed. Parents and alumni protested vigorously to the board of trustees, but the president and the faculty stood firm (Richardson, 1932b). Thus horning ended at Dartmouth, and faculty authority over student discipline has not since been questioned there.

The Harvard incident has been admiringly described by a German philosopher who taught as an exchange professor during two of the last years of President Eliot's administration:

> Two students, members of the two university boat crews which were just then making ready for the annual contest with Yale, had been suspended for a serious violation of the University rules, and this dropped them from their crews almost on the eve of the race. The victory over Yale, until then joyfully and confidently expected, was put in question. An extraordinary excitement took hold of alumni and students, and turned against Eliot. Then President Roosevelt and First Assistant Secretary of State Bacon, both of them loyal Harvard men, telegraphed to Eliot expressing their astonishment at the severity of the punishment and asking him to modify it so as to permit the men to row. Eliot telegraphically declined the request "since both men did a dishonorable thing" [Kuehnemann, 1909, pp. 81–82].

Robert Bacon wired Eliot in his capacity as a Harvard overseer, and President Roosevelt had been an overseer and would be again. Such pressure could have persuaded a less sturdy administrator to urge his faculty to submit and thus to eviscerate two centuries of progress. But literally no one could persuade Eliot, at once a New England Puritan and a Boston Brahmin, to retreat from a judgment he considered legally and morally sound. His unwavering stand strengthened faculty control of student life not only at Harvard but also generally. Other presidents could cite Eliot's example—and some undoubtedly did—when trustees or alumni barraged them in comparable situations. "So shines a good deed in a naughty world" (*Merchant of Venice*, 5:1:90), especially when performed by a pivotal personage.

Over questions of admissions and degree requirements, few faculties appear to have had to fight with legal entities for ascendancy. On both counts, however, all have sometimes had to resist the goadings of individual trustees and alumni (if not groups of both) who have sought favors for promising athletes or for the offspring of friends, clients, or customers. Seldom, however, do these problems go to faculty governing bodies for decision. Administrators handle them resolutely or otherwise, depending upon the stiffness of their backbones. Those who capitulate lose the respect and support of their faculty colleagues; but, regardless, astute legal entities have unreservedly assigned to faculty governing boards the right to legislate conclusively concerning both admissions and degree requirements.

Nor do wise trustees today check personally on the teaching effectiveness of faculty members. Observe the qualification "today." Until the latter half of the nineteenth century, the governing boards of Harvard, Yale, Dartmouth, and undoubtedly other colleges appointed committees to examine students directly or to listen to the oral questions of their teachers. Harvard students called these ordeals "sitting solstices," but faculty members probably thought of themselves as sitting on hot seats (Morison, 1936c). With the reduction in the number of ministerial trustees (that is, of those who could give up two weeks or more each spring to be examiners) and also with the introduction of written examinations and the rapid proliferation of knowledge, this long-established practice disappeared. It seems safe to predict that this sector of the academic domain will continue unchallenged in the hands of the professoriate.

A comparable prediction cannot be made about curriculums or about instructional materials and methods. In these matters forward-looking boards of trustees of institutions unconnected with organized religion have long given faculties free rein, but churches have very considerable control in the colleges they control or help support. Accreditation associations and learned societies, however, have become so powerful that they dominate substantial segments of the educational programs of all American colleges and universities. Be this as it may, the generalization can here be made that, by and large, legal entities have ceded their educational powers to faculty governing bodies which have assented to their control by various external groups. Otherwise stated, if there be culprits here, they have not recently—except in a diminishing number of retarded institutions—been boards of trustees.

To the contrary, perceptive trustees, have, by and large, bent over backwards in their efforts to reduce if not to eliminate the causes of faculty resentments and protests. Exemplifying the increasingly dominant point of view of trustees, Charles A. Coolidge, while a member of the Harvard Corporation, gave the following advice to new trustees: "I can sum up the [rules of conduct for trustees] by a big 'don't'—DON'T MEDDLE. . . . You must realize that you are not expert in education. . . . As I see it, the job of a lay member of a governing board . . . boils down to this: Do your best to see that the organization is good, that it is well manned, and that it runs smoothly—but don't try to run it. Make your decisions on evidence furnished you by experts, and not on your own imperfect knowledge of academic affairs. If you do that, I think you will be of real help to the President, and that in my view is what you are there for" (Special Trustee Committee, 1957, pp. 23–24). Laird Bell, a former chairman of the boards of the University of Chicago and of Carleton College and for a period a member of the Harvard Board of Overseers, has written to the same effect: "Trustees had best bear in mind that they could not be a college faculty and that they should keep their hands off education. . . . Once overall policy is decided it ought to be true that the educational experts should determine how the policy is to be implemented" (Special Trustee Committee, 1957, p. 24). Bell's complete statement does include a caveat of enormous importance, namely, that trustees must not abdicate their legal responsibility for the educational programs of their institutions. Yet, even in this important area, trustees are advised to show constraint, as attested by the following statement from a committee of the board of trustees of Columbia University: "The legal supremacy of trustees and their final authority to act as they wish is unquestioned, but the most experienced trustees are themselves constantly warning their newer colleagues that overactivity in certain areas—particularly in the area of education itself—is as great a sin against the modern spirit of trusteeship as is neglect" (Special Trustee Committee, 1957, p. 9).

Presidents have likewise taken an amelioristic position toward faculty authority, Stanford's David Starr Jordan going so far as to propose that "the office of president . . . must be considered a temporary stage." He did not foresee its disappearance, however, until American higher education had achieved "permanent form." So long, he observed, as colleges and universities have "a forward urge" presidents will be needed. "We cannot do without them yet" (Jordan, 1922b, pp. 458–459).

President Jacob Gould Schurman of Cornell, a Canadian who had studied for several years in Britain and Germany and who admired their methods of academic government, agreed with Jordan about the at-least-temporary indispensability of presidents, but he believed that faculties should be represented by some of their own members on legal entities. After broaching this idea in his report for 1910 (Schurman, 1910), he spelled it out two years later, declaring: "What the American professor wants is the same status, the same authority, the same participation in the government of his university as his colleague in England, in Germany, and in other European countries already enjoys. He chafes at being under a board of trustees which in his most critical moods he feels to be alien to the Republic of Science and Letters. . . . The only ultimately satisfactory solution of the problem of the government of American universities is the concession to the professoriate of representation in the board of trustees or regents and [that] these representatives of the intellectual, which is the real life of the university, must not be mere ornamental figures; they should be granted an active share in the routine administration of the institution" (Schurman, 1912, pp. 9–10).

Because of Schurman's absence on a sabbatical, the Cornell board did not take action on his proposal until 1916 when it approved of the election of three faculty members for an experimental period of three years during which time they could participate in board discussions but could not vote. It added, however, an idea of its own, namely provision for other elected faculty members to meet with three pivotal board committees—general administration, finance, and buildings and grounds ("Trustees and Faculty of Cornell University," 1916). In an editorial captioned "Cornell's Magna Charta," a leading Boston newspaper hailed these actions as great forward strides in "the democratization of American university government" ("School and College," 1916), and so they were. So also were later actions: At the end of the experimental period the Cornell board made the arrangement permanent and, in 1956, by charter amendment increased the number of faculty trustees to four and gave them all the prerogatives of trusteeship, including the right to vote during their five-year terms.

Despite its merits, the Cornell *modus operandi* has been adopted by only a relatively few institutions. The chief deterrent seems to have been the maturation of the multicameral conception of academic government, which keeps professors, trustees, and students within their own separate governing bodies. Also significant has been the absence of enthusiastic support from the AAUP. Committee T, for example, disparaged it in its definitive 1920 report because: "(1) It seems undesirable that faculty representatives should vote on such matters as appointments, promotions, and salaries of their confreres; and (2) Faculty representatives are really in a stronger position to give information and advice if they are not members of the board" (American Association of University Professors, 1920, p. 26). Now and then a professor gives voice to his belief in the Cornell method, and in 1960 Committee T listed it as an approved method for facilitating communication between faculties and legal entities but did not select it for emphasis (American Association of University Professors, 1960). Consistently, the Committee has stressed the need of "statutory provisos for faculty participation in university government" giving professors "an effective part in determining the conditions under, and the manner in, which their services are to be rendered" (American Association of University Professors, 1920, pp. 24, 47). The AAUP has therefore especially applauded written constitutions that have spelled out faculty prerogatives. The move to collective bargaining has helped to ensure, of course, that such measures are written into contracts.

Four years before Committee T made its first report, such a constitution took effect at Reed College in Portland, Oregon. It had been written by a committee of faculty members at the request of President William T. Foster and had been approved by the unanimous vote of the board of trustees (Foster, 1916). A new institution, Reed lacked the traditions or statutes that might have protected the prerogatives of the faculty, but the new constitution served that function well. Foster recognized the need for such a document, and that which he and the faculty successfully promoted at Reed seems to have been one of the first such documents. In any case, he exemplified the enterprise of leading presidents of his period in expanding the governing role of faculty members. At Reed, this role has remained especially strong.

Long before the campaign for faculty constitutions and also

long before the organization of the AAUP, great advances relating to academic freedom and tenure in particular had been initiated by the presidents of leading universities. Highly significant, it seems to me, is the fact that the ad hoc committee on academic freedom and tenure appointed by the AAUP in 1915 declared that "in many universities and colleges the situation has come to be entirely satis- factory" (American Association of University Professors, 1915, p. 23). Further, it quoted former President Eliot of Harvard, the lodestar of contemporary presidents, in support of its efforts to edu- cate what Eliot called "barbarous" boards of trustees (American Association of University Professors, 1915, p. 23). That is to say, the committee turned to a university president to endorse and to help forward its campaign for academic freedom. The committee might also have quoted Eliot on the subject of tenure. He began as early as 1879 to affirm its importance and wrote about it as follows in the statement from which the AAUP committee quoted: "A long tenure of office is well nigh indispensable, if a just academic freedom is to be insured for them. . . . Teachers in every grade of public instruc- tion from the lowest to the highest, when once their capacity and character have been demonstrated, should hold their offices without express limitation of time, and should be subject to removal only for inadequate performance of duty or for misconduct publicly proved" (Eliot, 1907, p. 2). No professorial pronouncements concerning academic freedom and tenure of which I know surpass in vigor and clarity these and other statements of Eliot's. He made that just quoted, be it observed, six years before the beginning of the AAUP's embryonic period. Many, if not most, pre-AAUP presidents had parallel views. Certainly, the vast majority in office during the past several decades have as witness, first, such memorable declarations as Coffman's (1934) of Minnesota, Conant's (1936) and Lowell's (1918) of Harvard, and Wriston's (1949) of Brown; and, second, the adoption in 1925 and again in 1940 of a joint "Statement of Principles" by the AAUP and the Association of American Colleges (Joughin, 1969, pp. 33–38).

In sum, being loyal, in Aristotle's words, to "the established constitution" of the American system of higher education, professors, presidents, and trustees share a "joint responsibility and coopera- tion" in the affairs of their institutions.

FIVE

Student Voice

The College Student is not a class, he is a race, and he is a race which is the same, apparently, in all countries as in all climes.

Charles F. Thwing, 1906

Student agitations during the 1960s and 1970s awoke an interest in the student's role in academic government. This role, at various times through history, has proven strong. In Chapter One I described, for instance, the dominance of student guilds over the medieval University of Bologna. I also mentioned in Chapter Four the controversies at Harvard leading George Ticknor to propose changes at the Massachusetts institution. These controversies were in part stimulated by an especially unruly student generation at Harvard. Many other such instances have occurred through history, and they require attention in a book on academic government.

European Students

A thoroughgoing account of the relationship of students to academic government would need to deal with student affairs in the Hellenic, Hellenistic, Roman, Byzantine, and Muslim institutions of higher education which successively flourished during the 1500 years before the emergence of universities in Western Europe. Such a convoluted task cannot be undertaken here. However, before describing student governing activities since the students of Bologna lorded it over their teachers, a glimpse of the exploits of some of their fore-runners seems pertinent. For the sake of brevity, I comment only on the situation in the fourth century of the Christian era.

During that momentous era, institutions of higher education had spread over the length and breadth of the Roman Empire, and Christians attended them. Hostility to pagan learning by churchmen had already kindled but it did not burst into an overpowering flame until somewhat later. "In the east Christians read Homer and Plato," writes an authority on the period, "and in the west they steeped themselves in Virgil and Cicero, and in both east and west they were a match in all things pertaining to a liberal education" (Glover [1901] 1924, p. 68). Thus seven of the nine premedieval "Doctors of the Church" (eight of the nine being fourth-century prelates) were thoroughly grounded in the literature and philosophy of the Greeks and Romans through attendance at institutions of higher learning. Jerome and Ambrose studied in Rome, Augustine in Carthage, Athanasius in Alexandria, Basil in Constantinople and Athens, Chrysostum in Antioch, and Gregory of Nazianzus in both Alexandria and Athens.

Some fourth-century professors under whom Christians and pagans studied together received salaries from municipal authorities and some from both that source and the imperial government. Many, however, supported themselves as private teachers by collecting from students whatever they felt inclined to pay (*honoraria*) or, if well established, by charging fixed fees. As later at the University of Bologna, these primitive but sometimes highly profitable methods of compensation made them dependent upon student good will, but even salaried professors (many of who also charged fees to augment their usually large *salaria*) had to organize their students into loyal bands of disciples or be victimized both by them and by their fellow professors.

When, for example, the renowned Libanius arrived as a freshman in Athens with plans to study under a fellow countryman, the students of another professor held him captive "in a cell," he later recalled, "not much larger than a wine jar" until he swore allegiance to their mentor (Walden, 1909, p. 304). In another instance, a ship's captain "discharged in the middle of the night, a whole shipload of Asiatic students into the house of a rhetor who was a friend of his" (Marrou, 1956, p. 306). During his years as a teacher, Libanius and his associates never spoke approvingly of the ideas and work of "competitors" but, instead, habitually denigrated them in their lectures. Some of them also egged their students on to undermine unwelcome rivals by invading their lecture rooms and starting fights there, by throwing mud in their faces on the streets, by dragging them out of bed at night for a dousing in a fountain or pond, and by other such persecutions. Because of this kind of behavior, Augustine left Carthage and set himself up as a private teacher in Rome, but he found conditions no better there. Students behaved better in Rome but they had a reputation for not paying their teacher his fees (Augustine [397] 1961).

Because no effective means of central control developed until after the appearance of the medieval universities, neither professors nor students participated in academic government as it began to function centuries later. Students, however, managed their own rudimentary societies and also, by the pressure of their opprobrious behavior, forcibly influenced the content and methods of instruction. The patterns of student life they established would reappear and mushroom in the Middle Ages.

As described in Chapter One, students achieved ascendance at the University of Bologna and others in southern Europe. Those in the universities organized on the Parisian pattern also acquired extensive privileges by means of riot and rebellion. Outbreaks usually occurred spontaneously, and in most of the medieval universities student societies called "nations" espoused the cause of their members who got into trouble. Modeled on the pervasive and powerful craft and commercial guilds, these fellowships arose primarily because aliens had no political status in most medieval cities. Groups of such students therefore organized for camaraderie, for mutual aid of various kinds, and especially for the frustration of civil and academic restraints.

Supported by a succession of imperial and papal edicts and especially by those of Frederick Barbarossa in 1158 and Honorius III in 1217 (Kibre, 1948), the nations of Bologna early subjugated professors and also held city authorities and townsmen at bay. Thirty-three nations early took form there, seventeen of students from Italian and Mediterranean dominions and sixteen from those across the Alps. By 1244 (Coulton, 1913), these two clusters of societies had coalesced and became a brotherhood of Italian students and another of those from distant domains, France and Germany in particular. Each of these new groups yearly elected a rector from its typically mature membership, and these two officers and their subordinates cooperatively monitored the instruction offered and otherwise ruled the institution. Also, as earlier described, civil authorities, beginning in the fourteenth century, maneuvered students out of power by putting professors on their payrolls and by appointing the antecedents of modern external governing boards.

Nations arose in most of the universities of Europe, but undergraduates acquired governmental power only in those of the Bolognese type. Recall, however, that even these "undergraduates" at Bologna were mature men of some importance sent by their constituencies to study the law. At Paris, likewise, only those who had earned the degree of master of arts could be members of any of its four nations. This put control in the hands of those holding posts in the Faculty of Arts.

The teachers of the University of Paris fell into four categories (Mullinger, 1873, p. 358): (1) apprentice lecturers holding only the bachelor's degree, (2) regent masters in the Arts Faculty performing two years of "necessary regency," (3) regular members of the Arts Faculty or older masters of arts who continued on after fulfilling their regency obligations, and (4) the "mere handful" of teachers in the three "superior faculties" of theology, law, and medicine (Rashdall [1895] 1936a, p. 315). Students usually matriculated at the age of fourteen, earned the bachelor's degree at about eighteen, and the master's degree typically at twenty-one (Mullinger, 1873, p. 346). To provide instruction for the undergraduate and the bachelors who continued on for advanced work, the universities required every master of arts to lecture an hour a day, most of them devoting the remaining hours to studying for higher degrees. Their title of *regent master* evolved from the Latin verb *regere,* "to rule," hence to manage a class.

These young regent masters outnumbered by far, it must be emphasized, the other three groups of teachers at all the Parisian-type universities (Rashdall [1895] 1936a). Further, since only they and the much smaller number of permanent Arts Faculty teachers had votes in the nations, they dominated them. They also controlled the overall government of the University since the nations elected the rector, its chief administrator. Almost always they elected one of their own number who, like the equally immature heads of nations (proctors), also held teaching posts. Understandably, therefore, Paris never enacted controls over the faculty like those so prominent in Bologna.

Medievalists make a clear distinction between universities of students (the Bologna type) and universities of masters (the Parisian type). None that I have read emphasizes sufficiently, however, the fact that because regent masters were commonly young men doing their stint of "necessary regency" they differed very little in age and in psychological characteristics from the undergraduates and bachelors they taught. On this score, however, Rashdall has written the following brief but illuminating statement: "This system [necessary regency] must be borne in mind in order to realize how large, youthful, and fluctuating a body the masters of arts really were, and in order to appreciate the resemblances in spite of diversity between the master-university of Paris and the student-universities of Bologna" (Rashdall [1895] 1936a, p. 409).

In short, the "universities of masters" were not, as generally assumed, governed by mature and well-established professors but, rather, by men younger than present-day graduate students and conspicuously less self-controlled than modern undergraduates. Thus, though "members of the government," youthful regent masters and their juniors (and sometimes their seniors) did frequent battle among themselves and with civic officials, ecclesiastical administrators, and townsmen (Glover, 1943, p. 12). These embroilments, many of them "murderous affrays" (Rashdall [1895] 1936a, p. 407), led to almost constant disorder and to not a few cessations of teaching. The Great Dispersion of 1229, for example, emptied Paris of academics (about half the population) for two years and caused such economic havoc that, at the behest of the king and the pope, the city submitted to the conditions that the young regent masters stipulated for the resumption of instruction (Schachner, 1938).

Because of the decline in the number of foreign students at Paris during the fourteenth century, its system of nations began to weaken; and in the next century, the kings of France moved against the University (one of them with an army!) (Schachner, 1938), and "the spirit of the once haughty corporation was completely broken" (Rashdall [1895] 1936a, p. 430). Thereafter, the nations continued to function feebly until abolished during the French Revolution (Kibre, 1948).

The two English centers of higher learning followed the example of Paris, and hence each functioned as a university of masters. Their nations, however, disappeared early; and at neither institution did the continental rectorship emerge. Instead, their titular heads, called *chancellors,* were high-ranking ecclesiastics living at a distance. The office of resident vice-chancellor did not appear until later or take its modern form until the seventeenth century. Meanwhile, two proctors administered each university, and, as at Paris, the paramount Arts Faculty, the fief of the young regent masters, elected them (for annual terms) from among their own members.

The flooding into the cities in which universities developed taxed their housing facilities, and thus groups of students early organized self-governing hospices. These domiciles soon came under the supervision of university authorities who required that a master of arts reside in each of them to superintend its residents and its finances (Mullinger, 1873). Though individually short-lived, lodging units of this kind operated for several centuries, and each member, regardless of his age and academic rank, apparently had a voice in their affairs (Rashdall [1895] 1936b). The same procedure carried over into the endowed halls and colleges but with two differences: undergraduates usually lost the right to vote, and the transient regent masters gave way to permanent "heads." The first of these mutations has, down the centuries, precluded any significant undergraduate collaboration in the government of Oxford and Cambridge. The second has profoundly influenced every facet of subsequent English university history for the reason that it brought into the universities men of ripe years, some of them nonacademics. Fortified by their permanent tenure and high status, these college "heads" soon overshadowed the reigning regent masters, the proctors, and even the vice-chancellors. In sum, they became the most powerful figures in both universities.

As discussed earlier, the original American colleges and all others established until about a century ago adopted the administrative structure of the autonomous colleges of Oxford and Cambridge rather than that of the two universities. Thus the academic presidency, modeled after the headship of the English colleges, became standard in this country. Further, English precedents fostered no concept of student involvement in college government. None began to bud in the United States until the nineteenth century.

American Students

Present-day American students affect academic policy and operations in three general ways: (1) through their self-governing structures, (2) through their reactions to educational procedures, and (3) through the stands that groups of them take on public issues. These areas overlap but they can best be described separately.

Self-Government. Today American students enter into many of the decisions relating to academic government. The spread of self-government has helped bring about this transformation, a transformation that began with student responsibility for student discipline.

Down the centuries, five factors have chiefly precipitated student disorder: (1) the unharnessed vitality of youth, (2) boredom, (3) the conviction of injustice being perpetrated upon them as a group or upon some other group whose cause they have championed, (4) gloomy career prospects during periods of economic depression, and (5) intellectual and emotional involvement in academic and public controversies. The last two of these provocations came into play on several occasions during earlier periods but did not become crucial until the 1930s. The third factor has a long history extending to the middle ages. The first two, however, pervaded American colleges until about a century ago and inevitably invited persistent student turbulence. I comment on them first.

Pre-Civil War America offered few ready-at-hand recreational opportunities to anyone, and students, the majority of them away from home, had to create their own. Here, however, they encountered protracted lists of required and prohibited activities specified in codes of "laws" enacted by their stiff-necked mentors. Weekdays customarily began with chapel at 6:30 in the winter and an hour earlier through the rest of the year. Sunday included at

least two long church services, and during all hours of every day
and evening faculty members snooped for miscreants. "A law got
him out of bed and put him back again," a historian of the University of Georgia has written. "He ate by them, he studied by them,
he recited by them—they were with him always" together with an
awareness of the money fines listed for transgressions (Coulter,
1928, p. 60).

Students could usually throw and kick balls, but the heavy
penalties assessed for breaking windows or otherwise damaging
property discouraged such exercise. Walking, yes; but only in pairs,
never on Sunday, and always within limited boundaries that skirted
places housing "any public tavern, store, tippling shop or any other
place where spiritous liquors are retailed" (Coulter, 1928, p. 61).
Indoor games like backgammon, cards, and of course dice presum-
ably incited to gambling and incurred large fines. Dramatic per-
formances also allegedly induced profligate conduct, and all
colleges interdicted them.

The spelling out in the rule books of so many ways to mis-
behave inevitably encouraged adventurous spirits to taste forbidden
pleasures. Student chieftains also fomented noisy and sometimes
violent protests against the food served in commons, the tutors and
professors they disliked, the punishments meted out to fellow
students, and the attempts to curb their traditional prerogatives of
hazing freshmen and doing battle with townies. In short, rowdyism,
riot, and rebellion kept the old American college in almost perpetual
turmoil and made the professor "a detective, sheriff, prosecuting
attorney, and judge" (Richardson, 1932a, p. 462). It also turned
faculty meetings into criminal court sessions. The situation at Dartmouth typified that commonplace in all colleges:

> Faculty meetings consumed no small proportion
> of the teacher's time. For example, in the year 1828–29
> there were fifty-one of them, while in 1832–33 there were
> sixty-eight. . . . Cases of discipline occupied the greater
> part of the time. . . . It was also the practice at certain
> meetings to "read the catalogue," with a call for com-
> ments by any professor who had information concerning
> the "moral delinquencies" of any student, and an assign-

ment of those charged with such offenses to "individual officers for conversation, advice, and reproof." Moreover, at the beginning of the year, the village was divided geographically, and to each professor was assigned a section of it. It was his duty to visit the rooms of all students located in his area at least once a term, acting partly as a spy, partly as an inspiration to good [Richardson, 1932a, p. 462].

The two spheres of legitimate interest—study and religion—did not restrain student ebullience. Instead, both bred boredom, hooliganism, and organized opposition to authority. The narrow-ranged classical curriculum failed to engage the enthusiasm or even the serious attention of any but the most zealous; the juvenile recitation method of instruction triggered the invention of a multitude of devices for evading study and harassing instructors; and the oppressive concepts of religion in vogue quickened the Old Harry rather than quelling Old Adam. As a member of the Yale Class of 1861, who later became a famous publisher, wrote in his memoirs: "The most diabolical ingenuity could hardly have done more to make both religion and scholarship repulsive" (Holt, 1923, p. 34).

It would take many pages to report the reforms and counter-reforms undertaken to civilize students, humanize professors, and modernize American higher education. The subject exudes excitement, but only those segments of it bearing upon the part that students have come to play in academic government have present relevance. Consider first their governing structures. These may be classified as central and peripheral. The former deal with comprehensive student affairs, the latter with specific subdivisions such as athletics, dramatics, fraternities, publications, and college-owned residences. The peripheral structures can be bypassed with two summary generalizations. First, dormitories excepted, students have initiated and nurtured them in their endeavors to order and to enrich campus life. Second, although some of these undertakings function ineffectively and some unwholesomely, by and large they substantially benefit both students and the educational enterprise.

Efforts to establish central governing structures began before the Civil War but did not take hold firmly until late in the nineteenth century or spread widely until the early twentieth. The University of Virginia made the first attempt upon its opening in 1825. Envisioning an institution relieved of the historic problems of student uproar, Jefferson and his associates framed a plan under which a board of six student "censors" would assist the faculty in maintaining order ("College Instruction and Discipline," 1831). A series of riots during the opening months, however, demolished the plan. Three former presidents of the United States—Jefferson, Madison, and Monroe—who had administered the nation for twenty-four of its thirty-six years sat on the Board of Visitors when it met to restore peace, but not even their knowledge and prestige could breathe life into a scheme of self-government that collided with the deeply embedded tradition of student contumacy (Bruce, 1920a). Seventeen years later, however, a former president of the state's Supreme Court of Appeals, who had resigned that post to teach law at the University, won enthusiastic student cooperation in instituting Virginia's celebrated Honor System of Examinations. When it matured after Appomattox, it not only gave students complete jurisdiction in cases of academic dishonesty but also greatly improved the tone of student life in general (Bruce, 1920b, 1920c). No less significantly, its success animated other institutions over the country to initiate comparable codes—for example, West Point in 1871, the University of North Carolina in 1875, Princeton in 1893.

Amherst appears to have been the first Northern college to experiment with student self-government. Soon after its founding and three years after the debacle of the initial effort at Virginia, its students set up a remarkably wide-ranging program: "During the summer term of 1828, the students, with the approbation of the faculty, organized a sort of interior government. . . . A legislative body, called the House of Students, enacted laws for the protection of the buildings, for the security of the grounds, for the better observance of study hours, and similar matters. Then a court, with a regularly organized bench, bar, and constabulary, enforced the execution of the laws, tried offenders in due form and process, and inflicted the penalties affixed to their violation" (Tyler, 1895, p. 74).

This experiment remained in force for only two years, but the memory of it lingered on to inspire the adoption of a successful enterprise designed half a century later (1860) by an alumnus who had given up his seat in Congress to assume the Amherst presidency (Tyler, 1895). It attracted national attention, as had a somewhat comparable project set in motion at the University of Illinois but which its students decommissioned the year that the more durable "Amherst Plan" made its debut (Solberg, 1968).

Data about the spread over the country in more recent decades of comprehensive student governing structures seem never to have been gathered and published; but even were they available, recounting them here would be tedious. It suffices to mention these familiar facts: (1) they have appeared in one form or another in practically all colleges and universities, (2) they have been instrumental—along with athletics, coeducation, and epochal educational advances—in effecting improvements in student behavior, and (3) currently many of them (as well as the administrators who work with them) seek solutions for complex problems concerning the scope of their activities and the soundness of their procedures. The protests of the 1960s and 1970s swept over them with great force and left some of them shattered. From those difficult years came, however, closer ties between student government, the faculty, and the administration. Students sat on more faculty committees, had better access to the president's office, and (while they did not usually have the vote) participated more formally in the affairs of the governing board.

Reactions to Educational Procedures. Despite their historic unruliness, students have both expedited and instigated pivotal changes in the fundamental activities of American colleges and universities. The boredom that bred insurgence before the Civil War also provoked ambitious and imaginative students into two kinds of adventures designed to offset faculty obtuseness. First, they organized societies devoted to extracurricular intellectual development and camaraderie. Second, they facilitated, urged, and sometimes demanded changes in official programs and practices.

The societies sponsored debating, the communal ownership and reading of important books unheeded in their courses, the carrying on of modest scientific investigations, and the writing of papers for reading at their meetings. These adventures in self-education, well under way in the late eighteenth century, did a good deal more for many students than their formal studies. In his admirable biography of Mark Hopkins, Rudolph (1956) has described how the Lyceum of Natural History founded in 1835 by eight Williams students cultivated the underprivileged sciences there. The following passage from Rudolph's (1962, p. 138) history of American higher education sums up the vigor and value of the literary brotherhoods that arose in all the colleges: "The classroom, while officially dedicated to disciplining and furnishing the mind, was in reality far better at molding character and at denying intellect rather than refining it. The literary societies, on the other hand, owed their allegiance to reason, and in their debates, disputations, and literary exercises, they imparted a tremendous vitality to the intellectual life of the colleges, creating a remarkable contrast to the ordinary classroom where the recitation of memorized portions of text was regarded as the ultimate intellectual exercise."

The heyday of student literary and scientific groups ended in the middle of the last century because, in part, fraternities, athletics, and other extracurricular activities came to absorb student interest and, in part, because, to quote Rudolph (1962, pp. 143–144) again: "The colleges themselves took over some of their old purposes: built up broader collections of books, opened the libraries more than once a week, introduced respectable study in English literature, discovered history as a field of study, expanded the sciences."

Meanwhile, student agitators for change aided adult educational reformers and also campaigned independently. Until well into the twentieth century, student critics seem to have made few direct proposals for alterations in educational programs, but their frequent and sometimes violent expressions of disgruntlement enhanced the exertions of the faculty members and administrators who strove to update curricular content and methods of instruction. The most notable example of the interaction of student fractiousness and educational progress comes from the history of Harvard during the third decade of the last century.

Late in the summer of 1819, George Ticknor assumed the newly created Smith Professorship of French and Spanish at Harvard and immediately proposed changes in established procedures there. Because of his just-completed four years of study and travel in Europe, where he met many of the leading minds of the period, and also because of his wealth and social preeminence, his ideas got a respectful hearing. They led, however, to only a few minor changes; and so when the 1823 senior class staged one of the most egregious of all Harvard student upheavals, he took advantage of the opportunity it presented to play a strategic role in persuading the Board of Overseers and the Corporation to initiate the first—and probably the most productive—of all college self-surveys (Tyack, 1967).

Everyone agreed that something had to be done to suppress student insubordination. The rebellion fostering the agreement had led to the expulsion of forty-three of the seventy members of the Class of 1823, including one of the sons of John Quincy Adams, the nation's secretary of state (Morison, 1936c). Earlier convulsions had been hardly less grievous, and it seemed clear that the future of the College required that as many as possible of the causes of student ruffianism be eliminated. Four committees, therefore, went immediately to work: one committee of the Overseers, another of the Corporation, a joint committee of both bodies, and a committee of the Immediate Government (Morison, 1936c). Two years of give-and-take among these groups led to substantial changes, and although they disappointed Ticknor (Ticknor, 1825), they gave Harvard a leg-up to the position of leadership which Ticknor's nephew, Charles W. Eliot, solidified after becoming president in 1869. The reforms of 1825 would undoubtedly have been inevitable later, but the point for present emphasis is that student discontent and disorder hastened them.

The reconstruction of American higher education could not be avoided for a complex of reasons, one of the most insistent being the dissatisfaction of the parents of potential students: They steered their sons away from the colleges. The topic in hand is student pressures on academic policy, but the attitudes of parents—and also of the public at large—interlink so closely with it that they must be commented upon.

In 1850, President Francis Wayland of Brown submitted a report to his board of trustees concerning the problems of Brown and the other eleven New England colleges. The twelve institutions, he pointed out, enrolled a total of 1,884 students or an average

of 157 students. He also called attention to the fact that although
the population of the area had grown during the previous twenty
years from two to almost three million, the average increase in
their student bodies totaled only twenty-seven (Wayland, 1850, p.
30). He followed his statistical review with this comment (p. 34):

> It would seem then from such facts as these that
> our present system of collegiate education is not ac-
> complishing the purposes intended. . . . Our colleges
> are not filled because we do not furnish the education
> desired by the people. We have constructed them upon
> the idea that they are to be schools of preparation *for the
> professions.* Our customers, therefore, come from the
> smallest class of society; and the importance of the
> education which we furnish is not so universally
> acknowledged as formerly, even by this class. We have
> produced an article for which the demand is diminishing.
> We sell it at less than cost, and the deficiency is made up
> by charity. We give it away, and still the demand dimin-
> ishes. Is it not time to inquire whether we cannot furnish
> an article for which the demand will be, at least, some-
> what more remunerative?

Wayland put his finger on the cause of the failure of the colleges
to attract students: They limited their offerings to the classical
languages and to the elements of mathematics and ignored the
urgent need of the nation for trained manpower and for augmented
knowledge power. The country had, he continued, "land to be
surveyed, roads to be constructed, ships to be built and navigated,
soils of every kind, and under every variety of climate . . . to be
cultivated, manufactures . . . to be established." "In a word,"
he concluded, "all the means which science has provided to aid
the progress of civilization must be employed if this youthful republic would place itself abreast of the empires of Europe" (Wayland, 1850, p. 12).

The New England colleges, the most advanced in the country
at the time, paid little heed to Wayland's plea for a system of
higher education that would serve "all classes of society" (Wayland, 1850, p. 58). One finds it hardly surprising, therefore, that

twenty years later (in 1870) Harvard, the largest American college, enrolled only 655 undergraduates, Yale 644, Dartmouth 305, Amherst 200, and Williams 161. Colleges in other sections fared no better. Princeton had 328 students, Columbia 122, and Pennsylvania 134. Michigan, the largest of the state universities in 1870, had 446 nonprofessional students. Enrollments did not rise impressively until the mid 1880s; and then they began to grow largely because a procession of men younger than Wayland succeeded in making higher education equal to the demands of the fast-changing times. Students flocked into the colleges in ever-increasing numbers not only for the inviting kinds of instruction made available by the reformers but also for the social experiences and contacts provided by the booming extracurriculum. To the latter, most students gave all but a small and reluctant fraction of their attention, and neither they nor the majority of those committed to earnest study seriously questioned the new order of things.

A few undergraduates, however, found the extracurriculum inane and the curriculum unchallenging. The confirmed individualists among them went their private ways, but two small reformist groupings appeared on a number of campuses. One severely criticized prevailing educational concepts and practices and sought to change them. The other wrestled with some of the huge problems facing society at large. The latter came upon the scene first and, on occasion, has been vigorous over the past two hundred years; but before describing their activities, the campaigns of the educational reformers of the 1920s and 1930s must be summarized.

Barnard College students opened this neglected chapter in the history of American higher education with a report written during the academic year 1921–22. The following statement epitomizes its spirit and product: "Are college students persons, or are they pupils? Most colleges treat them as pupils. But in some places they seem to be demanding admission to the human race. Barnard College has a group of candidates for such a standing. The Student Curricular Committee has made public a curriculum worked out by the students which they have asked the faculty to consider as a possible substitute for the present course of study" (Barnard, 1922, pp. 217–218). This initial student report bore no fruit at Barnard, but two years later it provided an editor of the *Daily Dartmouth* with a focus for a dynamic editorial campaign. Hammering away persistently at the defects of his alma mater, he provoked President Ernest Martin Hopkins to appoint a committee of twelve seniors to make "a complete survey, review, and examination of [the College's] educational processes" (Dartmouth College Senior Committee, 1924, p. 5). A 1926 editorial in a leading New England newspaper describes the impact of the resulting pamphlet of forty-five printed pages:

> All our colleges now seem to be asking their students to assume . . . the task of teaching their teachers. Dartmouth led the way in this matter, soliciting from undergraduates a very complete report of their views of higher education as supplied them at Hanover, what they think is good about it and what they think is wrong. Bowdoin and Middlebury have likewise sought counsel of their seniors and sophomores, their juniors and freshmen. And now the ink has scarcely dried upon the report of the Harvard Student Council's "committee on education," when the students at Yale, at the direct instance of President Angell, begin making a similar canvass.
>
> What an extraordinary development this is in the collegiate world. Fifty or more years ago it would have been unthinkable. In an American college of the eighteenth and nineteenth century any proposal that the students should be asked to state in public what they thought of their teachers and teaching, would not merely have been considered horrible. It would have been horripilant. Chills and fevers of outraged authority would have shaken the whole faculty from the President down to the youngest assistant instructor [*Boston Transcript*, 1926].

Motivated by the Dartmouth Report and student criticism, fourteen institutions produced statements through the year 1931—six unitary liberal arts colleges, four private universities, and four state universities. Other statements followed during the decade before Pearl Harbor, the most meritorious being five produced by the committees of the Harvard Student Council. The effects of these documents cannot be measured, but that they were extensive cannot be doubted (Harcleroad, 1948). No less important, they strengthened the concept that students have useful things to say about their education and hence should somehow be associated with formulating the decisions that control it.

Stands on Public Issues. Some who knew about the student committees assumed that the veterans who surged into the colleges beginning in 1945 would renew and intensify the educational criticisms of the interwar period, but for two chief reasons nothing of the sort happened. First, the general expectation of a deep economic depression impelled the overage veterans in particular to rush through their studies so that they would be established in their careers before the crash came. Second, when a boom instead of a bust ensued, the students who were disillusioned with the postwar world almost unanimously turned their eyes and their energies to public rather than to academic issues. In so doing, they followed precedents that have been forgotten or were never known by those who believe that in the past American collegians have been indifferent to public questions.

These precedents began with the American Revolution. All of the nine existing colleges either closed down or greatly limited their operations because most of their eligible students had joined the militia or the Continental Army, but more relevant here are instances of students frustrating the British and discomfiting Loyalists. Two such events illustrate these numerous harassments: Harvard students drove out of Cambridge the tutor who directed British troops to Lexington and "the shot heard round the world"; the soapbox harangues and the pamphlets written by an eighteen-year-old Kings College undergraduate named Alexander Hamilton helped arouse the mob that, despite his pleas against violence, three weeks later forced President Myles Cooper to seek refuge on a British warship bound for England.

Next came the slavery issue, which began seriously to concern students, as it did Americans in general, during the third decade of the new century. The American Colonization Society, established in 1817 to resettle slaves in Africa, stirred their imagination, especially after the founding five years later of Monrovia, the nucleus from which Liberia developed. The Society's 251 auxiliary groups of 1832 faded away, however, after it became clear that the colonization formula could not solve the slavery problem (Nye [1949] 1963). Meanwhile, in 1828, John C. Calhoun had stated the principle of nullification, which rapidly solidified the South against federal interference with its affairs in general and with slavery in particlular. Three years later, William Lloyd Garrison began publishing the *Liberator,* the organ of the most fanatical wing of the abolitionists. Its program and tactics not only infuriated and frightened the South but also split the North into a score of wrangling factions.

Below the Mason and Dixon line, the attitude symbolized by the American Colonization Society eroded or went underground, and students joined with their elders in molesting antislavery visitors from the North and the rare Southerners who expressed even mild doubts about the sanctity of slavery. In 1856, for example, University of North Carolina students burned in effigy a professor who supported the newly organized Republican Party (Hofstadter and Metzger, 1955). In the same year, University of Virginia students cheered when their alma mater presented Preston Brooks with a cane like the one he used on the floor of Congress to beat Charles Sumner into invalidism (Beale, 1941).

Opinion in the Northern colleges ranged from the proslavery position of President Nathan Lord of Dartmouth to the ardent abolitionists of the Oberlin faculty. Between these extremes it took a variety of forms, the most common being the judgment that in the interest of order discussions of the slavery problem should be suppressed. At a few of the older colleges, students occasionally ignored the ban, but by and large they accepted it. In some of the newer institutions, however, they refused to be silent. The most notable example of intransigency occurred at the Lane Theological Seminary in Cincinnati. In 1835, its students scheduled eighteen meetings on successive evenings—nine on the colonization philosophy and nine on abolition. When the board of trustees ruled that further discussions should cease, forty students and two professors resigned, and eventually many of them transferred to Oberlin (Nye [1949] 1963, p. 88). Thereupon, that recently opened college became a fertile seedbed of antislavery propaganda, especially among the colleges of the Middle West and of the border states. It also maintained an intrepid station of the Underground Railway, an adventure in which students of other colleges similarly but less numerously engaged (Burroughs, 1911).

The confusion and indecision about slavery in the North, however, fettered most of its colleges and their students. Two inflammatory events at Bowdoin highlight the pressures upon them and the resulting diversity of thought and action. In 1852, Harriet Beecher Stowe, the wife of Calvin E. Stowe, a Bowdoin alumnus and professor who had been on the Lane faculty during the tumult there two decades earlier, published *Uncle Tom's Cabin*. Six years later, however, the College gave Jefferson Davis an honorary degree—probably at the suggestion of Franklin Pierce, Stowe's classmate, who had retired the previous year from the nation's presidency (Hatch, 1927). Bowdoin students similarly fluctuated. Some became antislave activists like the Stowes; some mildly opposed the South, like Henry Wadsworth Longfellow of the class behind that of Pierce and Stowe; and some ignored the horrendous problem, like Nathaniel Hawthorne, Longfellow's classmate.

Other than pacifists, most people will probably agree that serving in the armed forces of one's country during wartime constitutes an ultimate act of participation in public affairs. In any case, college students by the thousands joined the armies of the Union and the Confederacy; and many of them lost their lives. After the end of the conflict and after the initiation of educational reforms, the colleges—and more especially, the rising universities—started the climbs in public interest and in enrollments that continued for decades thereafter. As mentioned earlier, during the half century intervening before the outbreak of the First World War, most students succumbed to the seductions of the swelling extracurriculum.

Many of the new or augmented components of student life provided valuable intellectual experience (publications, debating, and managing student organizations, for example), but relatively few students worked at promoting self-government. Fewer still gave thought to the vexing economic and political problems of the era. One might expect that the dissatisfaction of the Middle West with the economic repression forced upon it by Eastern money interests would have provoked student discussions of the issues in the colleges of that section; but, by and large, their clienteles did not support the Grangers, the Greenback Party, the Populists, and other protesting groups. Further, until toward the end of the nineteenth century, the old-time classical curriculum held its own against the newer subjects even in the state universities. Robert M. La Follette of the Class of 1879 at the University of Wisconsin later wrote, for instance, that "there was then little teaching of sociology or political economy worthy of the name" (La Follette, 1913, p. 27). The denominational colleges did even less with the social sciences; and thus when, two years later, William Jennings Bryan graduated from Illinois College at the head of his class, he chose "Character" as the topic of his valedictory address (Bryan, 1909). Giving no hint of his later tenets, it reflected the emphasis on morals rather than intellect that continued to dominate college teaching.

La Follette, Bryan, and their Middle Western college contemporaries interested in public speaking memorized famous orations or those of their own composition. The oratorical tradition, however, had long been moribund in the East; and in the late 1880s, debating generally replaced it there. An undergraduate named Gifford Pinchot, who later became governor of Pennsylvania and a leading Bull Mooser, helped organize one of the earliest sponsoring groups—the Yale Assembly, founded in 1887 (" 'Pa' Corbin . . . ," 1937). With a comparable Harvard society, it staged a nondecision intercollegiate debate in Cambridge early in 1892 on the question, "Resolved, that a young man casting his first ballot in 1892 should vote for the nominees of the Democratic Party" (Ringwalt, 1897, p. 634).

This and a return engagement between youthful representatives of these two venerable institutions helped propel the establishment of debating societies in other colleges and also of intercollegiate forensic leagues across the country.

By 1910, however, debating had largely lost its appeal. In that year, a visiting editor writing of the Yale-Harvard debate reported: "There was a very tepid audience, mostly women and townspeople. Harvard won, but nobody seemed to care" (Slosson, 1910, p. 60). During their heyday, the debating societies had been sanctuaries for students interested in scientific and public affairs (Perry, 1935), but they had become too formal, artificial, and faculty dominated. Students troubled by the awesome problems facing society therefore organized new groups to study and—some of them—to champion various reforms. These groups had two chief foci: socialism and the Student Christian Movement.

Socialism first came to the pointed attention of the best-read students during the middle of the first decade of the century through the efforts of the Intercollegiate Socialist Society (I.S.S.). Upton Sinclair conceived it late in 1905, his seven cofounders including Clarence Darrow, graduates of three leading universities (Chicago, Harvard, and Yale), and Jack London, who had quit the University of California during his freshman year to seek fortune in the Klondike gold rush. The tremendous popularity of London's short stories and novels led the hundred or so present at the organization meeting to elect him president, and in that capacity he immediately set out on a cross-country tour of the colleges. Castigating a University of Chicago professor's definition of the purpose of higher education as "the passionless pursuit of passionless intelligence" (Foner, 1947, p. 75), London explained, during one of his well-attended speeches, that the I.S.S. desired "to arouse in the minds of the young men of our universities an interest in the study of socialism." He continued: "If collegians cannot fight for us, we want them to fight against us—of course, sincerely fight against us. But what we do not want is that which obtains today and has obtained in the past of the university, a mere deadness and unconcern and ignorance so far as socialism is concerned. Fight for us or fight against us. Raise your voices one way or the other; be alive" (Foner, 1947, p. 75).

London and his associates did arouse some of their hearers to "be alive" about socialism. During 1906, I.S.S. chapters formed at Columbia, Harvard, Wesleyan, and Yale. Soon thereafter, units were organized at an undiscoverable number of other institutions, among them Amherst, Barnard, City College of New York, Clark, Chicago, Illinois, Michigan, Oberlin, Princeton, Stanford, Wisconsin, and Vassar. Their memberships included not a few who would later become well known to many Americans: Paul Blanshard, Heywood Broun, Paul Douglas, Walter Lippmann, Edna St. Vincent Millay, Inez Milholland, Lewis Mumford, John Reed, and Norman Thomas. Because of the socialist stand against American participation in the First World War, the I.S.S. lost many of its early members and all but collapsed. It revived after the war, however, took the name of the League for Industrial Democracy, and—as I shall show later—became a potent force in the college life of the 1930s.

Most members of the I.S.S. and the Student League for Industrial Democracy (the student branch established in the early 1920s and referred to hereinafter as the S.L.I.D.) scorned organized religion, but a few joined the Student Christian Movement. Some of its numerous roots extended back many decades, but early in this century its stoutest branch propounded the Social Gospel under the leadership of such reformers as Walter Rauschenbusch, who, in his *Christianity and the Social Crisis* (1907) and *Christianizing the Social Order* (1912), fervently advocated socialism. The great majority of those associated with the Student Christian Movement, however, sponsored "the religion of humanity" (Gabriel, 1940, p. 214) rather than the destruction of the "capitalistic dragon" demanded by Rauschenbusch and his fellows. They urged—together with sundry secularists—the correction of such social maladies as child labor, industrial strife, poverty, and, above all else, war. Only a very small percentage of students joined even this ameliorative branch of the Student Christian Movement or supported its secular counterparts, and fewer still actively crusaded for their humanitarian ideals. In varying degrees, however, they colored the thinking of many alert students then and especially during the Depression.

Meanwhile, Americans in general largely ignored the overall sociopolitical scene. Obedient to President Harding's call for a "return to normalcy," they did not perceive that the country had entered upon one of the most baleful periods of abnormalcy in its history, to wit, the Roaring Twenties. They had neither ears nor eyes for the rumblings of a social unrest nor the grumblings of the social critics. Instead, on the college front, the rah-rah segments of the extracurriculum flourished more luxuriantly than ever; and the public avidly read about the revolt of the Younger (Lost) Generation. Its divergence from the concepts of its elders led to a cacophony of protests in sermons, speeches, and magazine articles which, however, served only to elicit such responses as the following:

In the first place, I would like to observe that the older generation had certainly pretty well ruined this world before passing it on to us. They give us this thing, knocked to pieces, leaky, red-hot, threatening to blow up; and then they are surprised that we don't accept it with the same attitude of pretty, decorous enthusiasm with which they received it, 'way back in the eighteen-nineties, nicely painted, smoothly running, practically fool-proof.

We're men and women, long before our time, in the flower of our full-blooded youth. We have brought back into civil life some of the recklessness and ability that we were taught by war. We are also quite fatalistic in our outlook on the tepid perils of tame living. All may yet crash to the ground for aught that we can do about it. Terrible mistakes will be made, but *we* shall at least make them intelligently and insist, if we are to receive the strictures of the future, on doing pretty much as we choose now [Carter, 1920, p. 302].

Abetted by the Coolidge Bull Market, the general disdain of Prohibition, and the libertarian concepts encouraged by the growing popularity of Freud and of behavioristic psychology, most students, like their seniors, did "pretty much as they chose." The symbols of their scorn of the Victorian verities included the hip flask, brawls at dances and football games, the flapper with her lipstick, bobbed hair, and flaunted cigarette, the Charleston, and unabashed necking and petting. Describing the change in college mores from those reverenced in *Stover at Yale, Frank Merriwell,* and other delineations of prewar student life, a writer in *Fortune* later addressed its typical upper-upper subscriber as follows:

Your son, born in 1903, went to college in the early 1920s. A sophisticated whelp, he joked about the fraternity system and regarded football games as an excuse for weekend binges. He was, so the newspapers and the magazines of the time informed you, part of the flaming youth of the jazz age that danced in the dark

and was ready to question all moral codes. He was vocal,
obstreperously and overwhelmingly vocal, about his
clothes, his gin from Billy Bender's, his [free-wheeling]
girls . . . and his general disrespect for all constituted
authority. Iconoclastic, exhibitionistic, ignorant, raucous,
socially irresponsible, and self-indulgent, he took the
country clubs by storm and remodeled the older generation in his own image. To find out about his antics you
bought and read F. Scott Fitzgerald's *This Side of Para-
dise*, Stephen Vincent Benét's *The Beginnings of Wisdom*,
and Percy Marks's *The Plastic Age*. And when somebody
saw the Marks novel on your living-room table and
murmured something about "the plastered age" you
knew what was meant ["Youth in College," 1936, p. 99].

Few readers of contemporary canvases of college life in the
1920s knew that beneath the surface other attitudes than those
exhibited in this quotation thrived among small clusters of thought-
ful students, many of them aligned with the S.L.I.D., the Student
Christian Movement, and (a corporal's guard) with communist-front
organizations. Some of these young men and women sought, as
earlier reported, to goad faculties into revising their educational
ideas and methods, but most of them devoted their attention to the
large problems gathering force beneath the happy-go-lucky surface.
As observed, the work of the former has been all but forgotten, but
that of the latter came to harvest in the Calamitous Thirties.

Americans generally think of the 1930s as predominantly
encumbered by the Depression, but long before the stock market
crash of 1929 political explosions abroad presaged the Second
World War: the 1922 coup of Mussolini in Italy, the 1923 Nazi
beer-hall *putsch* in Munich followed soon thereafter by the publication of Hitler's *Mein Kampf*, the 1924 accession to power of Stalin
in Russia, the 1927 and 1928 blockadings of Shantung by the
Japanese. No one forsaw where these events would lead, but discerning Americans reflected upon them and also upon lamentable
events and tendencies at home: the atrocious yet fascinating exploits
of Al Capone and other gangsters, the bitter and sometimes violent
disagreements between Capital and Labor, the Teapot Dome
scandal, the Scopes trial, the Ku Klux Klan, the scoffings at many

generally accepted characteristics and institutions of American life by such writers as H. L. Mencken and Sinclair Lewis, the departure for Europe of other writers like T. S. Eliot and Ernest Hemingway because they found the United States culturally barren, the soaring divorce rate, the plummeting of farmers' income, and a score of other such distresses.

Until the 1930s, American resilience had been equal, although somewhat tortuously, to the stubborn problems confronting the nation; but the Depression accentuated those unsolved in the twenties and added new and more grievous ones. Thus a mood of despondency overshadowed the country and produced a crisis of faith in the soundness and durability of the American way of life. Although this diagnosis relates most to the business community, in varying degrees the "crisis of faith" affected Americans in general—including college students.

During every period of stress, submerged dissidents among both reactionaries and progressives rise to the surface. Their agitations and especially their successes eventually bestir vigilant members of the moderate middle to protest and to initiate corrective measures. This process of action and reaction went on continuously during the Depression in all major areas of the national life, colleges and universities prominently included. Indeed, students became prime targets of both flanks of the extremists. I shall try to show how they responded and how their actions affected academic policies and operations.

In 1919, the revolutionary factions of the American Socialist Party withdrew and organized the Workers (Communist) Party, controlled by the Third International or Comintern. During the twenties, both parties and their affiliates sought recruits in the colleges. Through the S.L.I.D., the socialists had much greater success, but all the left-wing groups together succeeded in enlisting only a small fraction of one percent of the college population. The Student Christian Movement accounted for another five percent, and about the same proportions belonged to local discussion groups (the political unions on a number of the more cerebral campuses, for example) or to one or another of the miscellany of middle-of-the-road intercollegiate associations like the National Student Federation organized in 1925. In sum, during the twenties approximately one student in ten joined a group or groups devoted to examining broad societal problems, but only minuscule cadres embraced radical doctrines. The great preponderance of students went their unconcerned ways until the Depression jolted them and everyone else into sobriety and gradually into anxiety.

Even during the worst days of the Depression, however, the "crisis of faith" in the American Dream did not seriously weaken the deeply embedded optimism of most Americans. They accepted Herbert Hoover's promise that prosperity lurked "just around the corner"; and when events belied it, they elected Franklin D. Roosevelt and patiently followed his zig-zag quarterbacking. Roosevelt's tory critics, however, accused him of leading the country into socialism, and collectivists belabored him because he did not. Along with all other divisions of the body politic, the resulting tensions and torsions harried the colleges. There the reformist groups (red, pinko, and humanitarian) only slightly increased their memberships but they became so vocal and activist that they seemed to their critics to be growing with frightening rapidity.

A score or more of friction points perturbed student malcontents, but chiefly half a dozen or so spurred the especially bold into aggression: labor disputes, discrimination against blacks and Jews, loyalty oaths, the rise and growth of foreign-controlled and domestic fascism, the banning of critics of "one hundred percent Americanism" from many college platforms, compulsory military training, and—most important of all—the growing threat of war. On these issues they agitated vociferously, some of them going to jail for joining picket lines and for marching in protest parades. Most of their belligerencies involved very few students and attracted only local attention; but when the newspapers reported that many thousands participated in the campus peace strikes of the mid thirties, alarmed rightists launched retaliatory assaults on the colleges.

The S.L.I.D. and the National Student League, a further-to-the-left offshoot, organized the first peace strike (Wechsler, 1935). It occurred on Friday, April 13, 1934, its promoters appealing to students across the country to stay away from classes during the same mid-morning hour. Fifteen thousand New York City college and high school students complied, as did students on other campuses around the nation ("Nation's Students . . . ," 1934). It received considerable newspaper coverage too, and, together with a series of other incidents, raised the blood pressure of jittery ultraconservatives, especially when more thousands participated in the peace strikes the following year. Some of the other events of 1934 included the meeting in Chicago that summer of the United States Congress Against the War and Fascism, attended by over 3,000 delegates, college students among them, of organizations ranging from the Communist Party to the Y.M.C.A. ("Rather Than Be United . . . ," 1934); the International Fete of Socialist Youth held some weeks later in France, some of its participants being American collegians; the initial session of the American Youth Congress at New York University in August attended by representatives of 121 associations ("Youth Divides," 1934); the protests at Columbia and C.C.N.Y. against the receptions given that autumn to a group of visiting Italian Fascist students, twenty-one undergraduates of C.C.N.Y. being expelled for their ardor ("Twenty-One Students . . . ," 1934); the announcement by the Board of Regents of the University of Minnesota that R.O.T.C. training would henceforth be optional there; the student support given Upton Sinclair in his 1934 EPIC (End Poverty in California) campaign on the Democratic ticket for the governorship of California; the refusal of the Student Council of U.C.L.A. to sponsor a Navy League essay contest on "Our Navy" or to permit the American Legion and the R.O.T.C. to parade during the Armistice Day football game and to share in its receipts, as they had in the past (Wechsler, 1935).

These and other "plots against American ideals and principles" made "economic royalists" like William Randolph Hearst spitting mad. In the autumn of 1934, Hearst instructed his chain of newspapers to wage war against faculty and student "Reds." Other newspapers joined his crusade, along with congressmen like Samuel Dickstein and Hamilton Fish of New York and a long list of "patriotic" bodies including the American Legion, the American Liberty League, the American Vigilant Intelligence Association, and the Daughters of the American Revolution. Their clamorous remonstrances whipped up the passions of their growing number of partisans who moved on various fronts to check "the bolsheviks." Their primary drive against the colleges centered in the legislatures of a score of states, but I report only what happened in New York and Illinois and the reverberations of their defeats there.

In 1934, the New York Legislature enacted a teachers' loyalty oath, and that autumn a Hearst adherent introduced a bill to require a similar oath of all students attending the colleges and universities of the state wholly or partially financed by public funds. Affronted by the bill and by the accusations of the Hearst papers, a phalanx of Vassar students set to work to block the passage of the bill. Led by the daughter of a midwestern businessman, 80 Vassar girls carried to Albany a protesting petition signed by 800 of their 1,200 college mates. On two later expeditions, students from other colleges joined them bearing some 8,000 additional signatures; and during their picketing, they ("Vassar Goes to Town," 1935) replied to a Hearst editorial entitled "Keep Our Women Wholesome" by singing a song to the tune of "America the Beautiful" which began:

> Oh beautiful for motherhood and faith in Randolph Hearsed,
> We'll spill our blood for country's good; let Communists be cursed.

The New York Senate passed the bill; but the Assembly killed it in committee, the student opposition to it undoubtedly playing a definitive part in that outcome. In short, representatives of the Moderate Middle worsted the efforts of the Radical Right to curb the Radical Left with legislation that would discourage if not smother the rising flame of student interest in public affairs.

Several weeks before the New York denouement, a much more widely publicized battle began in Illinois. Probably because of what he had been reading in the two Chicago newspapers owned by Hearst and in the *Chicago Tribune*, the chain-store druggist Charles R. Walgreen questioned his niece about her courses at the University of Chicago. Her description of them together with her original defense of them led him to conclude that several of her professors were communists, and he therefore withdrew her. Press reports of his action provided the opportunity that some of the legislators at Springfield had been itching for, and the Senate appointed a committee of five of its members to investigate the University. It went to work immediately, its sessions providing such critics of the colleges as Mrs. Elizabeth Dilling (author of *The Red Network*, published a few years previously) with opportunities to denounce the University and, in turn, for its officers and professors to defend it. At the conclusion of the heated hearings, the committee voted four to one to exonerate the University, moderation again prevailing.

In most states, middle-of-the-roaders did not win, the passage of a faculty loyalty oath bill in Massachusetts especially pleasuring the Radical Right. Nor did the victories of Hearst and his frightened associates quiet the leftist firebrands. Developments everywhere, however, made it clear that the great majority of Americans and of college students repudiated both species of extremists. In 1940, for example, the voters elected President Roosevelt to an unprecedented third term, despite the argument of the Radical Right that he was leading the nation into socialism. Meanwhile, college students showed their repugnance for red-baiting doctrines and tactics by boycotting movie theaters that ran Hearst-Metrotone newsreels, a project backed enthusiastically at several dozen colleges and started at Williams (than which probably no American institution of higher education had a larger proportion of matriculants from upper-crust families). Many thousands joined the 1935 and 1936 peace strikes, but their radical organizers recruited few new collaborators. Instead, most students continued to be cool if not opposed to the avowed reformists among them. They similarly disdained those who sided with the superpatriots.

The refusal of the run-of-the-mill student to stick his or her neck out either to the left or to the right did not, however, signify indifference to the menacing problems confronting society. A 1936 *Fortune* survey of student opinion, for example, led to the following conclusion: "Sometimes quite palpably, sometimes indefinably it [the world crisis] colors nearly everything the student does and says. Fear of the future and a vague sense of imminent frustration have taken the Fitzgeraldian cockiness out of the average undergraduate. If he drinks less and wenches less, it is because the stuff of the newspaper headlines is on his mind. A few have been enormously stimulated by the uncertainty of these years, but they are the exceptions. However, both the timid ones and the zestful ones have been mulling over the same social and economic problems. This mulling has not yet produced a definite youth movement, but the campus is a little—a very little—to the left of the country as a whole ("Youth in College," 1936, p. 156).

The growing conviction that Hitler's aggressions and atrocities would lead to war and that the United States would become involved eradicated any possibility that a concerted American youth movement would develop. Then came Pearl Harbor and the mammoth youth movement into the armed forces that it vitalized. Thus ended the frenzied interwar period. During it and its aftermath, American students once again gave the lie to the oft-made accusation that—unlike their counterparts in other countries—they complacently disregarded the perplexities of the world at large.

With the war's end in 1945, the G.I. Bill of Rights deluged the colleges with several million veterans. Some of us expected that these much-matured students would be so critical of existing methods of instruction and the onrushing research emphasis of faculty members that they would rise in rebellion. We were much mistaken. Everybody predicted a depression, and the veterans were out to acquire their degrees and find jobs before it struck. A period of apathy resulted—the so-called Silent Generation. Then in 1960 the lid blew off again.

Much more complex than in earlier periods, the student activism of the 1960s and 1970s thrust into both the academic and public domains. Many of its leaders, moreover, operated simultaneously in both. Their criticisms—sometimes ameliorative and other times radical—received a hearing far beyond the campus. In some instances, those criticisms deserved a hearing. As a result, administrators and faculty members had to face up to the abounding impersonalism that has come to characterize higher education, the inadequacy of many teaching procedures, the devastations of the publish-or-perish syndrome, and the urgent need of establishing better methods of student participation in institutional policy making.

In these and other academic matters, ameliorative activism has paid dividends, and the same can be said about ameliorative activities in public arena. The students who joined the Peace Corps or Vista and who, while enrolled in college, worked with under-privileged children and youths, received relatively little newspaper publicity; but their numbers probably surpassed those of the radicals. Both groups, however, helped arouse the nation's con-science concerning a number of crucial social inequities.

What about the future? It seems to me that the events of the past make several predictions reasonable. First, student activism will continue to be a fact to reckon with. Second, unrest will take place both in the form of the visceral activity associated with the panty raids of the 1950s and the more cerebral form of the 1960s. Visceral unrest will continue to emerge on occasion but, in the United States at least, will seldom express itself violently. Third, student criticism of educational practices will be increasingly recog-nized as a valuable resource and will be facilitated by better channels of faculty-student communication. Fourth, during troublous times student idealists will take stands on public issues; and their ameliora-tive ideas that win popular support will be productive. Fifth, when these youthful Utopians join the ranks of those past thirty whom they have heretofore disdained, they—like so many of their predeces-sors—will either become important members of progressive move-ments or pessimistic reactionaries.

SIX

Alumni Participation

Balliol made me, Balliol fed me,
And the best of Balliol loved and led me.
Whatever I had she gave me again;
God be with you, Balliol men.

Hilaire Belloc, 1910

Alumni constitute still another group involved in academic government. Their role, like that of students, professors, presidents, trustees,
is often misunderstood. Nevertheless, they have had a voice in institutional affairs for centuries.

In a 1908 series of lectures of Northwestern University on
academic government, President Eliot of Harvard devoted the
second of his six papers to the topic "An Inspecting and Consent-
ing Body—Alumni Influence" (Eliot, 1908). Therein he chiefly
reported and applauded the situation at Harvard which, as noted
earlier, has two external legal entities. One of them, the Board of
Overseers, has been made up entirely of graduates since 1866.
Alumuni participation has considerably increased meanwhile, and
especially since Eliot gave his Northwestern lectures, but it has a
long history fashioned in part by English antecedents that reach to
the Middle Ages. I review British backgrounds and present practices in the opening pages of this chapter and then proceed to
canvass American alumni involvement in the affairs of Alma Mater.

British Sources and Current Practice

Alumni prerogatives in British academic government derive from the medieval obligation of "necessary regency." Graduates of the Parisian-type universities were required to teach for a period upon taking their degrees. During these years, they were called *regents,* a status they continued to hold as long as they taught or held any of various kinds of administrative posts within the institution. Upon completion of their regency stints, many graduates entered other occupations but, called *nonregents,* they retained suffrage rights in the government of the universities. Thus—to limit the discussion to Oxford for the moment—two governing bodies evolved: the Lesser Congregation of Regents and the Great Congregation of Regents and Nonregents, today respectively referred to as Congregation and Convocation. In sum, the right of Oxford alumni to share with members of its permanent staff in making university policy has a long lineage. The same statement can be made about Cambridge, which also has two comparable and historic governing bodies—Regent House and the Senate.

During the course of time, the specifications for nonregency status in both Oxford and Cambridge have been markedly tightened, and the powers of nonregents have also been drastically limited. Nevertheless, it remains that alumni have shared in the government of both universities since the medieval era. It should also be observed that the University of Paris and its continental offspring operated in the same general way for several centuries, but since British practices have had a significant impact upon the basic characteristics of American academic government, the wearing away of alumni governing rights in other countries need not be enlarged upon. Concerning the present-day situation in countries other than those within the Anglo-American orbit, the following observation made in 1922 still holds: "For the graduate of a continental university, the word *alumnus* has little meaning. Practically no ties of sentiment bind him to his alma mater. It is the outstanding teacher, of course, that attracts the student, who passes easily from one university to another. In Germany, whatever university sentiment the graduate has is reserved for his corps, the equivalent of our fraternities, or for the partly academic, partly convivial *verein* which centers about the branch in which he is specializing. Even these slender ties are lacking for the French university man. Save as a citizen, he has no voice in the management of his university, nor does it ordinarily even seek to keep in touch with former students" (Shaw, 1922, p. 680). Despite the antiquity of alumni partnership in the government of Oxford and Cambridge, the last sentence in this quotation, slightly modified, also applies currently to the universities of Britain. The amended sentence reads: "Save as citizens, alumni have *little* voice in the management of the universities, nor do the universities ordinarily even seek to keep in touch with former students." I amplify this statement for Oxford and Cambridge and later for the Scottish and newer English universities. Between these two brief expositions comes a description of the devoted, although extralegal, solicitude of the alumni of the resident colleges of Oxford and Cambridge.

Convocation at Oxford and the Senate at Cambridge continue to function, but their powers have been so effectively curtailed during the past century that they may fairly be called anachronisms. Until 1854 these bodies, about 90 percent of whose members were nonstaff alumni, dominated institutional decision making so thoroughly that they largely controlled the appointment of professors; and until 1922 they continued to hold the whip hand in fiscal matters. The famous William Osler, who became Regius Professor of Physic after having taught medicine for thirty years in Canadian and American universities, described the situation there in 1910:

> That no conservatism is so strong as in a democracy is well illustrated by Oxford and Cambridge, the two oldest democracies in Europe, which today, as in the Middle Ages, are in control of the Masters of Arts, whose voice decides everything from the election of a Chancellor to the disposal of a five-pound note. In Oxford the resident M.A.s and professors, with the heads of the colleges, form a body called Congregation, and these, with all M.A.s, resident and nonresident, on the books of the colleges, form Convocation. The former has 526 members, the latter about 7,000. Every Tuesday in term

at 2:00 P.M. these bodies meet to transact university business, prepared by a smaller body called the Hebdomadal Council. As a rule, the attendance is small—a handful of men—but when an important question is before the university several hundreds may be in Congregation, while the outside M.A.s from all over the country may swarm to Oxford (even in special trains!) to *placet* or *non placet* a contentious measure [Osler, 1910, p. 544].

Because the majority of the alumni who took the time to exercise their suffrage in Convocation and Senate stubbornly resisted change, commissions, appointed by the national government in 1919 and 1923 further whittled down the functions of both assemblies to these innocuous two: (1) the election for life of a distinguished public figure to the Chancellorship, largely a ceremonial post, and (2) the consideration of statutes passed by the resident governing bodies (Congregation at Oxford and the Regent House at Cambridge) by no less than two thirds of those present and voting, a prerogative that has never been exercisable at either university since the constitutional changes made in 1919 and 1923. At Oxford, Convocation also elects a distinguished literary figure to the professorship of poetry for a short, nonrenewable term. The post carries an honorarium of £300, its incumbent lecturing when and if the spirit moves him.

Although they have long since passed into desuetude, Convocation and Senate meet half a dozen times each term, but alumni per se seldom attend. Consider Oxford, for example. Since resident staff members belong to both Congregation and Convocation, they fill the seats at the meetings of both bodies. "Fill," however, serves poorly in the last sentence because typically only a few of the members of Congregation trouble to appear at its sessions; and these same regulars make up the bulk of attendance at Convocation. The same situation prevails at Cambridge. In short, organized alumni collaboration has all but vanished from the government of both universities. Neither of them, moreover, keeps in touch with former students through alumni associations, alumni magazines, or any of the other means employed in the United States. Such activities they leave to their autonomous colleges, none of which exploits these devices with the persistency displayed in American colleges and universities.

In the government of Oxford and Cambridge, *college* alumni have never had a legal voice. Departed students, however, have always had very great influence, especially in protecting their colleges from those who have sought to abridge their privileges. Well over a century ago, John Henry Newman chronicled the power of their alumni in the following graphic passage:

> There is no political power in England like a College in the Universities; it is not a mere local body, as a corporation or London company; it has allies in every part of the country. . . . It [a college] is a second home, not so tender, but more noble and majestic and authoritative. Through his [the alumnus's] life he more or less keeps in connection with it and its successive sojourners. He has a brother or intimate friend on the foundation, or he is training up his son to be a member of it. When he hears that a blow is levelled at the Colleges, and that they are in commotion—that his own College, head and Fellows, have met together, and put forward a declaration calling on its members to come up and rally round it and defend it, a chord is struck within him, more thrilling than any other; he burns with *esprit de corps* and generous indignation; and he is driven up to the scene of his early education, under the keenness of his feelings, to vote, to sign, to protest, to do just what he is told to do, from confidence in the truth of the representations made to him, and from sympathy with the appeal. He appears on the scene of action ready for battle on the appointed day, and there he meets others like himself, brought up by the same summons; he gazes on old faces, revives old friendships, awakens old reminiscences, and goes back to the country with the freshness of youth upon him. Thus, wherever you look, to the North or South of England, to the East or West, you find the interest of the Colleges dominant; they extend their roots all over the country, and can scarcely be over-

turned, certainly not suddenly overturned, without a
revolution [Newman (1856) 1902, pp. 227–228].

Several strong "revolutionary" efforts have been made to
overturn the power of the Oxford and Cambridge colleges but,
until the recent past, they have largely failed. Commissions appointed by the national government have coerced them into trans-
ferring some of their income and a few of their functions to their
parent universities, but they continued strong until the 1960s, when
large government grants directly to the university proper gave new
authority to the umbrella organization.

To describe the government of the Scottish and of the newer
English universities, I must recall a fact about the University of
Edinburgh reported in Chapter Two; namely, that it opened in
1583 with a lay governing board. The three older universities of
Scotland operated somewhat similarly after their post-Reformation
reorganization, but in none of the four did alumni have governing
rights comparable to those of their Oxford and Cambridge counterparts. Graduates, however, began to share in their management
after Parliament in 1858 reconstructed the four institutions by
assigning the government of each to a small board called a *court*,
supplemented by a much larger body called a *general council*. On
the latter, alumni have continuously been predominant in numbers
but apparently not in influence.

The court of a Scottish university consists of somewhat
fewer than twenty members, four or five of whom have been chosen
by the faculties from among their own number. The remainder are
administrators and nonacademics, four of them (called *assessors*)
being elected by the general council. To the latter also belong faculty members below the rank of professor, but alumni greatly out-
number them because they automatically become enrolled upon
paying the registration fee imposed when they take their degrees.
Through these general councils the graduates of the Scottish universities can, when and if they so desire, influence their policies.

In neither the Scottish nor—for that matter—the newer
English universities, however, do alumni usually or potently affect
policy. Few attended the meetings, and only occasionally are grad-

uates per se elected as representatives on the courts. In brief, alumni have the means to affect policy but seldom use it. Nor do their voluntary-membership associations (usually called *guilds of graduates*) often project themselves into university affairs. Rather, they largely limit their activities to promoting camaraderie.

The American Scene

I have sketched the evolution of the part played by alumni in helping determine the policies of British universities in order to controvert the widespread belief that they are Johnny-come-latelys in academic government. Apparently, however, American practices have developed independently of historic precedents abroad. Neither alumni nor the college presidents and trustees who sought their assistance seem to have drawn consciously upon the experience of Britain. They began *de novo* but undoubtedly with at least a subliminal awareness of the prerogatives of Oxford and Cambridge degree holders.

The Latin word *alumnus,* "pupil, foster son," emerged in English in the mid seventeenth century. It derives from the infinitive *alere,* "to nourish," and many of those nourished by Alma Mater (fostering mother) have not only ministered to her but also to her blood relatives, that is, to other colleges and universities. Thus the principal founders and key members of the governing boards of Harvard and William and Mary had attended English, Scottish, and Irish institutions; and nine of the ten "Partners and Undertakers" who launched Yale, the third college to be established, had been educated at Harvard. Upon the death of these precursors, alumni predominated among their successors; and, in turn, their successors have chiefly been former students. The same generalization can be made about the lay governors of many other institutions, including some financed by legislatures. These trustees do not serve, however, as official representatives of the alumni but, instead, have been chosen because of their personal qualities. In such ways, the products of higher education have always been actively engaged in American academic government.

Similarly, alumni in general have diligently promoted the development of their own and of other colleges and universities.

For example, the General Court of the Massachusetts Bay Colony
—long presided over by an alumnus of Trinity College, Cambridge
—accelerated the cause of higher education in accepting a gift of
about £800 and about 400 books made by a master of arts of Em-
manuel College, Cambridge, named John Harvard. A century
later, graduates of the Collegiate School of New Haven introduced
the legislation in the General Court of Connecticut which converted
it into Yale College, thereby honoring the memory of a noncollege
man whose patronage had been solicited by a graduate of Harvard.
Alumni have also taken the initiative in the founding of most later
institutions, including state universities, Jefferson's helmsmanship in
the establishment of the University of Virginia being but one of
many cases in point. Alumni, in sum, have been the chief cham-
pions not only of the colleges that they attended but also of other
institutions, both private and public.

From the very beginnings of American higher education,
moreover, alumni have contributed support of private colleges and
universities; and, as legislators, lobbyists, and molders of public
opinion, they have strategically influenced the subsidizing of higher
education. For instance, in association with two younger graduates,
two members of Harvard's first class of seven bachelors of arts
(1642) purchased and gave the College a small parcel of land on
which now stands a portion of Widener Library (Morison, 1936c).
Direct alumni benefactions did not become a major factor in academic financing until late in the nineteenth century, but they have
hoary precedents. So has alumni facilitation of legislative support
of higher education, zealous alumni being assiduous stimulators of
such support in all states of the Union.

Not until the late eighteenth century did alumni begin to
organize formally, and not until the mid nineteenth did they first
participate as representatives of their fellows on college and university governing boards. I scan these developments in preparation
for examining the present scene.

The college class long constituted the primary academic and
social unit of American institutions of higher education. Especially
before the adoption of the elective principle and before the onset
of soaring enrollments, the members of a class primarily looked to
one another for companionship and confidantes. The associations

thus formed often continued through life, and this inevitably led members of closely knit classes to facilitate their fellowship by means of group meetings at commencement and later by the election of class secretaries to keep records and to circulate news among members. Commencement reunions go back to the earliest days, but the Yale Class of 1792 appears to have been the first to create the office of secretary. Later classes at Yale and at other colleges followed suit, and the post—like the concept of the class that it fortifies—continues to be significant in many institutions.

Associations open to all former students rather than classes, however, soon became the paramount foci of most alumni activities. Williams organized the first of these in 1821 under circumstances that illustrate the worth of alumni interest. Williams opened in 1793, but various considerations, including its location in the remote and thinly populated northwest corner of Massachusetts, halved its small student body from a maximum of 115 to 58 in 1815–16 (Spring, 1917, p. 99). This led to a series of efforts to move it to a more promising locale, but the Massachusetts legislature vetoed the idea. Soon thereafter the pro-removal president resigned and accepted the headship of the academy then in the process of becoming Amherst College. Worse, he took a fifth (fifteen) of Williams' students with him (Tyler, 1895, p. 26). These blows threatened the survival of the College; but "a number of gentlemen educated at the Institution," led by a recent graduate who later became governor of the state, called a meeting to learn "the true state of the college" and to organize the alumni for its "support, protection, and improvement" (Rudolph, 1956, p. 201). Those who assembled on September 5, 1821, inaugurated the Society of Alumni of Williams College, the country's and probably the world's first such association.

Bowdoin and Columbia followed the Williams lead in 1825, Princeton in 1826, Miami and Rutgers in 1832, Georgia in 1834, and the University of Pennsylvania in 1836. Thereafter the idea took hold generally, as witness the score of groups formed by 1850. Comparable organizations have long been commonplace across the nation. Alumni energies, variously coordinated, have long been harnessed in the interests of American colleges and universities.

Especially between the first and second world wars, sharp

criticisms of alumni, expressed not only by academics but also by some of themselves, abounded. Before then, however, few thought organized alumni activities inimical; and of late the number and severity of criticisms have waned.

As earlier remarked, alumni have always had seats on the governing boards of American colleges and universities, but not until 1865 did any assume office as representatives of their fellow graduates. The change began at Harvard in the spring of that year through legislation passed by the Massachusetts General Court. It provided that as vacancies occurred on the Board of Overseers they should be "annually supplied by ballot of such persons as have received from the College a degree of Bachelor of Arts, or Master of Arts, or any honorary degree, voting on Commencement Day, no member of the Corporation, the administration, or of any of the faculties being eligible" (*Charter of the President and Fellows of Harvard College*, 1976, p. 15). The plan went into effect the following year, and later legislation has extended suffrage and potential membership to holders of degrees from the Harvard professional schools. Thus, since the Board of Overseers must approve of all major decisions of the Corporation, the "ultimate responsibility" for the government of Harvard has been in the hands of its alumni for over a century (Conant, 1939, p. 23). A statement made by President Eliot epitomizes the role played by the alumni in Harvard affairs: "When the President and Fellows [the Corporation] led by the Faculties, are too rapid or too experimental in their action, the Board of Overseers will serve as a brake; but if the President and Fellows become inert or too conservative, the Board of Overseers will provide the needed stimulation" (Eliot, 1908, p. 64).

Unicameral institutions could not follow the same plan as bicameral Harvard, but several of them soon adapted it to their situations: Cornell in 1867, Bowdoin, Oberlin, and Wesleyan in 1870, Williams and Yale in 1872. A bit later, others also turned over some board places to alumni: Amherst in 1874, Dartmouth in 1875, Rutgers in 1881, Princeton in 1900, Columbia in 1908, Brown in 1914. The leading women's colleges followed the pattern too—Vassar in 1887, Smith the next year, and Wellesley in 1894. No authoritative data seem to be available about the number of boards that now include elected alumni members, but among private institutions the proportion appears to be one in every two.

In twenty state institutions, alumni qua alumni sit on legal entities by legal right. Governors appoint the alumni trustees of eight of these institutions, in three instances from among the nominees proposed by alumni organizations. An alumni representative serves ex officio on four boards, and the alumni bodies of eight universities elect their own representatives. Alumni trustees, it should be observed, differ little from their fellows because most boards have alumni members regardless of legal requirements (Cartter, 1964).

Several other developments paralleled the assignment of board posts to alumni beginning during the late decades of the nineteenth century. These included the appointment of full-time officers to administer alumni affairs, the establishment of annual money-raising campaigns usually called alumni funds, the publication of magazines to foster alumni interest and to interpret and influence institutional programs, the allocation of places to alumni on standing committees, especially those concerned with athletics, and on ad hoc groups concerned with educational and administrative problems, the use of the alumni of publicly financed institutions in legislative relations and those of private institutions in seeking gifts and bequests, and the organized employment of alumni in recruiting students. More recently, colleges and universities have actively promoted the opportunity for alumni to enroll in courses especially designed for them and taught by members of the institutions' faculty.

Critics of Alumni

I believe I have demonstrated the dynamic impact of alumni upon institutional policies, and hence the chapter could be ended at this point. Criticisms of alumni, however, have not been wanting; and some of them have been so derisive that they need to be exhibited and commented upon. Here are seven excoriations, one written during each of the first seven decades of this century:

Distinguished Essayist, 1907: I used to care somewhat about Harvard College; but since those circulars

about Eliot's seventieth birthday and the three million
fund, and all of that bombast and vulgarity, I cannot
bear to be called "a loyal son of Harvard." This chest-
thumping, back-slapping, vociferous and cheap emo-
tionalism, done to get money and land money, is too
much like everything else. . . . Everything seems to be a
baseball team—jollying, rough good-feeling, and a thoroughgoing belief in money and us [J. J. Chapman,
quoted in Howe, 1937, p. 226].

Editor, 1910: When "the old grad" of any university sits by the open fire of the commons or fraternity
house and the young men gather around in an attitude
of disciplehood that they rarely show to their official
teachers, what does he talk about? Is his conversation
apt to be of a character that could be called edifying?
Does he help along what the president and faculty are
trying to do with these boys, or does he counteract their
influence? What sort of an idea would they gather from
his stories of the college life of his day about the educational influences which have contributed to his successful career?

Of course he is merely lying, but that is only a
partial justification of his conduct. He is telling the most
harmful kind of lies. In order to make himself solid with
the boys he is making himself out unfit to associate with
anybody [Slosson, 1910, p. 78].

Socialist Muckraker, 1922: I asked one of the
most eminent of American scientists, a man who has
lived most of his life in universities, what is the matter
with these institutions, and his answer came in an ex-
plosion: "It is the semi-simian mob of the alumni! They
have been to college for the sake of their social position;
they have gone out utterly ignorant, and made what they
call a success in the world, and they come back once a
year in a solid phalanx of philistinism, to dominate the
college and bully the trustees and the president" [Sin-
clair, 1923, p. 363].

University President, 1934: All alumni are dan-
gerous. They see their Alma Mater through a rosy haze
that gets thicker with the years. They do not know what
the college was like. They do not want to know what it is

like now. They want to imagine that it is like what they think it was like in their time. Therefore they oppose all change. If changes are made without their approval, they are resentful. Since no useful change could ever be made with their approval, few useful changes have been made in higher education [Hutchins, 1936, p. 87].

College President, 1942: Anyone who has opportunity to meet and study in large numbers the alumni of the American colleges is likely to have attacks of depression. In spite of the vast investment of money and energy in these institutions, it is only too clear that in a great many cases education has failed to take, or the infection has been so slight that few traces are to be perceived after five or ten years of the wear and tear of American life [Nielson, 1941–42, p. 4].

Professor of English, 1954: The familiar symbol of the lamp of learning whose flame enlightens the mind of men, and the common motto of *Lux et Libertas,* might, I suggest, more appropriately be replaced by the figure of a fullback *couchant* before the goal posts *rampant.*

And when we cease to render lip service to the myth we no longer believe, we might in the tone of university-alumni relations, rewrite our diplomas in the new style: "Hiya, ol Pal, We Gonna Win, Our Grads make Good, Our Gals Got Glamour, We Build Big Buildings, Gimme!" [Shockley, 1954, p. 487].

Social Psychologist, 1962: The trouble with students, the saying goes, is that they turn into alumni. Indeed, a close look at the college-educated people in the United States is enough to dispel any notion that our institutions of higher learning are doing a good job of liberal education [Sanford, 1962, p. 10].

If this were a treatise on alumni and alumni affairs per se, a detailed analysis of these criticisms would be in order, but only three or four comments concerning their bearing upon academic government have present relevance. First, they—and most other such blasts—ignore the meritorious characteristics and activities of alumni. Some administrators *do* employ lamentable methods in soliciting funds from alumni. Some alumni *are* perpetual sophomores clamoring for never-losing football teams. Some *do* try to project themselves into academic affairs and snipe at professors whose ideas they oppose. Some *are* so loyal to Old Nostalgia that they do their damnable best to obstruct essential change. Such administrators and such alumni, however, have always been a minority, even though criticisms such as those quoted give a contrary impression.

Second, few changes in American higher education have been as pronounced as the growth of alumni serious-mindedness not only about the affairs of their own colleges but also about the world in general. At alumni meetings, speakers typically used to talk more about athletics than about education and the intellectual concerns of Alma Mater, but an invitation received in more recent times from the University of Chicago illustrates the huge change that has taken place in our day. It came from the San Francisco Bay Area Alumni Club of the University and described a meeting scheduled to begin early in the afternoon and to continue through the evening. The invitation listed seven faculty members from Chicago, Stanford, and the University of California who would speak, not about alumni affairs, but about their academic specialties—anthropology, business administration, English literature, and so forth.

Since President Ernest Martin Hopkins of Dartmouth urged in his 1916 inaugural address that institutions of higher education should assume the responsibility for the continuing education of their former students, scores of institutions have been offering their alumni fare similar to that of the meeting just cited. Many of them have organized what they originally called *alumni colleges*, which meet during the spring or summer over a period of several days or even weeks; many publish reading lists; some operate book-lending services for their alumni; and several on occasion display alumni paintings and sculpture. These enterprises have done much toward puncturing the stereotype of the alumnus as a peghead who stubbornly refuses to understand the activities of egghead professors and hence of colleges and universities. Indeed, studies by social psychologists and sociologists of college graduates show substantial changes in alumni attitudes and interests during recent decades (Freedman, 1962).

Third, two of the criticisms quoted refer to the backslapping, athletic-stressing techniques employed by administrators and alumni secretaries; but anyone familiar with alumni affairs knows how markedly attitudes and methods have changed. Some retarded institutions still employ the rah-rah approach in nurturing alumni interest and soliciting funds, but the better institutions have long since outgrown their Stover-at-Yale adolescence. Anyone who doubts this should read such alumni magazines as the *Harvard Alumni Bulletin*, the *Dartmouth Alumni Magazine*, and the *Ohio State University Monthly*.

Fourth, the volume and vehemence of criticisms made of alumni and of alumni officials have very substantially abated during recent years. Thus I have had to search long and hard to find remonstrances published since the end of the Second World War. Their paucity witnesses the spreading belief that alumni are better qualified than during any earlier period to have a voice in deciding college and university directions. Some academics, of course, hold strongly to the opinion that, qualified or not, alumni should have no governmental rights, but both the medieval precedents and the American experience reviewed in this chapter undermine their thesis. In any case, alumni participation is today a deeply embedded fact in American academic government and seems certain to grow in significance and, I believe, in value.

One final point about the relationship of alumni to institutional government must be made, to wit, that the notion occasionally expressed—and notably in a peppery book of the early fifties by a Yale graduate (Buckley, 1951)—that alumni should be the ultimate authorities in the determination of policy has no justification either in fact or in sound theory. Alumni constitute important, and indeed essential, participants in college and university decision making, but final authority has never been and never should be theirs.

SEVEN

Association Influence

One of the most valuable services performed by voluntary agencies is accreditation. The national and regional accrediting associations do essentially what ministries of education do in most countries. Their work is outside the framework of law but is almost as compelling as if it were law. Their decisions are accepted as the voice of authority.
U.S. President's Commission on Higher Education, 1947a

Thousands of academic associations encircle and variously act upon American colleges and universities. A complete listing and authoritative categorization of these voluntary groups would be a difficult task but, aside from those interested in alumni and student affairs, they fall into the following fifteen categories, with some examples of each:

1. Accrediting bodies, both regional and professional: Northwest Association of Schools and Colleges, National Council for the Accreditation of Teacher Education
2. Subject-matter societies: the American Chemical Society, the American Economics Association
3. Broad subject-area councils: the American Council of Learned Societies, the Social Science Research Council

145

4. Organization of analogous institutions: the Association of American Universities, the Association of American Colleges

5. Societies of administrators: the National Association of College and University Business Officers, the American Association of Collegiate Registrars and Admission Officers

6. Organizations of college and university trustees: the Association of Governing Boards of Universities and Colleges

7. Fund-raising agencies: the Council for Financial Aid to Education, Washington Friends of Higher Education

8. Agencies performing various services for colleges and universities: the Educational Testing Service, the Teachers Insurance and Annuity Association, the American College Testing Program

9. Subdivisions of religious denominations: the Association of Southern Baptist Colleges and Schools, the Association of Jesuit Colleges and Universities

10. Groups devoted to furthering various educational enterprises: the Institute of International Education, the National University Extension Association

11. Councils and associations concerned with higher education in general either nationally or regionally: the American Association for Higher Education, the Southern Regional Education Board

12. International bodies: UNESCO, the International Association of Universities

13. Groups devoted to the advancement and preservation of faculty prerogatives: the American Association of University Professors, the National Education Association, the American Federation of Teachers

14. Honorary fraternities: Phi Beta Kappa, Sigma Xi

15. Honorific academies: the American Academy of Arts and Sciences, the National Academy of Education

In varying degrees, all these kinds of organizations influence college and university policy making, and in a thoroughgoing assessment of American academic government all would need to be considered. That would require a long book; and so I discuss only those that most powerfully affect teaching and research, namely, the first two listed above: accrediting bodies and subject-matter societies.

Accrediting Bodies

As it relates to education, the term *accreditation* signifies three kinds of endorsement: of schools and higher educational institutions, of college and university departments and schools, and of individuals trained vocationally therein. These enterprises have come upon the academic scene to facilitate the transfer of students from one institution to another, to protect society against fraudulence and incompetence, to enforce minimum standards, and to encourage educational and professional upgrading. Because of the American federal system of civil government and the resulting absence of national controls on education, voluntary associations superintend the first and second of these kinds of accreditation; but each of fifty-five American legal jurisdictions (the fifty states, the District of Columbia, Guam, Puerto Rico, and the Virgin Islands) administers its own specifications for the certification of individuals. The three varieties of accreditation interact, however, and hence I shall comment on all three.

Institutional Accreditation. Building on European precedents that go back many centuries, the older colleges on the eastern seaboard employed examinations (oral until about a hundred years ago) to judge the qualifications of candidates for admission. This method, however, proved too onerous for the newly organized secondary schools of the Middle West; and so in 1871, the University of Michigan inaugurated what came to be called the Certification System and which soon became standard over the country except in the East. It had these characteristics: (1) colleges and universities accepted an applicant for admission to the freshman year on the say-so of the secondary school he had attended; (2) state universities annually sent "school visitors" (faculty members in various subjects) to inspect the schools and to help them improve their curriculums and methods of instruction; and (3) higher educational institutions admitted only those applicants who had attended schools that visitors had certified (accredited). The organization in

1895 of the North Central Association of Colleges and Schools led eventually to that group's assuming the accreditation function throughout the nineteen North Central states between the Alleghenies and the Rockies.

Meanwhile, two Eastern groups of schools and colleges had formed for the purpose of discussing admissions and related topics —the New England Association, organized formally in 1886 after half a dozen years of preliminary activities, and the Middle States Association, established in 1888. Both backed entrance examinations in opposition to the Middle Western certification plan, and their deliberations led to the creation in 1900 of the College Entrance Examination Board. These three bodies and the three other regional associations that now span the country did not get into the business of accrediting colleges and universities until later. More prestigious structures initiated that function, namely, the Association of American Universities for both graduate schools and undergraduate colleges and the American Medical Association for medical schools. David Starr Jordan has recorded how the former got started: "With the beginning of 1900 there was inaugurated an important movement for cooperation in higher education. This began at the University of Chicago in the conference called by the University of California at the instance of Dr. Armin O. Leuschner, professor of Astronomy, and made up of representatives of American institutions providing for research. Its occasion was the receipt from the authorities of the University of Berlin of a request for data to enable them to reach a just valuation of American degrees, the standards in this regard among our 575 colleges being very unequal" (Jordan, 1922b, p. 1). The conference to which Jordan refers took place at the end of February, 1900, representatives of eleven leading American universities foregathering to discuss how "to secure in foreign universities . . . such credit as is legitimately due to advanced work done in our universities of high standing" (Association of American Universities, 1901, p. 11). Reaching tentative conclusions on this question, they "went on to discuss various other matters of common interest and enjoyment" (Jordan, 1922b, p. 1) and decided to organize the Association of American Universities "for the purpose of considering matters of common interest to graduate study" (Association of American Universities, 1901,

p. 14). They also extended invitations to three institutions not represented, bringing the number of original members of the association to fourteen.

The plans made during the early years of the Association of American Universities (AAU) for informing the universities of other countries (Germany in particular) about the institutions whose work they should credit turned out to be discriminatory against universities not among its members and also against all unitary colleges. This led the association in 1913 to prepare a list of 119 colleges and universities, including its own members (increased to twenty-two), that met its standards, for transmission to the "Prussian Kultusministerium and corresponding ministers of other German states" (AAU, 1913, p. 59). Four years later, it published an augmented enumeration of 138 institutions for the use of registrars in evaluating applicants for admission to American graduate and professional schools (AAU, 1917). In this fashion, the AAU produced the first lists of nationally accredited colleges and universities. It continued as the country's most authoritative accrediting agency until 1948 when, after publishing a list of 283 approved institutions, it abandoned the function (AAU, 1948). Since then no other body has appraised the quality of colleges and universities the country over. Instead, the six regional associations referred to earlier have assumed the task for their territories. Three of them had been so engaged for many years (Selden, 1960), the North Central Association having published its first list eight months before the AAU made its original national enumeration in 1913 (Kelly and others, 1940).

Accreditation of Substructures. Before we examine the impact of overall institutional assessments, attention needs to be given to the accreditation of university substructures. This enterprise got under way earlier than the comprehensive enterprises dealt with earlier, the medical profession taking the lead. Other professions traveled over much the same road somewhat later, and so a sketch of the evolution of medical accreditation will serve to delineate the general pattern.

Two anecdotes about the Harvard Medical School, established in 1782, illustrate the sorry state of American medicine until late in the nineteenth century. The first tells of how William James, after having attended a three-month course of lectures repeated almost verbatim during three successive years, passed his final examination in 1867 and simultaneously became a doctor of medicine and a licensed practitioner:

> In a large room a number of professors sufficient to examine in the nine principal subjects disposed themselves at suitable intervals. The students circulated singly from one to the next and were quizzed on a new subject at each station of the journey. Every ten minutes a presiding functionary sounded a bell and the candidates moved along. When the bell had pealed nine times . . . the examiners were expected to be ready to vote. This they did without consultation. . . . Each had a piece of cardboard that was white on one side and marked with a black spot on the other. The Dean called the name of a candidate and pronounced a formal question and a command—"Are you ready to vote? Vote!" The nine examiners simultaneously thrust forward their cards. If the Dean counted not more than four black spots, the candidate received his degree. . . . When the candidate had thus captured his degree . . . he could hang out his sign and work his ignorant will on the patients who came to him, for under the laws as they then were a School diploma conferred the right to practice [James, 1930a, pp. 275–276].

The second anecdote reports an event that occurred three years later when Harvard's recently inaugurated young president, Charles W. Eliot, attempted to introduce written examinations in place of the orals just described. The Faculty of Medicine vetoed the proposal, the Dean conveying the decision to Mr. Eliot: "Written examinations are impossible in the Medical School. A majority of the students cannot write well enough" (Eliot, 1924, p. 127). Small wonder since no American medical school at that time required any college work for admission, and many students entered without having graduated from secondary school. In fact, the great majority of practicing physicians had never attended medical school: They got their training as apprentices. This situation so appalled Eliot that he wrote in his 1871–72 report to the Harvard governing boards: "The ignorance and general incompetence of the average graduate of American medical schools . . . is something horrible to contemplate" (Eliot, 1873, p. 25).

Medical leaders, most of them the products of European schools and hospitals, had for some decades been attempting to do something about the low state of their profession. Thus, in 1846, they organized the American Medical Association (AMA), including among its plans creation of "a uniform elevated standard of requirements for the M.D. degree" (Kelly and others, 1940, p. 66). Progress toward that goal, however, depended upon the improvement of medical education which, despite the efforts of Eliot and other presidents, did not begin to make strong forward strides until the opening of the Johns Hopkins Medical School in 1893. Associated with the world-renowned Johns Hopkins Hospital, having a faculty of brilliant titans, stressing the sciences underlying medicine, and requiring an undergraduate degree for admission, it inaugurated the modern era of American medical education.

Columbia, Harvard, Pennsylvania, and the schools of a few other universities had been pushing ahead steadily if also slowly. The program of Johns Hopkins gave them all—and the Association of American Medical Colleges (AAMC), organized in 1890—a tremendous shot in the arm. It also fortified both the designers of the new schools being established by universities and the reorganizers of those being appropriated. Then, in 1902, the AMA, supported by the AAMC, took the first steps toward the accreditation of medical schools and hospitals by appointing a committee of five which two years later became the Council on Medical Education (CME). The developments thereafter can best be summarized in a chronological table:

1905: First report of the CME summarizing the initial inspection of medical schools undertaken by the AAMC in 1903.

1906: A four-group classification established by the CME, the primary criterion being the percentage of a school's failures on state board examinations.

1908: The weeding out from its membership by the AAMC of proprietary schools and of schools offering the bulk of their instruction during the evening.

1910: (1) Publication of the Flexner study, *Medical Education in the United States and Canada*, leading to the closing of many of the 156 schools still in operation among the 457 historically organized; (2) 66 schools accredited by CME; (3) admission requirements set at eight years of grammar school, four years of high school, and at least one year of college.

1911: The Federation of State Medical Boards (FSMB) organized.

1913: (1) A year of premedical work in college added to admission requirements; (2) a year of hospital internship encouraged.

1918: (1) Two years of college work required for admission; (2) the FSMB accepts the accredited list of the CME and the AAMC; (3) 59 schools accredited, all but 3 as Class A.

1919: Joint inspection begun by the CME and AAMC.

1920: The CME becomes the CME&H, the "H" signifiying Hospitals.

1927: The CME&H begins to certify hospitals for residencies.

1930: The AAMC recognized by the FSMB as the standardizing agency in all matters relating to medical and premedical education.

1934: A new survey of medical education begun and published in 1937.

1938: Three years or more of college work for admission strongly urged.

1942: The work of the CME&H and the AAMC coordinated through the establishment of the Liaison Committee.

1953: A minimum of three years of college work for admission required and four years strongly recommended.

Since 1953 the requirement of four years of college work for admission to medical school has become standard, and other expectations have grown apace. Issues in recent years have included the encouragement of medical students to prepare for primary care rather than specialization, the similar encouragement of graduates to consider practicing in regions (usually rural or inner city) not currently well served by the medical profession, constitutional questions over the admission of minorities to medical schools, and calls for earlier clinical experience than now occurs. Perceptive observers of medical education, noting the apparent success of medical schools in gearing their curriculums to the scientific demands stated in the Flexner report, are now beginning to wonder if a better balance might include more attention to the social sciences and humanities (Odegaard, 1966).

Much the same process of upgrading has occurred in architecture, dentistry, law, pharmacy, and other professions and also in the academic disciplines (such as chemistry) which have established accrediting agencies. Despite, and indeed because of, their effectiveness, however, these groups have come under attack for reasons that can more appropriately be considered after reviewing the third type of accreditation.

Accreditation of Individuals. Since at least the first century of the Christian era, individuals trained vocationally in higher educational institutions have been subjected to accreditation or, to use the more frequently employed synonyms, have been certified or licensed to practice the occupations for which they have studied. Vespasian, Roman emperor from A.D. 69 to 79, and his successors during the next two centuries, for example, accredited in three ways: (1) by licensing professors of law, (2) by limiting the legal practice of medicine to those who had studied in state-supported medical schools, and (3) by bringing distinguished professors of rhetoric to Rome and paying them high salaries (Durant, 1944). Later Valentinian, in 329, set up qualifications for teachers in the higher schools of the empire, and the Theodosian code of 438 extended them. These precedents undoubtedly influenced medieval licensing practices, and Paulsen (1906) has shown how Prussia drew upon them in establishing state examinations for lawyers in 1693.

The decline of higher educational institutions and of the professions that resulted from the dissolution of the Roman Empire in western Europe put accreditation into the hands of the medieval Church, professional practitioners all being ecclesiastics except in Italy, where laymen still practiced law and medicine. Teaching in particular came under the control of the Church; and in each diocese the chancellor or archdeacon, acting for the bishop, issued teaching licenses. This led to the controversy between the Parisian guild of masters of arts and the chancellor of the Diocese of Paris discussed earlier.

Diocesan chancellors issued the *licentia docendi* or license to teach after a candidate for the masters degree had been examined by representatives of the faculty in which he had studied. Although the approval of the chancellor became *pro forma* after Gregory IX promulgated his famous bull of 1231, he continued to endorse teachers until the secularization of the universities in the sixteenth century. Meanwhile, the license evolved into the academic degrees that have been in use ever since. Concurrently, admission to recognized status in the practice of law and medicine or as theologians to a prelate depended upon one's having an advanced university degree.

An American term still in use in the twentieth century signifies the method of licensing that superseded the authority of the Church, namely, the *diploma privilege*. It denotes the right of an individual to practice the occupation for which he has studied because of the fact that an educational institution has given him a degree in the subject. The diploma privilege has largely lapsed in Europe for a complex of reasons, including the spread of nationalism and the decline of privileges of universities, state examinations replacing it. Prussia established such examinations for law in 1693, for medicine in 1725, and for school teachers in 1810 (Paulsen, 1906). Napoleon codified the system of state examinations for the professions in France, and during the middle of the last century Britain supplemented its long-established licensure statutes and oral scrutinies by requiring written demonstrations of intellectual competence.

In the United States, the diploma privilege continued to be the major method of licensing professionals into the twentieth century. It will be recalled from earlier in the chapter that William James acquired his license to practice medicine in 1869 merely by passing a number of ten-minute oral quizzes given by members of the Harvard medical faculty who also certified him to the University's governing boards for the degree of doctor of medicine. No state established effective regulations for medical licensure until ten years later, Massachusetts not until 1895, and the majority of jurisdictions not until after 1900. Since then, all jurisdictions have abrogated the diploma privilege in medicine, and it has largely disappeared in law and other professions. In short, civil government has all but completely taken away from higher educational institutions the function of accrediting individual practitioners. In the process, further, civil government agencies have acquired strategic influence over curriculums and teaching methods in all schools and departments whose products they examine for licensure.

It must be observed that because universities and not civil governments confer degrees, and also because of the cordial relationships that usually exist between state boards and professional faculties, the latter have considerable freedom of action. The fact remains, however, that the points of view of those who examine the products of an educational program definitively influence its nature and, indeed, frequently make the vital decisions concerning it. "It must not be forgotten," wrote President A. Lawrence Lowell, "that examinations essentially control the content of education" (Lowell, 1921b, p. 272). He might have added that teaching methods are also affected. Having initiated comprehensive examinations and the tutorial system at Harvard, Lowell knew whereof he spoke.

Criticisms of Accreditation. The licensing of individuals by civil government comes in occasionally for criticism, but protests against the activities of the voluntary agencies that accredit institutions and their substructures have been extremely sharp. They bear upon a dozen or so considerations, but four stand out prominently: (1) by requiring governing boards to spend funds for buildings, equipment, and staff under threat of losing their endorsement, accrediting agencies force institutions to neglect programs in areas not under accreditation control; (2) by requiring that certain courses be taught (often by means of specified methods), they limit educational experimentation and progress; (3) by decreeing that undergraduates planning to enter professional schools take stipulated preprofessional courses, they limit the opportunities of students to become broadly educated; and (4) by basing their standards on proven practices of the past, they have difficulty adjusting to non-

traditional practices (such as those found in external degree programs) that do not fit the conventional mode.

The reiteration of these and other criticisms by college and
university presidents of high prestige led the American Council on
Education to call a conference of accrediting agencies early in 1939.
Samuel P. Capen, Chancellor of the University of Buffalo and an
early enthusiast for accreditation, addressed them. In 1931, he had
applauded accreditation heartily, commenting that "the standardizing movement is some twenty-five years old." "When it began,"
he continued, "there were literally hundreds of institutions, colleges,
academies, medical schools, law schools, and dental schools that
were selling to the public—often at considerable profit to their
backers—educational gold bricks." Accreditation, he pointed out,
had curtailed these practices. "No such brilliant success," he concluded, "has ever attended any other movement in American education" (Capen, 1931, p. 96). At the 1939 conference, however,
Capen reversed himself:

> I shall now hoist the black flag. I have made it
> my mission in life to prey on you and all your kind. I am
> against standardizing, any standardizing whatever, and
> against all accrediting. I am persuaded that it would be
> better for the future of higher education if you were all
> to disappear as of tomorrow and if your places were left
> permanently vacant. The necessary job of vigilance com-
> mittees—and I freely admit that it was once necessary—
> has been done. The crooks are under lock and key, or
> they have already tasted hemp and are no more.
>
> The issue is plain. Is the American university sys-
> tem to be dominated by competitive blackmail, or is it to
> be conducted in accordance with the best judgment of
> the boards and administrative officers charged with this
> responsibility through charters and through legislative
> enactments? [Capen, 1939, pp. 10, 17]

Capen overstated the case against accreditation, but the fact
remains that academic associations exert significant and often in-
exorable pressures upon college and university governing bodies.
Among these external bodies, accrediting agencies bulk large. Con-

tinuously and consequentially, they limit the freedom of action of professors, presidents, and trustees.

Subject-Matter Societies

Incalculably more potent than accrediting agencies in shaping college and university policies are the learned societies. Zealously devoted to research, these organizations have been prime agencies during the past century in broadening and deepening knowledge of the nature of the universe and of man, in improving living standards by fostering the acceleration of technology, and in spurring the modernization of education. Since I know of no account of their history to which readers may be referred, I survey it briefly before commenting on how they affect academic government.

Among the national audits made during the centennial year of 1876, a number of scientists and scholars assessed the status of American intellectual achievement, a prominent chemist writing, for example:

> America, when compared with other first-class nations, occupies a low position in science. For every research published in our country, at least fifty appear elsewhere. England, France, Germany, Austria, Russia, Italy, and Sweden outrank us as producers of knowledge. Our original investigators in any department of learning may almost be counted on the fingers. Fifteen or twenty chemists and physicists, as many mathematicians and astronomers, and a somewhat larger number of zoologists, entomologists, botanists, and geologists, would fill out our meagre catalogue. Among these few discoverers a comparatively small proportion are of high rank. There may be in the United States, all told, twenty men of really actual achievements with Sir William Thomson, Helmholtz, or Regnault. In geology we make a pretty fair showing, perhaps, because of the great facilities for research offered by our surveys and exploring expeditions. The newness of our country has also been of advantage to our zoologists, who have not failed to improve their opportunities. But in chemistry and

physics, the two sciences most intimately connected with our greater industries, we have accomplished very little [Clarke, 1876, pp. 467–468].

Simon Newcomb, the country's leading astronomer, wrote in the same vein and declared that "the development of the higher branches of the sciences [is] marked by the same backwardness which characterizes the higher forms of thought in other directions: and that however eminent we might stand in the lower branches, we . . . find ourselves far behind in the higher ones." This "comparatively imperfect development of our thought in the direction of science is not due," he observed, "to any lack of native ability," but rather could be accounted for by the absence of government support, by the failure of Americans to give their lives to continuous scientific investigation, and by the meagerness of facilities for the publication of scientific literature (Newcomb, 1876, pp. 92, 101).

The ink had hardly dried on these laments before two events occurred that set in motion enterprises that would help markedly to correct the situation—the establishment of the American Chemical Society and the opening of Johns Hopkins University.

A few learned societies had been organized in the United States before the establishment of the American Chemical Society on April 20, 1876, but they had small memberships and limited scope. Few professors, moreover, belonged to them, colleges and universities, as I shall show directly, having little interest in research. The action of the chemists together with the animated endorsement of research by Johns Hopkins University, however, signaled an irresistible change of direction; and during the next three decades, hundreds of associations came upon the scene. At least one took form in every subject-matter field and often in their subdivisions. The following typify the major groups now flourishing:

Society	Date organized
American Chemical Society	1876
Archeological Institute of America	1879
Modern Language Association of America	1883

American Historical Association	1884
American Economics Association	1885
American Mathematical Association	1888
Geological Society of America	1888
American Psychological Association	1892
Botanical Society of America	1893
American Physical Society	1899
American Philosophical Association	1900
American Anthropological Association	1902
American Political Science Association	1903
American Sociological Association	1905
American Classical League	1919

Aside from the American Chemical Society, most of whose members hold governmental and industrial positions, the majority of those belonging to these societies teach in colleges and universities; and the leadership of them all has come largely from the professoriate. This has resulted primarily from the shift to the research emphasis initiated by Johns Hopkins upon its opening in 1876. Daniel Coit Gilman, its first president and the author of its trend-changing program, "had in view the appointment of professors who had shown their ability as investigators, whose duties as teachers would not be so burdensome as to interfere with the prosecution of their best work, and the fruit of whose labors in the advancement of science and learning should be continually manifest in the shape of published results. With this general purpose in view, Mr. Gilman's first tasks were to lay hold of a set of picked men who should give just the impulse that was wanted for the making of this new departure in the higher education in our country, and at the same time to add to his own knowledge of the methods and the ideals prevailing in European centers of learning" (Franklin, 1910, p. 196).

Among the college and university presidents in office in 1876, Gilman alone emphasized the urgency of research, but the achievements of the Johns Hopkins faculty rapidly convinced others that they should follow his leading. In his inaugural address seven years earlier, President Eliot had observed that Harvard had "not a single fund" for research except the small endowments of its astronomical laboratory; and he also asserted that "the prime business of American professors in this generation must be regular and assiduous classroom teaching" (Eliot [1869] 1961, p. 617). "The most devoted professors will contribute something to the patrimony of knowledge," he conceded; but until Gilman stirred up the academic waters, Eliot did little to encourage such men. Witness his response to a young chemist on the faculty who asked for some free time to do research. "What will be the result of these investigations?" the President asked. "They would be published," was the reply. The President wanted to know where. The professor named a German chemical journal. "I can't see that that will serve any useful purpose here," said Eliot, who dismissed the professor with no further comment (James, 1930b, p. 19).

Developments at Hopkins, however, soon revised Eliot's point of view; and when somewhat later a Harvard biologist made a comparable request, Eliot approved and thereafter earnestly encouraged research (James, 1930b). Other presidents took their cues from Hopkins, more specifically William Rainey Harper at the University of Chicago and David Starr Jordan at Stanford, who had the exhilarating challenge of designing new universities. Both made research the preeminent function of faculty members, Harper requiring each appointee to sign an agreement that his promotions in rank and salary would depend chiefly upon his research productivity. In turn, Jordan asserted that "a professor to whom original investigation is unknown should have no place in a university. Men of common-place or second-hand scholarship are of necessity men of low ideals, however carefully that fact may be disguised. A man of high ideals must be an investigator" (Jordan, 1888, pp. 8–10).

In swinging over American higher education to the new research emphasis, Gilman, Eliot, Harper, Jordan, and their fellows had the continuing support and, indeed, the persistent stimulation of the waxing subject-mattter societies. These organizations had been organized primarily to promote the advancement of knowledge, and they have remained constant to that purpose. Only occasionally and briefly do they turn their attention to problems of education.

Foundations, individual benefactors, industry, and government have furnished the bulk of research funds, but the societies have been the supreme agencies in changing the attitudes of professors, presidents, and trustees about research and hence in making it the sovereign function of universities and increasingly of colleges. They have been able to accomplish this deep-cutting change because the spectacular fruits of scientific investigations in particular have convinced even the proverbial man-on-the-street of the value of research. Building on this pervasive conviction, the learned societies have effectively diverted the loyalties of an ever-growing proportion of academics from the institutions that pay their salaries. This shift in allegiance has been inevitable because of, first, the huge prestige attached to research; second, the inability of any but one's peers to judge the significance of an inquiry; and third, the fact that the societies constitute organized groups of such peers. Since this book has to do only with academic government, the ramifications of this epochal academic mutation cannot here be explored. I seek only to describe it and to show how it affects the policy making of colleges and universities.

In 1924, an administrator who during his career headed three universities discerned a subtle but pivotal change in faculty values. "It seems to me," he commented, "that individual faculty members today are less deeply rooted in the soil of the institution they serve, less complete in the identification of their interests with its development, less concerned about it as an institution, than were the men who came into university faculties a generation ago. There are, of course, numerous and outstanding exceptions, but I do believe that, while we have gained enormously in the competency of instruction, we have lost something of the deep sense of personal attachment of an earlier day. And this loss seems to me to constitute an important problem for those who are concerned about the most effective functioning of universities" (Chase, 1924, p. 66). Two years later, President Chase discussed the trend again and suggested that the learned societies had become the cynosure of professorial fealty. In his words, "Their [faculty members'] audience is no longer that of their immediate classroom. It is rather their own craft, scattered throughout the academic world. It is by impressions made on these fellow-specialists that the future is more to be determined than by the quality of teaching that goes on in their present jobs. . . . I do not mean to minimize the devotion and unselfish-ness of large groups of men and women on college faculties. But it remains true that there has been a change in the typical satisfac-tions of the academic life. They have come to center more about professional recognition, with a consequent tendency toward les-sened interest in the immediate problem of good teaching and the individual needs of students" (Chase, 1934, pp. 290–291).

These problems aside, the learned societies and area councils are making strong and occasionally successful efforts to develop interdisciplinary research and teaching and hence to counterbalance the divisive specialism that has become such a dominant character-istic of colleges and universities. These enterprises have great prom-ise, especially in research, but they have not significantly changed teaching practices. Nor have they made much impression on the proclivity of academics to consider themselves "professors of chem-istry, psychology, and political science" and as such to vote on policy questions as the representatives of special interests. In short, faculty members by and large give their allegiance not to the higher learning in the broad but, instead, to their departments and to the learned societies that reinforce them. Their colleges consist, in the words of one observer, of "leagues of more or less amicable sover-eign states, each of which is intent on preserving its own sovereignty unsullied and unimpaired. The only issue on which the league itself is inclined to act cooperatively is the opposition to presidents or trustees proposing measures that threaten their separate or cor-porate sovereignties" (Millett, 1945, pp. 18–19).

Interdisciplinary efforts may in time mature sufficiently to change the prevailing fragmental commitments of professors, but meanwhile few will deny that departments and the learned societies undergirding them extensively influence the educational and re-search programs of colleges and universities. Together with accredit-ing bodies and most of the other clusters of academic associations listed earlier, they continuously circumscribe and often cripple insti-tutional policy decisions.

EIGHT

Philanthropic Impact

Frederick T. Gates early this century to John D. Rocke-
feller: "Your fortune is rolling up, rolling up like an ava-
lanche! You must distribute it faster than it grows! If you
do not, it will crush you and your children and your chil-
dren's children."

Nevins, 1940

Those who pay the pipers do not call all, or even a majority of, the tunes played by colleges and universities. The patrons who provide them with capital resources and other funds, however, decide upon many of their selections and have a good deal to say about the arrangements they employ in rendering their repertoires. Among these congeries of sponsors, philanthropists have been conspicuous for the magnitude of their support and for the weight of their influence. I shall try to show that they have had and have at least as much to do with shaping institutional policies as the professors who assert that "primary responsibility" in such matters must be theirs.

Individual donors have both nurtured and helped mold higher education since its inauguration in the Western World. Plato endowed the Academy with funds that continued to yield income until its dissolution almost 900 years later; the benefactions given Oxford and Cambridge during the Middle Ages estab-

163

lished the college system that dominated their histories for centuries thereafter; and the "colledge" created by the Massachusetts Bay Colony in 1636 two years later took the name of the first of the great host of men and women who have contributed their mites and their millions to American colleges and universities.

John Harvard's bequest of about £800 ensured the success of the nation's initial adventure in higher education, and the approximately 400 books that it also included made it possible for the new college early to gain acceptance of its degrees at Oxford and Cambridge. For about 250 years, the major private patrons of American higher education were individuals like John Harvard, but during the present century philanthropic foundations have become transcendent. Generous individuals, however, continue to be numerous and highly significant. I discuss their impact upon colleges and universities first.

Individual Donors

An earlier chapter summarized the contributions of alumni to their colleges and to higher education generally, and hence they need not be dealt with here. Some of the individuals to be cited in the following pages attended the institutions they aided, but the majority did not. All sorts of people, educated and uneducated, have helped—literally "rich man, poor man, beggarman, thief; doctor, lawyer, merchant chief." Their gifts have ranged from subscriptions of a few pence during colonial times to the princely gifts more recently acquired by persuasive presidents, trustees, and their unquenchable agents.

During early times and often much later, most benefactors gave their little or their much to establish colleges and to keep them afloat rather than to support particular studies. Since they buttressed rather than deflected established conceptions of education, they have little relevance to the topic in hand; but a few examples will help set the stage for later program-shaping gifts and bequests.

Although several of the colonial colleges had financial assistance from civil government, private persons chiefly supported them. During its first century or so, Harvard, for instance, received about £20,000 from the public treasury but nearly £56,000 from individuals. In turn, Massachusetts authorities conveyed 3,300 acres of land to the College in comparison with 3,793 given by individuals (Bush, 1891, p. 66). Private persons also supplied the College with building materials, equipment, and a miscellany of contributions such as sheep, cotton cloth, a pewter flagon, and such silver goods as fruit dishes, silver spoons, and jugs (Peirce, 1833). They also contributed produce, a large number of New England families from 1644 to 1652, for example, annually donating a peck of wheat or its equivalent in money. The proceeds amounted to enough to pay faculty salaries and to support about a dozen needy students (Morison, 1936c, p. 15).

Virginia supported William and Mary, the wealthiest of the colonial colleges, by assigning it portions of the duties collected from exports such as distilled spirits plus a fraction of the license fees paid by surveyors and peddlers. Its chief income, however, came from its large land holdings. The monarchs after whom it took its name gave 2,000 acres; and before the Revolution other benefactors, including the executors of the primary organizer of the Royal Society, Robert Boyle, supplied 18,000 more. Its first president, incidentally, had an alert financial nose, as evidenced by the following anecdote told by one of his successors:

> Some years before Dr. Blair's visit to London, the English authorities had caused it to be made known that any pirate coming into port by a certain time should be forgiven his past transgressions and permitted to retain a part of his ill-gotten treasure. Many availed themselves of this concession to make their peace with the government; but there were three pirates—Edward Davies, John Hinson, and Lionel Delawafer—who came in after the date set by the law, and, as a consequence, were arrested and put in jail. They sent a humble petition to the privy council for pardon, alleging that they did not know of the proclamation till it was too late to come in by the day appointed. Dr. Blair saw his chance, hunted the pirates up, and offered to use his influence in their behalf, if they would consent to give the sum of £300 of the goods under seizure to the use of his proposed college. This the pirates readily agreed to do, and, through

the intervention of Dr. Tillotson and Dr. Compton, the
pirates were pardoned, and an order was entered by the
privy council on March 10, 1692, for restoring to them
their treasure, minus the amount promised to the college
in Virginia [Tyler, 1907, pp. 9–10].

What later came to be called "tainted money" also made it
possible for the third American college to emerge from its cocoon.
A dozen plus years after the founding of Connecticut's Collegiate
School, its agent in London (one Jeremiah Dummer, a Harvard
graduate and the first native-born American to earn the Ph.D.
degree) interested Elihu Yale, a former official of the East India
Company, in its welfare. Yale had made a fortune from his "on the
side" trading ventures, an investigation of which led him to restore
some of it to the company. With the remainder he returned to
England and, as proper for a follower of John Calvin, became a
philanthropist. Dummer, seconded by Cotton Mather, who strongly
disapproved of the theology in vogue at his alma mater, laid before
Yale the needs of the Collegiate School. Yale's resulting gifts, valued
at £800, so delighted the trustees that they immortalized their
benefactor by renaming the institution in his honor.

Neither Elihu Yale nor John Harvard changed the programs
of the colleges they assisted, but other individuals have helped to do
so. Most donors designate how their money shall be spent, but the
majority sponsor ideas suggested to them by professors, presidents,
and trustees. Such ideas frequently run counter to those of the
majority of people within the recipient institution, and they become
operative only because the new funds given to support them over-
ride opposition. In short, to be launched, the plans of internal
minorities often require the pressure supplied by external backers
who play secondary but essential roles in these maneuvers.

Campus-conceived projects, it should be noted, differ markedly from those directly proposed by donors who have strong con-
victions of their own and who are able to persuade an institution
to accept them. A not inconsiderable proportion of the enterprises
underwritten by philanthropic foundations fall today in this latter
category, but most individual benefactors apparently take their cues
from institutional representatives. In the examples of personal

philanthropy to be reported in the next few paragraphs I shall, where possible, indicate the sources of the conceptions they have subsidized; but in most cases, the relevant facts have not been published or even recorded.

A London merchant named Thomas Hollis appears to have made the first program-changing gifts to an American college. Jeremiah Dummer solicited funds from Hollis for Yale, but Hollis preferred the more liberal theology simmering in Cambridge. In 1721, therefore, Hollis offered to endow a professorship of divinity at Harvard; and, being a Baptist, he stipulated that none be refused the chair "on account of his belief and practise of adult baptism" (Morison, 1936c, p. 66). The orthodox members of the Harvard governing boards, however, rebelled against this and other conditions of the donation, one overseer declaring that "Mr. Hollis could not bribe *him* to say that infant baptism didn't matter." The ensuing politicking led to the appointment to the professorship of a young ministerial alumnus who declared his adherence to all the doctrines held dear by the theological stalwarts but who, during his forty-three years' tenure, "proved the vanity of academic oaths and tests" by leading "the way out of the lush but fearsome jungles of Calvinism" (Morison, 1936c, p. 68). Thus did a donor accelerate a salient change in Harvard's teaching and, to boot, in the direction of American religious thought.

Hollis, "to whom Harvard owes more," one of its historians has written, "than to any other benefactor outside her alumni" (Morison, 1936c, p. 66), also vitalized the teaching of science. The year after he provided funds for the creation of the Hollis Professorship of Divinity, he gave Harvard a twenty-four-foot telescope and other astronomical apparatus (Morison, 1936c). Somewhat later, he financed the establishment of the Hollis Professorship of Mathematics and Natural Philosophy held by a succession of distinguished men of science, one of them a Nobel Prize winner (Morison, 1936c). Hollis selected the first incumbent who, along with his immediate successors, introduced experimental science into the Harvard curriculum. Most other colleges continued until the next century to offer their students outmoded textbook fare, and thus here too a perceptive philanthropist significantly helped fashion academic policy.

A frequent problem of many nonprofit institutions throughout most of their history has been the finding of revenues to inaugurate new activities and methods. This problem has often vexed higher education which, conservative because of its essential nature, must ceaselessly deal with widespread antagonism to change not only among the general public but also among its staff, governors, and friends. Since colleges and universities cannot in the main raise venture capital through the means available to commercial enterprises, they must employ the circumscribed devices at their disposal. The most productive of these until the present century—that is, before legislatures and philanthropic foundations became such conspicuous cornucopias—were generous, far-sighted individual benefactors. They have been and, indeed, continue to be key fulcrums in lifting American colleges and universities to higher ground. Thus it would be possible to show, I believe, that the great majority of advances made by American higher education until the relatively recent past have resulted from the assistance given by individuals. Thomas Hollis, in short, has had hundreds of history-making successors; but their energizing contributions in only four areas can be sketched here, namely, agriculture, engineering, business administration, and medicine. I have chosen the first three of these subjects because their advocates collided with deeply entrenched academic traditions which funds provided by private philanthropists helped initially to counteract. As I shall show in due course, medical education, though a respected university study since ancient times, languished until the wealth of perceptive benefactors vivified it late in the last century.

The Hellenic and Hellenistic thinkers whose ideas until quite recently pervaded all institutions of higher education everywhere deplored all studies related to the work of the world. Almost to a man, academics unyieldingly believed that only banausic (vulgar, menial) men engaged in such activities; and hence they would have been shocked at the suggestion that agriculture, engineering, and commerce should be studied in universities. Not until the nineteenth century would these subjects be reluctantly admitted to lowly status in European universities, and only recently have those of Germany included them. The same attitudes hampered their cultivation in American colleges, but the passage of the Land Grant College Act led to suppressing the antagonism of all but small clumps of sullen diehards who still believe that these studies do not belong in universities. Like-minded men all but monopolized higher educational policy at the time that President Lincoln signed the Act in 1862; and thus its promoters succeeded in their arduous campaign for its passage and for the remodeling of American colleges only because the terrain had been readied by pioneer educators and laymen, cheered on by discerning men of wealth.

During the late eighteenth and early nineteenth centuries, Benjamin Frankin, Thomas Jefferson, Benjamin Rush, and a number of other leading Americans resolutely advocated what later came to be called technical education; but not until Stephen Van Rensselaer provided funds did it begin to make headway. Impressed by the work of Amos Eaton, whose lectures and investigations in New England and New York aroused a swelling interest in science, Van Rensselaer in 1824 established a school in Troy, New York, headed by Eaton, "where people would receive instruction . . . in the application of science to the common purposes of life" (Baker, 1924, p. 6). Toward this end, he then and later gave something over $20,000 to found what developed into Rensselaer Polytechnic Institute (R.P.I.). It opened primarily devoted to agriculture but soon became famous as a civilian engineering school, the first in the English-speaking world.

A decade earlier, that extraordinary American expatriate, Count Rumford (Benjamin Thompson), bequeathed Harvard funds to extend the industry, prosperity, happiness, and well-being of society by "the useful arts." He stipulated the founding of a "new institution" related to Harvard which would train applied scientists like himself; but the Corporation decided to assign the income of the bequest to a professor of medicine for delivering occasional lectures on technology. Had Rumsford's intention been honored, Harvard would have become the first American institution of higher education to foster engineering and allied subjects. That distinction, instead, belongs to R.P.I.

Van Rensselaer, a Harvard graduate and one of the promoters of the Erie Canal, glimpsed the momentous importance of applied science; and so did the second philanthropist to subsidize it, namely, Abbott Lawrence, a Boston merchant, textile manufacturer, and railroad builder who had not attended college. In 1847, he gave Harvard $50,000 with which it established the Lawrence Scientific School. That same year, two young enthusiasts contributed their meager savings and all their time to projecting what developed into Yale's Sheffield Scientific School. Since they illustrate a kind of philanthropy that occurs more often than is generally known, I narrate briefly their feat and its remarkable consequences.

The two pioneers were John Pitkin Norton and Benjamin Silliman, Jr., twenty-two and twenty-nine years old, the latter the son of Yale's distinguished Professor of Chemistry, Mineralogy, Pharmacy, and Geology who began his teaching career there in 1799. In the summer of 1846, the elder Silliman presented to the Yale Corporation a document, written by his son, entitled "Proposals for Establishing a Chair of Agricultural Chemistry and Vegetable and Animal Physiology." The Corporation approved the proposal in August and a year later appointed Norton to the professorship named in the proposal. It also named young Silliman "professor of chemistry and the kindred sciences as applied to the arts."

Yale, however, gave no money for the support of the venture; and, in the words of one of its historians, "it is more than doubtful if it would have given it" since the impression "seemed generally to prevail that chemistry, like virtue, must be its own reward" (Kingsley, 1879b, p. 106). Norton and Silliman therefore used their own funds to rent a house for their laboratory and to buy equipment. Their income consisted of the fees paid by their students—eight the first year and eleven the second. They called their project the Yale School of Chemistry which, to give the two young adventurers faculty status, the Corporation made a division of the created-for-the-purpose Department of Philosophy and the Arts. Their little school constituted "the arts," a term which in those days referred more frequently to the utilitarian than to the liberal arts.

Young Silliman withdrew from the enterprise in 1849, and Norton, debilitated by overwork, died of tuberculosis three years later. Happily, two other young men were available to carry on the project: John A. Porter and William A. Norton. The former, a chemist, continued the agricultural emphasis of the original two-man team, and the latter, an engineer not related to John Pitkin Norton, initiated engineering instruction. They worked under the same no-salary, no-support plan of their predecessors, but the Corporation permitted them to use Yale's name in soliciting funds. In these endeavors they prospered spectacularly primarily, it seems, because Porter successfully courted the daughter of New Haven's richest citizen, Joseph E. Sheffield. Sheffield's gifts to Yale of more than a million dollars during the following two decades led the Corporation to acknowledge the Cinderella of applied science and to recognize the Sheffield Scientific School as an integral part of the University. Porter, of course, became the School's first dean.

Like most other men of wealth in the United States before the Civil War, Sheffield had started his career as a merchant and then became interested in building and financing railroads. He made the bulk of his fortune, for example, in developing what grew into the New York, New Haven, and Hartford and the Chicago and Rock Island. Understandably, the school that bore his name promoted engineering education. It continued its concern in agriculture, however, and as late as 1890 Sheffield stood out as the nation's leading producer of fundamental research in the subject.

Meanwhile Harvard, impelled by the largest benefaction it had to date, also inaugurated work in agriculture. The donor, Benjamin Bussey, a Boston merchant whose son had been a member of the Class of 1803, bequeathed Harvard in 1835 securities and real estate worth almost half a million dollars, about two thirds of which he stipulated should be used for agricultural education. Legal and other complications delayed the opening of the school (the Bussey Institution) until 1871. Eight years later, Harvard graduated its first Bachelor of Agricultural Science.

Agricultural education, however, waned at both Harvard and Yale, in part because of the reproaches poured upon it by faculty members who taught the traditional subjects and in part because of the huge sums of money being spent for it in the institutions created by the Land Grant College Act. Thus Yale closed out its program in 1903, and six years later Harvard converted the Bussey Institution into a unit for advanced instruction and research in biology. Beyond doubt, both institutions as well as other private universities would have developed into important centers of agricultural education had not the Land Grant College Act been passed; but the point to be emphasized here is that neither academics nor civil government but, instead, private philanthropists introduced the subject into American higher education. The great majority of academics, in fact, thundered against the "cow colleges" and the admission of "bumpkins and yokels" to the hallowed groves of Academe. They did their bitterest best, in fact, to harass the enterprise even in the land-grant institutions.

Engineering education encountered the same hostility. For example, the Yale authorities would not permit Sheffield students to live in the same dormitories as the students of Yale College, or to belong to the same fraternities, or, until the mid 1880s, to play on Yale football teams. President Noah Porter and most faculty members recognized the necessity of technical education but they insisted that it be completely isolated from the classical education given in Yale College. An event of 1886 emphasized this segregationist attitude: Yale included no members of the Sheffield faculty among its delegates to Harvard's two hundred and fiftieth anniversary celebration even though its director, George J. Brush, had long been a close friend of President Eliot (Canby, 1936).

This "what is useful is vulgar" bias continued to dominate Yale until 1920 when the College and Sheffield merged. It also accounted for the rise of a score of pioneering engineering schools unconnected with universities and financed by public-spirited men of wealth, including, for example: (1) Armour Institute of Technology (now Illinois Institute of Technology), founded in 1892 as the result of a gift of $2.5 million made by Philip D. Armour; (2) Case Institute of Technology (now Case-Western Reserve University), established in 1880 with funds, eventually totaling $2.35 million, provided by Leonard Case; (3) Massachusetts Institute of Technology, chartered in 1861 and opened four years later after two Boston citizens contributed $50,000 to initiate its phenomenal career; (4) Stevens Institute of Technology, began in 1870 with the $650,000 plus a city block in Hoboken bequeathed by Edwin A. Stevens; and (5) Throop Polytechnic Institute (now California Institute of Technology), organized in 1891 by Amos G. Throop with a gift of $100,000.

Following the examples of Lawrence and Sheffield at Harvard and Yale, philanthropists also expedited technical education in established colleges and universities, as witness the fact that the engineering schools of Cornell, Dartmouth, Pennsylvania, Princeton, and a number of other institutions memorialize their names. State universities, including those resulting from the Land Grant College Act, did not in general become significant centers of applied science until after the beginning of the twentieth century. Hence the vital enterprise of engineering education got under way in the United States primarily because private benefactors subsidized it.

The statement just made also applies to schools of business administration, vigorous opposition to which came not only from academics but also from run-of-the-mill businessmen. A gift to the University of Pennsylvania in 1881 of $100,000 (later increased to half a million) by a Quaker entrepreneur named Joseph Wharton led to the establishment of the first such structure—the Wharton School of Finance and Commerce. Not until 1912, however, did it achieve enough status to have its own faculty and dean (Pierson and others, 1959).

After 1898, other universities ventured into the direct education of the increasing numbers of college graduates who were entering upon business careers. During that year, the daughter of one of the Comstock Lode "Bonanza Kings," Cora Jane Flood, gave the University of California half a million dollars for "the general purpose of commercial education," its School of Business resulting. Concurrently, the University of Chicago organized its School of Commerce and Administration, which made little progress, however, until fortified by a portion of the $10 million "final gift" of John D. Rockefeller to the University in 1910. During the year in which these two schools got under way, an English literary man who some years later became Britain's Minister of Education sneered at the education of intending businessmen in universities, declaring that "three primary forces" would provide all the training needed—"ambition, necessity, and greed" (Birrell, 1922, pp. 304–305).

Happily, a few wealthy American businessmen disagreed with the Englishman and provided the funds for the creation of the first group of university schools of business administration to be established in the United States and, indeed, anywhere in the world. For decades now, most American businessmen and academics have accepted them as proper higher educational enterprises; and, although the majority of them now in operation are divisions of state universities, they originally came into American higher education through the efforts of open-minded and open-handed outsiders. The same generalization applies to modern medical education, to which I now turn.

The University of Pennsylvania, Columbia, Harvard, and Dartmouth instituted medical departments during the last third of the eighteenth century; but, like the more than 400 medical schools established between then and the publication of Flexner's history-making exposé of American and Canadian medical education in 1910, they functioned essentially as proprietary enterprises. That is, their faculty members operated them for profit, distributing student fees among themselves. In the previous chapter, I touched upon the barbarous results of this system and upon the crusade that President Eliot began in 1869 to upgrade the Harvard Medical School. He ended the proprietary era of the School by paying salaries to its professors, and he enforced notable revisions in admission requirements and in curricular procedures. Faculty opposition and lack of funds, however, made other urgently needed changes impossible. American medical education, therefore, did not begin to make significant forward strides until the opening in 1893 of the nation's first modern medical school and teaching hospital in Baltimore.

In his will, probated in 1874, the Baltimore Quaker merchant-financier, Johns Hopkins, bequeathed $7 million, half of it for a university, the other half for a hospital. The university opened in 1876, but the hospital board took about a decade to consummate its plans. By that time, the university trustees found themselves in such deep financial straits that they could not organize the medical school that Hopkins had stipulated should be under university control rather than that of the hospital board. Thus half a million dollars of new money had to be raised, and into the breach came five young feminists whose wily generosity made it possible for the medical school to open but under conditions that coerced two history-making changes in medical education.

The leader of the five young feminists, all about thirty-five years of age, was Mary Elizabeth Garrett, the daughter of a Hopkins trustee who had died some years before President Gilman approached her for assistance. She and her friends (one of them being the indomitable president of Bryn Mawr College, M. Carey Thomas) agreed to contribute $100,000 but only on the condition that the medical school admit women. The board of trustees had no choice but to accept, even though it and the faculty had stubbornly opposed coeducation to the point, so the story goes, of requiring Miss Thomas during her student days to sit behind a curtain in the classes they permitted her to attend. But $100,000 was insufficient. Having won their first point, the group decided upon a second condition before making up the needed balance of $306,000: The Hopkins board would have to agree to require a bachelor's degree of all students admitted to the medical school. Urgently needing the money, the board again gritted its collective teeth and submitted. Thus, the Johns Hopkins University Medical School opened in 1893 not only to accelerate the beginning of the modern period of American medical education but also to manifest the policy-shaping power of strong-minded donors.

As earlier observed, during the previous quarter of a century, President Eliot had been striving valiantly to improve medical education at Harvard. In his efforts he had the enthusiastic assistance of Calvin Ellis, the dean of the Medical School, and of the members of the faculty who helped counteract the opposition of the Old Guard. Ellis continued to promote progress after his death in 1883 by leaving the Medical School $150,000, the first gift of substantial size that it had had to date. The big push forward, however, had to await the example of Johns Hopkins. It motivated Harvard in 1900 to solicit $5 million for the building and endowment of a new medical plant and for the establishment of new professorships. About a hundred individuals made contributions, three giving a little more than half the total: John Pierpont Morgan a million and a third, John D. Rockefeller a million, and Mrs. Collis P. Huntington a quarter of a million. Andrew S. Draper, president of the University of Illinois at the time, reported some years later the circumstances of the Rockefeller subscription:

Half a dozen years ago the richest man in the country became suddenly ill. In the absence of his regular physician he called in a young graduate of the

Harvard School of Medicine [William B. Coley, M.D., 1888] and impulsively assured him that if he would get him out of that scrape he would pay any charge that he might make. The case was not serious to an educated man. The young man understood the difficulty and soon he wrought the needed cure. No bill was sent and in time it was asked for. The young physician reminded the multimillionaire of the promise. "Oh, yes," he said, "but I assumed, of course, that your charge would be within reason." The doctor's time had come. He said: "I shall make no charge, but I shall ask you to do something for me. The Harvard School of Medicine needs help. I would help her if I could. Under the circumstances I feel warranted in asking you to look into the matter with a disposition to aid her justly, as you easily may." The old man said, "Would you like to bear a message to President Eliot?" "Yes." "Ask him to come and tell me all about it." In a week the man of wealth had given his pledge to the president of Harvard for a million when the balance should be raised, and in a month five millions had been assured which have erected and equipped the finest plant for a medical college that is to be found in the wide, wide world [Draper, 1907, p. 75].

In his narrative Draper bent the facts a bit; but be that as it may, the story reveals the pivotal role played by unitary givers in vitalizing American medical education.

During the nineteenth century, individual donors—typically against fervid faculty objection—animated not only the four subjects treated here but also every sector of American higher education. Further, they continue to be incalculably important agents in opening up new roads and in widening old ones. During the present century, however, philanthropic foundations have become such fabulous and influential dispensers of largesse that they have thrown private patrons into the shadows.

Foundations

Beginning in 1940, I served a term on the Problems and Plans Committee of the American Council on Education, and I well remember a discussion at one of its sessions concerning the influence of foundations on education. In particular, I remember the observation of a distinguished university president in the group that he would much rather be the head of a leading foundation than of any university in the world. Why? Because, he said, foundation officers (philanthropoids) wield incomparably more policy-molding power than university presidents or, indeed, than any other group in the academic world.

Soon after the expression of this judgment, the Ford Foundation orbited into the foundational firmament to become its Jupiter, and those who have dealt with the philanthropoids on its staff can testify to their magisterial proclivities. *Ipse dixits*, however, need not alone be depended upon in describing the prowess of the foundations. After a brief rundown on their rise, I give some examples.

The eleemosynary trusts commonly referred to as philanthropic foundations have a long history reaching back in this country to two established by Benjamin Franklin, but they did not become numerous or conspicuous factors in American academic affairs until the creation early this century of those organized by Andrew Carnegie and John D. Rockefeller. Beginning in the 1880s, these prolific Mascenases gave many millions to churches, colleges, hospitals, and various other social institutions; but, seeking help in bestowing their benefactions, soon after 1900 they turned over large sums to foundations. Each of them created about ten such bodies, but the following four in particular have been concerned with education:

- *The General Education Board*: Established in 1902 by Rockefeller with an initial grant of a million dollars and a total of $129 million before his death in 1937. In 1960, its trustees voted to expend their last remaining funds, thus closing out an agency that "had appropriated nearly $325 million for the promotion of education in the United States" (Fosdick, 1962, p. 1).

- *The Carnegie Foundation for the Advancement of Teaching*: Projected in 1905 with an endowment of $10 million for the purpose of providing pensions for American and Canadian professors. Carnegie's letter to the trustees he appointed to direct the Foundation barred members of the faculties of state-supported and also "sectarian" institutions from participation in the pension program, but in 1908 he provided an additional $5 million so that the former might be included. I shall later describe the furor caused by this pioneering adventure in philanthropy and also the high-yield results of the $1.25 million that Mr. Carnegie gave the Foundation in 1913 for the creation of its Division of Educational Enquiry.

- *Carnegie Corporation of New York*: Carnegie made his first large gift in 1896—a million dollars to the Carnegie Institute of Pittsburgh. Between then and his seventy-fifth birthday in 1910, he gave away some $200 million, but he still possessed a large fortune which, following his dictum that "the man who dies rich dies disgraced," he wished to dispose of benevolently. Thus, in 1911, he established Carnegie Corporation with an endowment of $125 million to which he later added another $10 million. According to the words of its charter, the Corporation contributes to "the advancement and diffusion of knowledge and understanding among the people of the United States," Canada, and "the British Colonies." In contrast to the two Rockefeller bodies here being sketched, it holds its principal fund in perpetuity.

- *The Rockefeller Foundation*: Rockefeller began his philanthropies in the mid 1880s, the University of Chicago and the Rockefeller Institute for Medical Research being the largest recipients of his liberality until he created this major foundation in 1913 with an initial endowment of $100 million. Before his death in 1937, he added another $135 million; and in 1929, the Foundation acquired the assets (just short of $59 million) of the Laura Spelman Memorial Fund, organized in 1918 in memory of Rockefeller's wife. Established "to promote the well-being of mankind throughout the world," it has especially emphasized assistance to public health and medical education. Among the recipients of fellowships awarded by the Foundation are many Nobel Prize winners.

These four giants dominated higher educational philanthropy until the Second World War, but since that time a number of other foundations have joined them in support of higher education. Notable among this list are the Danforth Foundation, W. K. Kellogg Foundation, Esso Foundation, Ford Foundation, Kettering Foundation, Lilly Endowment, and Rockefeller Brothers Fund.

Inevitably those who distribute such large sums have enormous influence upon those they assist. "They say that knowledge is power," Lord Byron wrote a friend a century and a half ago; "I used to think so; but now I know that they meant *money*" (Byron [1822] 1966, p. 11). Money has been called the sinews of war, of life, and of innumerable other pursuits, and certainly today, more than ever before, the bastions of knowledge called colleges and universities need it in ever-increasing quantities. That the philanthropoids who supply it have influenced the institutions they favor —and those too that they neglect—I shall try to illustrate through the remaining pages of this chapter.

Carnegie Pensions. Carnegie established the Carnegie Foundation for the Advancement of Teaching in April 1905 primarily for the purpose of providing pensions for professors. As a trustee of Cornell, he "was shocked to discover" that they "were paid only about as much as office clerks" and that "for a professor to save for old age from his small salary was next to impossible" (Lester, 1941, p. 45). In his letter setting up the Foundation, he instructed its trustees to determine how the institutions whose faculty members were thus to be assisted should be selected. This gave three members of the board (Charles W. Eliot, the first board president; Nicholas Murray Butler, a member of its small executive committee; and Henry S. Pritchett, the Foundation's first president) the fateful opportunity to use the Foundation to help accelerate a campaign in which Eliot and Butler had long been engaged, namely, upgrading American secondary and higher education. That project, in fact, immediately became the prime business of the Foundation and accounts for the words "the advancement of teaching" in its name. Carnegie had, in effect, given the trustees a steel-engraved invitation to reform American education; and Eliot, Butler, Pritchett, and their like-minded associates accepted it enthusiastically.

Early in their deliberations, the trustees of the Foundation (all but three of the twenty-five were presidents of higher educational institutions) decided that pensions should be available only to professors of institutions with high academic standards and sound financial footing. Since the recently organized associations of colleges and schools had not yet begun their accreditation activities or even constructed authoritative definitions or norms, the Foundation essayed that momentous, future-shaping task. Acceptable higher educational institutions must, they declared, have four minimal characteristics: (1) six full-time professors, (2) a four-year curriculum for the bachelor's degree, (3) a requirement for admission of four years of sound secondary education, and (4) an endowment of $200,000 (Pritchett, 1907, p. 79). These specifications seem ridiculously meager today; but when the Foundation promulgated them, only a small proportion of the colleges and universities of the country could meet them and hence be available for participation in the Carnegie pension program. For example, of the approximately 500 higher institutions in the United States providing data in 1905, only 158 had annual incomes of $50,000 or more (Pritchett, 1907, p. 100); and the majority had scandalously low admission requirements. Thus, at the outset, the Foundation could find only 52 nonstate, nondenominational institutions possessing its four prescribed characteristics (Pritchett, 1907, pp. 7–24).

The exclusion by Carnegie of state-financed and "sectarian institutions" from participation in the Foundation's pension program partially accounted for the smallness of its accepted list of institutions. The National Association of State Universities (NASU) almost immediately succeeded in persuading Carnegie and his trustees to revoke the ban on professors of its member institutions; but the blazing criticisms of religionists did not change his mind about denominational colleges. Thus, in order to be able to share in the Carnegie manna, about a dozen of them swiftly dropped their church connections. In short, for weal or for woe, a philanthropic body originated a pivotal change in the policies of such key colleges as Bowdoin, Dickinson, Swarthmore, and Wesleyan.

Actuarily, however, the Carnegie pension plan proved impracticable; this led Pritchett to recommend the organization in 1918 of the Teachers Insurance and Annuity Association (TIAA). The excoriation of the Foundation for having discriminated against denominational colleges probably accounted for the TIAA policy of offering its services from the beginning to all American and Canadian colleges and universities regardless of their allegiances. The Foundation throughout most of its history has struggled under the financial burden of the original pension plan, often requiring transfusions from Carnegie Corporation in order to continue its various activities. Only in the past decade have the pension burdens lessened to the extent that the Foundation has found it possible to fund its work independently.

Educational Inquiry and Reform. Well before the organization of TIAA, the Foundation had conceived of itself as an investigatory agency bent on gathering data toward the end of upgrading higher education in Canada and the United States (Pritchett, 1907). This self-image accounted for the first venture of President Pritchett in educational reform, namely, the improvement of college admission standards and of the interlinked high school curriculum. Undoubtedly, Presidents Eliot and Butler had a good deal to do with this decision since they had been grappling with these problems for many years—Eliot as early as 1879 when he got the New England colleges (Yale excepted) to agree on admission criteria in English. He had also been the prime force in effecting the appointment by the National Education Association of its famous Committee of Ten on Secondary School Studies which he chaired and the members of which Butler nominated (Butler, 1893, p. 754). This committee, one of the most productive in the history of American education, set the academic world on fire with a desire to improve secondary education; and it also gave the budding accreditation associations the impetus they needed to blossom. Up until the inauguration of the Carnegie Foundation, however, improvements both in secondary education and in admission requirements had been spotty and insufficient, the essential reason being that no agency existed with power enough to establish standards the country over. The Foundation decided to become that agency—and did (Pritchett, 1907).

The day before the Foundation trustees held their first meeting in Carnegie's New York home, the NASU, meeting in Washington, authorized its executive committee to call together representatives of the four regional associations of colleges and schools along with members of its own organization and representatives of the two entrance examination boards initiated by Eliot and Butler. The resulting group, known as the National Conference Committee on Standards of Colleges and Secondary Schools, held its first session in Williamstown, Massachusetts, with the United States Commissioner of Education and Pritchett attending as guests. Later meetings convened in the offices of the Foundation, Pritchett apparently having become the central figure in the deliberations. In any case, the Conference in 1909 defined the standard unit of high school instruction as a minimum of four class meetings a week over a period of thirty-six weeks, each session being of no less than forty minutes' duration. The regional accrediting associations and the entrance examination boards immediately accepted this definition as their standard; and because of the strategic part played by the Carnegie Foundation in hammering it out, the gauge overnight became known throughout the educational world as the Carnegie Unit.

In sum, the Foundation served as the catalytic agent that resolved a ruinous confusion, thereby uplifting the quality of secondary and higher education over the country. Be it observed that professors, presidents, and trustees per se did not accomplish this far-reaching and long-overdue advance. Instead, a group of educational associations effected it and largely, it seems clear, because they had the resolute assistance of a philanthropic foundation. This course of action has been repeated scores of times since.

While the Carnegie Unit pot brewed, Pritchett put several others on the fire, namely, investigations of American professional education. The Foundation had "an opportunity as none of you have," he told the members of NASU in 1909, "to tell the truth about you" (meaning educational institutions in general) and added that the scrutiny of medical education had already begun. The country could no longer tolerate, he declared, "low standards in law and low standards in medicine" or in the other professions (Pritchett, 1909, pp. 61, 65). Meanwhile, he had selected Abraham Flexner to inspect each of the 155 medical schools in the United States and Canada. Flexner's celebrated report, published by the Foundation in 1910, made headlines in both countries and gave medical education the shot of adrenalin that its leaders had long known it urgently needed. Among other things, his shocking findings hastened the closing of sixty schools within the next five years. It also led to Flexner's appointment a bit later to the staff of the General Education Board where he became the chief Rockefeller deputy in distributing some $50 million to medical schools.

The Flexner study had such propitious results that the Foundation decided to establish a unit to conduct, or to contract for, others like it; and so in January, 1913, Carnegie added $1.25 million to its endowment for the creation of the Division of Educational Enquiry (Pritchett, 1913). Using the income from this fund together with grants made to it by Carnegie Corporation, the Foundation fathered, during the next four decades, several dozen explorations of higher education in particular. The General Education Board, which began making studies of Southern education immediately after its founding in 1902, also established a Division of Studies. Meanwhile, Carnegie Corporation and the Rockefeller Foundation financed scores of investigations by selected experts, and other foundations appointed research committees of professors and administrators to gather data for them. All of them employed consultants to help determine what fields should be plowed or to assess harvested data.

Merely to list the major studies undertaken or financed by foundations would require a score or more of pages. I submit instead the generalizations that they have been made in every academic area and that the successful ones have had revolutionary results. None has been as spectacular as those that followed the Flexner ventilation of the defects of medical education half a century ago, but some of the seemingly pedestrian inquiries have been no less productive of vital changes. In brief, through these studies the foundations have directly or indirectly altered the policies of every American college and university—sometimes, it should be added, without the enthusiastic approval of the majority of their faculty members, administrators, and trustees.

The essential power of the foundations resides not, however, in the investigations they have sponsored but rather in their ability to appropriate money for enterprises they consider desirable. Almost everyone has heard the definition of the Ford Foundation as "a large body of money completely surrounded by people who want

some" (Macdonald, 1956, p. 1). Implicit in that definition is the
fact that some people receive the money for which they ask and
others do not. In my opinion (shared, I think, by most other students of higher education), the majority of foundation decisions
have been eminently productive; but since the task in hand is to
show the potency of their influence rather than to make value judg-
ments, some of their denials of petitioned funds and the effects
thereof must be recorded along with their affirmations.

The Favored and the Unfavored. Some pages back, I referred to the distribution by the General Education Board of $50
million to medical education and research. These grants, all made
before the Depression of the thirties, went to "no more than two
dozen institutions" (Fosdick, 1962, p. 167), most of them in the
Eastern states. The Board doubled this sum before disbanding in
1960, Middle Western medical schools becoming the chief overall
beneficiaries. Vanderbilt University got $17.5 million, the Univer-
sity of Chicago $14 million, and Washington University in St. Louis
a similarly high figure. Only two Western universities profited—
the University of Colorado and the University of Oregon, which
together garnered $1,393,000. Several considerations determined
which institutions should be assisted, especially the slogan "Make
the Peaks Higher" frequently enunciated by Wickliffe Rose, president of the Board during most of this period. One factor, however,
topped all others in importance, namely, the willingness of a school
to accept or promote the Board's campaign to replace practicing
physicians and surgeons with full-time clinical professors (Fosdick,
1962).

In his autobiography, Flexner emphasized the fact that the
idea of full-time clinical professors had been proposed to him by a
member of the Johns Hopkins Medical School faculty (Flexner,
1940), and he also insisted that the General Education Board did
not make the acceptance of the idea mandatory for a grant. Nevertheless, he and his associates vigorously and with considerable success pushed the concept. Arguments still continue in medical circles
about the desirability of this Rockefeller-backed method of medical
instruction. The essential point in this discussion is that the medical
schools that agreed with the concept got favorable treatment from
the Board and also, I believe, from other foundations. Differently
stated, those schools that were willing to change their policies to

accord with a foundational judgment—or to indicate a willingness to try hard to change them—got help. Others did not.

Philanthropy for medical education during this period concentrated, as previously remarked, east of the Mississippi, only one Pacific Coast university (Oregon) receiving a small grant. For years I wondered about this lopsidedness, especially since in 1916 Stanford chose a physician in the person of Ray Lyman Wilbur. Recently I ferreted out the reason: In 1913, Stanford and the University of California invited Pritchett of the Carnegie Foundation to come to San Francisco to look over their situations, and he concluded that the state of California needed only two medical schools—one in San Francisco and one in Los Angeles (Fosdick, 1962). The governing boards of the two institutions bowed to his judgment, but they could not agree about how to merge the two schools. Thus neither institution got the Foundation's support. Later the state poured huge sums into the two medical schools of the expanding University of California, located at San Francisco and Los Angeles, but until the very recent past every nonmedical unit of Stanford University suffered because the medical school absorbed a quarter of the institution's endowment income. This situation eloquently illustrates the imprint of such decisions upon university programs and upon the activities of their faculty members.

So too does the fact that the most favored areas of the foundations, prior to 1960, were professional education and scientific research. During its life of fifty-eight years, for example, the General Education Board appropriated about $100 million for medical education and related sciences and almost $20 million for the sciences, but only $2 million for the social sciences and $7 million for the humanities. Such imbalances the federal government, which also gave the major portion of its support for scholarly work to the sciences, has since moved to correct with its National Endowments for the Arts and the Humanities. Foundation support occasionally moves in those directions as well.

Imbalance aside, few will deny that a large share of the credit for the huge strides that colleges and universities have made during this century belongs to foundations. This widely held opinion, incidentally, summarizes the effects of their benefactions upon the designers of institutional policy.

NINE

Government Involvement

The powers not delegated to the United States by the Constitution, nor prohibited by it to the States, are reserved to the States respectively, or to the people.

Bill of Rights

Many in academe today are appalled by the forceful role played by the federal and state governments in the affairs of higher education. This role strikes academics as inappropriate and out of keeping with the historic autonomy which they believe higher education has heretofore enjoyed in its relations with civil government. A closer look at that history will show, however, that civil government has long played a role in the affairs of colleges and universities. In earlier chapters, for instance, I discussed the emergence of lay boards in Italy, Switzerland, Holland, Scotland, and Ireland, in which government representatives often dominated institutional decision making. I have shown too how the kings of France took over from the papacy the external control of the University of Paris. In England, likewise, one can find frequent instances of the government's meddling in the affairs of Oxford and Cambridge (Karp and Duryea, 1979). All of these precedents occurred prior to the establishing of the first colonial colleges in this country.

The Colonial Period

During the colonial period, religion and civil government cooperated in promoting higher education. Most of the colonies, until late in the period, had their own dominant religious orientation, and representatives of that denomination worked together with government officials in fostering and controlling the new colleges. In Massachusetts and Connecticut, the religious orientation was Congregational, in Virginia and New York Episcopalian, in New Jersey Presbyterian, and in Rhode Island Baptist. Only Pennsylvania and New Hampshire opened colleges in which no denomination had a majority of memberships. With the founding of a second college (Rutgers) in New Jersey, however, this close tie between colonial governments and a single denomination weakened, and the period after the Revolution is marked by the emergence of a greater distinction between public and private higher education (Herbst, 1974,1976a).

Civil government and not the churches created the nine colonial colleges. William and Mary had a royal charter written by crown officers in Whitehall. Princeton, Columbia, Rutgers, and Dartmouth functioned under royal charters drawn up by colonial officials and endorsed in England. The four remaining colleges— Harvard, Yale, Pennsylvania, and Brown—began with charters issued by colonial authorities and accepted in Britain. Both ministers and lay churchmen, however, had been involved in the founding of all nine colleges; and with rare exceptions ministers headed them and constituted their teaching staffs. Nothing in the charter of any of the colonial colleges, however, required that control remain in the hands of the denominations that had initial preponderance; and only three charters specified the necessary religious affiliations of the president: Columbia's had to be Episcopalian, Brown's Baptist, and Rutgers' a member of the Dutch Reformed Church. In sum, sectors of the religious community acquired sundry institutional advantages.

Even before the colonial period ended, some of these advantages would be challenged. The attacks came from civil government directly and from members of underprivileged denominations who, critical of the existing priorities, persuaded civil authorities to take action against them. Both varieties of attack had their immediate source in the premise that civil government should have a large voice in the institutions it aided financially, but behind this point of view lay the belief that all institutions of higher education should be controlled by the state. The General Court of Massachusetts, for example, played a dominant role in the early affairs of Harvard, thus establishing a precedent for the other colonies. The Court, in fact, directly removed Nathaniel Eaton, the first head of Harvard, and it appointed his successor, Henry Dunster. It kept tight reins on the College, and delegated little of its authority to the governing board it had established. Even after appointing the capable Dunster and naming a new board, a majority of whom were government officials, the Court continued its supervisory role (Herbst, 1974).

Yale, in its early years, enjoyed greater autonomy than did Harvard, but it eventually lost that autonomy because of its need for funding from the Connecticut government. The change began in 1740 with the inauguration of a new president, Thomas Clap. A severely orthodox Calvinist minister endowed with intelligence and an indomitable will (Tucker, 1962), Clap succeeded in expanding the enrollment of the College, in raising funds for new buildings, and in getting the General Court to approve the charter of 1745 which he had drafted. His successes led him, however, into controversies with the warring factions vivified by the religious agitations of the times.

The strong resentments caused by Clap's religious point of view and his propulsive personality, together with smoldering discontents about the absence of public checks upon the College, led in 1755 to the discontinuance of the financial assistance that the colony had given since its founding. Between 1758 and 1763, moreover, "four distinct appeals were made to the legislature, through the fellows [trustees], the graduates, and the students of the College" to investigate its management (Clews, 1899, pp. 158–159).

These culminated in a formidable memorial addressed to the legislature in 1763 by nine leading citizens (Trumbull, 1818, pp. 327–328). It reviewed the legal history of the College and challenged its right to freedom from visitation. The memorialists included several Yale alumni, and the group chose as its counsel "the two most famous and learned attornies in the colony," both of them Yale graduates (Smith, 1908, p. 50). President Clap, no lawyer but intellectually brilliant, undertook the defense of the College. In his history of Connecticut, Trumbull has described the conflict: "Great expectations were formed by the enemies of the college from this measure, and the great ability of their counsel; and its friends were not without fears and anxieties. Gentlemen from different parts repaired to Hartford to hear the pleadings. That class of people who had been so long and so strongly opposed to the college flattered themselves with the pleasing prospect of bringing the college to their feet" (Smith, 1908, p. 50).

The attack failed, however. Clap maintained that by donating books a year or two before the Act of 1701 the ten founding ministers had established the College and that therefore the General Court had merely confirmed its existence. No evidence of such donations has ever been discovered, and at least two Yale historians have implied that Clap's fertile imagination may have fabricated them (Baldwin, 1882; Smith, 1908). In any case, Clap made the book donation the core of his argument, and his learned exposition of English law succeeded in winning his point. Thus ended the controversy of 1763, but Clap had won a Pyrrhic victory. The legislature did not reinstitute its semiannual grants, and disaffection among both faculty and students soon forced him to resign. Failing to find a successor, the Corporation appointed an acting president of limited competence. He served for eleven years during one of the most disheartening periods of Yale's history.

After a long search, the Corporation in 1777 settled upon two candidates, both alumni and Congregational ministers. Urgently in need of funds from the public purse, a committee of the Corporation met with members of the General Assembly of the new State of Connecticut to learn which of the two would be the more acceptable. The legislators expressed their preference for Ezra

Stiles, and it became clear that if Elizur Goodrich were chosen the Assembly would organize a new state-supported college to compete with Yale (Stiles [1777]1901). That knocked Goodrich out of the running, but Stiles took six months to decide whether or not he wanted to project himself into such a hornet's nest. Eventually he decided in the affirmative, but meanwhile he made what seems to be the most thorough study on record of a proffered college presidency.

Stiles talked with everyone who could throw light on Yale's dilemma, namely, how to get state support without submitting to state control. His talks with the governor and leading legislators led him to believe that a solution could be found, and hence he took office in 1778. The Revolution and the uncertain political situation following it, however, prevented an agreement until 1792 when a plan suggested in 1777 by Governor Trumbull took effect, to wit, the addition of representatives of the state to the Yale Corporation (Stiles [1777]1901). Thus by adding the governor, the lieutenant governor, and six state senators to its legal entity, Yale forfended state control and once again had state aid (Kingsley, 1879a).

Like Yale and Harvard, many of the other colonial colleges had government representatives on their boards. Four government officials, plus the governor as an ex officio member, sat on the Princeton board. Columbia's board, in like manner, consisted in part of city and court officials (Herbst, 1976b). Such a pattern grew after the American Revolution ended. Several of the colonial colleges, in fact, found themselves actually being converted into state universities.

The Period After the Revolution

The move to take over a colonial institution began in Pennsylvania in 1777. In that year, the Pennsylvania legislature investigated the affairs of the College of Philadelphia (the antecedent of the University of Pennsylvania), revoked its charter, established a new institution which it named the University of the State of Pennsylvania, and put on its board the six highest officials of the state together with six ministers and thirteen laymen. This closed the College of Philadelphia, but ten years later its board of trustees succeeded in having their charter renewed. For a brief period, the two institutions operated side by side, but adroit negotiations between the two boards soon led the two institutions to combine. In 1791, therefore, the University of Pennsylvania emerged in the form that has continued until the present. From that day to this, the governor of Pennsylvania has sat on its board of trustees, and the state has contributed to its support even though it continues to be a private institution.

Meanwhile, the state of New York expropriated the property of King's College (renamed Columbia in 1787) and assigned it to the Board of Regents of the University of the State of New York. Under this arrangement, Columbia would operate at the head of a state system of education reaching into the secondary schools. The arrangement insofar as Columbia was concerned, however, lasted only three years, the College trustees successfully persuading the legislature to return the property and to grant them an unencumbered charter. Several other states—Maryland, Georgia, and Kentucky among them—sought to organize state systems of education like that in New York. Benjamin Rush proposed such a plan for Pennsylvania. Dartmouth College president John Wheelock proposed to develop such a system for the state of Vermont. And in Virginia, Thomas Jefferson led a concerted effort to make his alma mater, William and Mary, a state university (Herbst, 1976a). Jefferson's efforts did not bear fruit, however, leading him to turn instead to the founding of a new institution, the University of Virginia. Before that institution could open, however, the efforts to remake Dartmouth College into a state university in New Hampshire ran into legal obstacles. From the situation at Dartmouth, therefore, emerged limitations on the capacity of states to assume control of private institutions without their approval.

The situation at Dartmouth reflected a chorus of criticisms that had come to focus on the colleges of that time, criticisms that labeled them "synods of pensioned bigots" (Morison, 1936c, p. 175) and "nurseries of Inequality, the Enemies of Liberty" (Hansen, 1926, p. 232). Elmer Ellsworth Brown in 1903 epitomized the attitude of a large portion of the public concerning the colleges:

About the time of the Revolution, there was growing up a widespread distrust of the colleges as then
conducted. This took many forms, and was shared by
men of the most diverse political and religious convic-
tions. But it all came back virtually to this: That no one
of the colleges fully answered the public need as regards
higher education. Every one of them was the college of
a faction, of a section, or of a sect, within the commonwealth, and failed therefore to be a college of the commonwealth in its entirety. The democratic spirit, which
had been rising, very slowly, since the beginning of the
eighteenth century, and the interest in civic affairs,
which increased rapidly as the Revolution drew on, both
tended to accentuate this feeling of distrust [Brown
(1903) 1924, p. 280].

The compromise reached in various states could, as observed, be overturned. Those who believed that higher education
should be a state function desired just that, and the opportunity
to push their idea came in the state of New Hampshire where
Dartmouth College had been in operation since its chartering by
George III in 1769. There President John Wheelock, a Presbyterian and a Jeffersonian, broke with his board of trustees, a majority of whom were Congregationalists and Federalists. In 1815,
the board dismissed Wheelock, whereupon he appealed to the New
Hampshire legislature which, predominantly holding religious and
political views sympathetic with his, rallied to his support. It revised
the College charter, established a new state-controlled institution
called Dartmouth University, and made Wheelock its president
under the direction of a reconstituted board of trustees supplemented by a board of overseers modeled on Harvard's.

After the trustees displaced from the College had unsuccess-
fully contested the action in the New Hampshire courts, they appealed to the United States Supreme Court which, early in 1819,
by a vote of five to one handed down its history-making conclusion. The official summary of the judgment reads in part as follows:
"The charter granted by the British crown to the trustees of Dartmouth College . . . is a contract within the meaning of that clause
of the constitution of the United States [Art. 1, S. 10] which de-

clares that no state shall make any law impairing the obligation of contracts. The charter was not dissolved by the Revolution. An act of the State of New Hampshire altering the charter without the consent of the corporation in a material respect is an act impairing the obligation of the charter, and is unconstitutional and void." (U.S. Supreme Court, 1819:4 Wheat. 518, 4 L. Ed. 629)

The termination of the Dartmouth College case ended the efforts of the states to commandeer the existing private colleges, and it undergirds the hundreds of other cases established since. It also constitutes one of the bulwarks of the American version of political pluralism, that is, the distribution of social functions and powers to governments other than civil government: to educational institutions, churches, business corporations, and scores of other kinds of private enterprises.

Meanwhile, the federal government during the period just after the Revolution began to explore its role in the support and control of higher education. One idea, advocated by George Washington, Benjamin Rush, and a host of other national leaders during subsequent decades, would have led to the founding of a national university (Madsen, 1966). This idea, although its advocates would continue to endorse it as late as the twentieth century, did not reach fruition. But the national government did begin to assist the states in the interest of higher education a year and a half before the Constitution replaced the Articles of Confederation. Contrary to many published statements, the Northwest Ordinance of 1787 did not make grants of land for education or for any other purpose (Rainsford, 1972). It did, however, include the following celebrated passage: "Religion, morality, and knowledge being necessary to good government and the happiness of mankind, schools and the means of education shall forever be encouraged (Commager, 1949, p. 131).

Few American governmental documents have been so highly praised or so influential as the Northwest Ordinance, but nonetheless the famous sentence just quoted had no force in law. Three months later, however, the Board of Treasury of the Confederation began to implement the history-shaping vision of the ordinance by means of a contract with a group of New Englanders organized as the Ohio Company of Associates. This instrument effected the sale to the Company of a million and a half acres of the newly acquired national territory north of the Ohio River and east of the Mississippi; but the original draft included no acreage in support of "religion, moralty, and knowledge." The members of the Ohio Company, however, had patriotic, commercial, educational, and religious motives. Their leader, the Reverend Dr. Manasseh Cutler of Massachusetts, especially emphasized the latter two, believing not only in their importance but also that land especially designated for education and religion would encourage settlers. Cutler felt so strongly about education and religion that he refused to sign the draft of the contract that did not include the acreage designated for them. He therefore "packed his trunk, made his parting calls, said he should leave town immediately, and make his purchase of some of the States. This was somewhat of a ruse on his part, and it turned out as he expected" (Poole, 1876, p. 262).

After three months of bartering, Cutler and his associates succeeded in getting the acreage for education and religion included in the contract, but this necessitated a deal with Colonel William Duer, Secretary of the Board of Treasury, and some of his friends. It involved Cutler and his associates in a second contract for more than four million additional acres which were to be conveyed by the Ohio Company for speculative purposes to a syndicate, headed by Duer, called the Scioto Company. Cutler and Winthrop Sargent signed both contracts for the Ohio Company on October 27, 1787, fifteen weeks after passage of the Northwest Ordinance. The Scioto Company soon failed, but the chicanery that led to its launching illustrates the oft-made observation that Virtue on occasion consorts with Vice to advance her cause.

Under terms of the contract negotiated by the Ohio Company, provision was made for (1) "two complete townships [46,080 acres] to be given perpetually for the purposes of an university," (2) a lot [640 acres] in each township for a public school, and (3) another such lot "for the purposes of religion." Two and a half years later, Congress endorsed the contract, and soon thereafter the new national government issued a patent for the land to the Ohio Company. It bears the signatures of George Washington and Thomas Jefferson (Peters, 1910).

The funds accruing from the sale of the acreage allocated

for higher educational purposes under the contract made possible the founding of Ohio University in Athens in 1804, and the precedent thus created led to later grants to most of the new states thereafter admitted to the Union for universities or "seminaries of learning." The sale of these acres opened the way for the founding of seventeen state universities not in the "agricultural and mechanic arts" category created by the Land Grant College Act of 1862. These seventeen state universities are just one of five categories of American institutions of higher education that have benefited from the land grants initiated in 1787. The five categories are:

1. The seventeen universities created as the result of land grants made to their states for "the purposes of a university" or for a "seminary of learning" without any stipulation about their instructional programs. Examples: Alabama, Michigan, Washington.
2. The thirty-seven institutions resulting from or buttressed by the legislation of 1862 and its supplements, each being required to teach "agriculture and the mechanic arts." Examples: Michigan State, Texas A&M, Washington State.
3. The thirteen universities that have been recipients of both kinds of assistance described above. Examples: Arkansas, Minnesota, and Wyoming.
4. The seventeen black agricultural and mechanical colleges, the University of Puerto Rico, and the University of Hawaii subsidized by funds linked with the legislation of 1890 commonly referred to as the Second Morrill Act.
5. The institutions resulting from the approximately three million acres given by the federal government to ten Western and three Southern schools of mines, and other specialized higher educational structures. Those still in operation include the Colorado School of Mines, the New Mexico Military Institute, and the Montana College of Mineral Science and Technology.

State universities did not emerge in the New England and Middle Atlantic states until the 1862 act spawned them. Two circumstances accounted for this delay: first, private colleges flourished in most of these states, and second, the thirteen original states and those partitioned from them received no pre-1862 federal land grants for education. Without benefit of federal aid, however, the legislatures of the four Southern states that had been British colonies (Georgia, the two Carolinas, and Virginia) established public higher educational institutions soon after the Revolution.

In sum, three systems of roots have nourished "the state university idea": (1) federal land grants to new states for non-A & M institutions, (2) the universities set in motion by four federally unassisted Southern states during the early decades following the Revolution, and (3) the Land Grant College Acts of 1862 and 1890. The concept of the state university did not begin to prosper, however, until legislatures undertook to promote it by means of continuous financial aid. Surprising as it may seem to some, three of the four Southern states that early established public universities without federal assistance pioneered the method of systematic appropriations to them, South Carolina being the first. Starting in 1805, it began contributing $6,000 annually to what developed into the University of South Carolina. Georgia followed in 1815 with $8,000 yearly to the University of Georgia, and Virginia in 1818 with $15,000 to the University of Virginia. North Carolina provided for the establishment of a state university in its 1776 constitution and incorporated the University of North Carolina in 1789. It opened in 1795, but the legislature almost completely neglected its offspring until 1881, when it voted an annual appropriation of $5,000.

The restricted economic base of the South, the havoc caused by the Civil War, and changes wrought by the Reconstruction era stifled the advantage that the state-supported institutions of the South had had from their legislative grants. The state university idea, therefore, flowered more luxuriantly in the Middle West and later in the Far West. This did not happen, however, until after the Civil War for the reason that no state north of the Mason-Dixon line began making regular appropriations to its publicly controlled university until 1867. During that year, Michigan allotted the income of a mill tax (about $15,000) to the University of Michigan, Indiana $8,000 from its general income to Indiana University, and Missouri $2,000 from the same source to the University of Missouri.

The immediately preceding paragraphs highlight regularized cash subsidies to state universities, but all states that had established public universities, or that had chartered institutions later becoming such, made occasional subventions for buildings and for various special purposes. Some—notably Minnesota and Texas— also endowed their universities with valuable acreage. The state university idea did not, however, start to flourish until the method of systematic money appropriations became standard practice and, further, until the appropriations increased substantially. To illustrate, in 1887–88, the nation's "state universities" had an average income from state government of $31,769 or 3.2 percent of Harvard's revenues of $985,954 for that year (U.S. Commissioner of Education, 1889, pp. 625–627). Among these, the University of Wisconsin had the highest total income—$319,611 or less than a third of Harvard's—and the combined incomes ($854,785) of the three front-running state universities fell short of Harvard's by 12.3 percent. Soon after 1887–88, legislative appropriations began to increase, but the pace of that increase did not accelerate vigorously until after the Second World War.

As shown earlier, the federal government rather than the states primarily supported all but four state universities by means of land grants until, after the Civil War, the states began to make annual or biennial appropriations to them. Not until 1887 did Congress begin to make money appropriations to state institutions, namely, $15,000 annually to the institutions created by the Land Grant College Act for the support in each of an agricultural experiment station. Thus modestly did Washington begin to contribute funds to state universities. Later money grants for other special purposes continued to be small until after the Second World War.

The Situation in the Twentieth Century

During the twentieth century, five levels of civil government—the nation, the states, counties, municipalities, and local tax districts—have come in various ways to affect education. Among these five, the states until the present period have long been the chief dispensers of funds for the support of higher education. The mammoth increase of federal funds made available to colleges and universities since the end of the Second World War has tended to obscure this fact and also three others: first, that the Constitution allocates responsibility for education to the states; second, that until the recent past federal monies have had minor budgetary significance for colleges and universities; and third, that the great bulk of federal support goes into student financial aid and *research* and not into *teaching*.

During the Second World War, cooperative arrangements between higher education and the federal government were forged which continued and expanded during the decades that followed. Appropriations emerged from Congress aimed at supporting research, facilities construction, graduate and professional study, student financial aid, developing institutions, academic libraries, the improvement of instruction, and a host of other undertakings. In accepting federal money for these purposes, however, colleges and universities also became responsible in the 1960s and 1970s for following civil rights/affirmative action guidelines established by Congress. Meeting those guidelines required special efforts on the part of administrators and professors, who suddenly became aware of the federal presence in a new form. As shown, the colleges and universities have shared the federal presence since the eighteenth century, but the impact it made in the decades of the sixties and the seventies struck them especially hard.

Similarly, the state governments, whose associations with higher education are as old as higher education itself, have increased their financial support dramatically since the Second World War. Meanwhile, their chief vehicles for controlling higher education—the budget and the state coordinating board—have on occasion bitten deeply into the affairs of local institutions. College and university officials have voiced their resulting concerns loudly.

The fact remains that civil government, which has created through the chartering process every higher education institution in the land and which remains in most cases today its primary benefactor, has final authority over higher education, as it does over most of the institutions in our society. People in higher education have a long history of relating to government. Moreover, their counsel is widely sought whenever new legislation affecting higher education comes under consideration. Perhaps, under the circumstances, leaders in colleges and universities do best to cultivate this search for counsel.

TEN

Conflict and Interdependence in Academic Government

The academic executive and all his works are anathema, and should be discontinued by the simple expedient of wiping him off the slate; and . . . the governing board, in so far as it presumes to exercise any other than vacantly perfunctory duties, has the same value and should with advantage be lost in the same shuffle.

Thorstein Veblen, 1918

Disputes flare periodically, as previous chapters have illustrated, over the legitimate role of students, alumni, professional associations, foundations, and civil government in academic policy making, but the steadiest fires of controversy involve the proper relationship of professors, presidents, and trustees. Proposals regarding this relationship take several forms. One group of proponents, whom I term the "radical reconstructionists," has adopted the position, championed so bitingly by Thorstein Veblen, that external governing boards and presidents be abolished. Another, the "medial reconstructionists," has embraced the point of view of

199

James McKeen Cattell and propagandized for a plan under which
lay boards and presidents would be retained but with greatly
diminished powers. A third group, the "ameliorists," represented
historically by such groups as the American Association of University Professors, has endorsed the general outlines of the American
system of academic government but sued for greater participation
by the professoriate.

These three positions developed during the late nineteenth
century in the conflict between an emerging new breed of professors and the new breed of corporate businessmen. They found
their clearest expression in the second decade of the twentieth century—specifically, between 1913 and 1920. To understand the
roots of today's controversies, it is necessary to examine the origins
of these conflicting points of view.

The New Professoriate Versus the New Trustees

In 1870, the number of college faculty members throughout
the country totaled 3,201, but during the next forty years it multiplied almost eight times to 24,667 or nearly three times faster than
the growth in national population (U.S. President's Commission on
Higher Education, 1947b, pp. 36–38, 128). The changing characteristics of faculty members, however, betokened infinitely more
than their increase in numbers. Until well after the Civil War,
teachers in even the best colleges functioned almost universally as
drillmasters and recitation hearers rather than as teachers. Witness,
for example, the following report by Andrew Dickson White on the
Yale teaching staff of a century ago:

> The worst feature of the junior year was the fact
> that through two terms, during five hours each week,
> "recitations" were heard by a tutor in "Olmstead's
> Natural Philosophy." The textbook was simply repeated
> by rote. Not one student in fifty took the least interest in
> it; and the man who could give the words of the text
> most glibly secured the best marks. . . . Almost as bad
> was the historical instruction given by Professor James
> Hadley. It consisted simply in hearing the dates from
> "Putz's Ancient History." . . . It amazes me to remem-

ber that during a considerable portion of our senior
year no less a man than Woolsey gave instruction in history by hearing men recite the words of the textbook
[White, 1907, pp. 27–28].

The new breed of teachers, an accelerating proportion of
them trained in German universities and in the newly established
graduate schools of this country, deplored and abandoned such
pseudo-instruction. Possessing the research-focused Ph.D. degree,
they refused to engage in the time-consuming and puerile business
of policing student behavior. William Lyon Phelps of the Yale Class
of 1887 has written the following poignant contrast on this score
between the 1880s and the 1930s:

Teachers were often chosen for their ability as
policemen. Now the question of order and good be-
haviour is never even considered, because there is no
occasion for it. Students are as well-behaved in the classroom as in church. In those days, it was so customary
to throw coal through a tutor's window, that he used to
say, "My salary is a thousand dollars and coal thrown
in." When I was an undergraduate, it was part of every
instructor's duty, if he had a room on the campus, to
maintain order. It was not an uncommon sight, in the
midst of an uproar at night, to "spot" a professor in his
nightgown, hiding behind a tree, and taking down names
of those unfortunate students who were revealed by the
bonfire. Then someone yelled "Faculty!" and there was
a scattering [Phelps, 1939, pp. 329–330].

Students have continued their agitation, both visceral and cerebral,
but faculty members have increasingly turned their concern away
from student discipline and toward their own specialties. In the
process, they have changed from broad-gauged disciplinarians to
intense specialists, as witness this comment by Dean Charles S.
Slichter of the University of Wisconsin Graduate School: "We not
only have 'scientists,' we have 'chemists.' We not only have 'chemists,' we have 'colloid chemists.' We not only have 'colloid chemists,'
we have 'inorganic colloid chemists.' We not only have 'inorganic

colloid chemists,' we have 'aerosol inorganic colloid chemists.' We not only have 'aerosol inorganic colloid chemists,' we have 'high temperature aerosol inorganic colloid chemists,' and so on indefinitely until the scientist is fractionated to a single paragraph of his doctor's thesis" (Slichter, 1933, pp. 97–98).

These new professorial specialists who emerged at the turn of the century championed professional specialization among their students and the creation of academic associations, such as those discussed in Chapter Seven, to promote their disciplinary interests. They bridled at restrictions on their professional status and, although the statutes of most institutions gave them considerable authority over student discipline, most of them believed that they should have a greater say over educational policy, faculty appointments and promotions, the choice of administrators, budgetary decisions, and institutional affairs generally. Also, they realized that the courts were generally viewing presidents and professors as employees of governing boards who could be dismissed at their pleasure. Earlier, as John E. Kirkpatrick has noted, "the professor was not entirely without rights and dignities of office. The common law accorded him the right of a hearing upon specific charges and the courts were ready, in part at least, to defend these rights." Now, he observes, "rights of office, free holds, dignities, judicial powers, legislative powers, once the possession of the teacher in the school world, had passed to a new class—the lay governor of the school" (1931, p. 200).

Faculty members had lower status than they wanted not only in academic law and public law but also in the eyes of a new group of trustees who held virtually as narrow a view of professorial prerogatives as their clerical predecessors: businessmen and their associates who represented the interests of the giant new corporations. By the turn of the century, these interests were coming to dominate boards of trustees. In 1917, Scott Nearing, a former professor of the University of Pennsylvania, found that businessmen or lawyers made up 58.5 percent of the trustees at 143 of the 189 colleges and universities throughout the nation that in 1915 had enrolled more than 500 students. "A new term must be coined to suggest the idea of an educational system owned and largely supported by the people but dominated by the business world," he argued. "Perhaps 'plutocrized education' will prove as acceptable as any other phrase" (1917, p. 141).

Similarly, Evans Clark, a young Princeton faculty member, found that, in 1922, 56 percent of private college boards and 68 percent of public college boards consisted of "bankers, manufacturers, merchants, public utilities officers, financiers, great publishers, and lawyers." He further reported that "of the other great economic groups in society there is little or no representation. The farmers total between 6 percent in private and 4 percent in public boards, while no representative of labor has a place on any board, public or private." Clark warned: "We have allowed the education of our youth to fall into the absolute control of a group of men who represent not only a minority of the total population but have, at the same time, enormous economic and business stakes in what kind of an education it shall be (Sinclair, 1923, p. 28).

In the same vein, Thomas E. Will, the former president of Kansas State Agricultural College who lost his position in a clash with his board of trustees, wrote: "If education in America is to be maintained by the Rockefellers and Stanfords, rest assured it will be controlled by them. If controlled by wealth, the influence of our colleges will favor the maintenance of triumphant plutocracy. If the people are not willing that those who control their industries, their fortunes, and their lives shall also control their thinking and thus control permanently their national policies, it is needful that from their own small earnings and savings they shall furnish the means that will make at least one institution in America independent of the millionaire who today controls so largely both private and public colleges and universities—the one through the bludgeon of the endowment, granted or withheld, and the other through the might of the party 'boss' " (Will, 1901, pp. 19–20). Additionally, John J. Chapman, a severe alumnus critic of President Eliot of Harvard in particular, observed: "As the Boss has been the tool of the businessman in politics, the college president has been his agent in education" (1910, p. 41).

Clark, Nearing, and others bespoke the fears of an increasing proportion of Americans who were appalled by the public-be-damned attitude of railroad and banking magnates, by the philosophy of "grab and hold" (Gabriel, 1940, p. 145) of the trusts, by such pronouncements as that of a leading industrialist during the 1902 coal strike that it was to feudal lords like himself that "God in his infinite wisdom has given control of the property interests of the country" (Sullivan, 1927, pp. 425–426), and by such abrasive statements about faculty members as this made in 1897 by James H. Raymond, a trustee of Northwestern University: "As to what should be taught in political science and social science, they should promptly and gracefully submit to the determination of the trustees when the latter find it necessary to act. . . . If the trustees err it is for the patrons and proprietors, not for the employees, to change either the policy or the personnel of the board" (Shibley, 1900, p. 294). That other trustees, even of leading institutions, agreed with Raymond's doctrine seems clear in the light of the study made by George H. Shibley, a member of the staff of the Bureau of Economic Research of New York. With Raymond's statement in hand, he interviewed members of the governing boards of a number of universities, including Chicago, Columbia, Johns Hopkins, Pennsylvania, and Yale. His report does not tell the size of his samples, but "of the trustees that I have interviewed," he wrote, "the opinions agreed with Mr. Raymond's almost unanimously" (Shibley, 1900, p. 296).

Such opinions goaded the new professors into action—especially those who had studied in Germany where professors had permanent tenure, all but unassailable academic freedom, and lofty social status. The most radical among them set out to reconstruct American academic government in their favor along German lines.

Radical Reconstructionists

Americans had become aware of the efflorescence of the German universities as early as the second decade of the nineteenth century. During that period, George Ticknor, a recent Dartmouth graduate, and three Harvard graduates—Edward Everett, Joseph G. Cogswell, and George Bancroft—went to Göttingen and then to Berlin for advanced instruction. After the middle of the century, many other Americans followed their example. By the end of the 1870s, the number of Americans studying in Germany passed the

Veblen also wanted the traditional undergraduate college to be disassociated from the university because Germany had none and because the college "is chiefly an establishment designed to give the concluding touches to the education of young men who have no designs on learning beyond the close of the college curriculum. It affords a rounded discipline to those whose goal is the life of fashion or of affairs" (Veblen [1918] 1965, p. 99). University educators had attempted to reorganize the entire structure of American education by pushing the freshman and sophomore years back into the secondary schools, thus making it conform to German procedure. No drive for change in the history of American higher education has been more persistently pursued than this (Cowley, 1942). In Veblen's day it had a number of advocates, some of them presidents. Veblen went further than most in that he wanted not only to bisect the traditional college but also to evict all undergraduate work and all professional schools from universities. The German universities had never engaged in general education or admitted agriculture, business administration, engineering, or any of the other newer utilitarian subjects; and Veblen held that the United States ought to go even further than the German example. Universities, he asserted, should be concerned only with the higher learning—by this he meant "esoteric knowledge" as contrasted with "matter of fact" or utilitarian knowledge. In short, he declared that universities should devote all their resources to the advancement of pure as distinguished from applied knowledge.

Only by the acceptance of his proposal, Veblen maintained, could universities and their administrative staffs be kept small and their sychophancy to business interests ended. Businessmen, he asserted, imposed upon higher education "decorative real-estate, spectacular pageantry, elusive statistics, vocational training, genteel solemnities, and sweatshop instruction" (Veblen [1918] 1965, p. 128). Boards of trustees controlled by businessmen were "of no material use in any connection; their sole effectual function being to interfere with the academic management in matters that are not of the nature of business, and that lie outside the range of their habitual interests" (p. 48). He castigated presidents who modeled themselves after corporation executives and conducted themselves accordingly as "captains of erudition." Among other things, he accused them of hornswoggling senates and other faculty groups by requiring them to discuss inconsequentials while retaining executive authority over all important matters. He admitted that faculties had "proved themselves notable chiefly for futile disputation; which does not give much promise of competent self-direction on their part, in case they were given a free hand," but he contended that "this latterday experience of confirmed incompetence has been gathered under the overshadowing presence of a surreptitiously and irresponsibly autocratic executive, vested with power of use and abuse, and served by a corps of adroit parliamentarians and lobbyists, ever at hand to divert the faculty's action from any measure that might promise to have substantial effect" (p. 206).

Needless to say, a sizable fraction of the professoriate both before and after have agreed with Veblen's diagnosis. A 1913 article by Professor Joseph Jastrow of the University of Wisconsin entitled "The Administrative Peril" reflected the tenor of many another. "The paramount danger, the most comprehensively unfavorable factor affecting ominously the prospects of higher education," he wrote, "is the undue dominance of administration" (Jastrow, 1913, p. 318). In the same vein, when the Scottish sociologist and city planner, Sir Patrick Geddes, designed the plant of the proposed new University of Jerusalem in 1919, he allocated a quite small structure to administration and placed it in an inconspicuous and inconvenient place behind the main building. He justified the arrangement by declaring: "The administration exists only to serve universities. . . . Hence I have segregated the administrators where they may be good servants, for when they usurp the central position of a university . . . they become the very worst masters" (Boardman, 1944, p. 359).

After the end of the Second World War, a former rector of the University of Munich visited Stanford and, in a public address, contrasted German and American higher education. Among other things, he observed that German universities pay little heed to administration and administrators and that, in his judgment and that of his associates, American colleges and universities overemphasized both. To illustrate the difference between the practices of the two countries, he told about a visit that an American educator had paid to his institution. He showed his guest through the libraries, laboratories, and other buildings of the University. When the tour ended, the American, he reported, turned to him and queried: "You've shown me everything but the administration building; where is that?" The German replied that he did not understand what the American meant; and when the latter amplified, his host exclaimed: "Oh, you mean the janitor's quarters."

Veblen himself, in the last paragraph of his *Higher Learning in America*, confessed that his proffered panacea of abolishing administrators and lay boards of control was impractical. But he and other radical reconstructionists readied the way for another, more pragmatic wing of the movement.

Medial Reconstructionists

From the beginning, the more practical-minded among the reconstructionists knew that the German model of academic government could not be imported to America. Some of them, therefore, formulated a plan that associated a number of German practices with others from England and Scotland. Their leader was James McKeen Cattell, a Columbia psychologist and, not incidentally, the son of a former college president.

Criticizing presidents has always been an academic pastime, but early in this century Cattell badgered them relentlessly in speeches and in the pages of *Science*, which he owned and edited. Among his needlings were such statements as this: "I once incited one of my children to call her doll Mr. President, on the esoteric ground that he would lie in any position in which he was placed. Of course, the president is by nature as truthful, honorable, and kind as the rest of us, and is likely to have more ability or enterprise, or both. But he really finds himself in an impossible situation. His despotism is only tempered by resignation; and in the meanwhile he must act as though he were a statue of himself erected by public subscription" (Cattell, 1913b, p. 31).

Cattell made public his plan for reconstructing academic government in a 1906 article in *Science*. Five years later, he republished it and distributed reprints with an accompanying questionnaire to leading American scientists, most of them professors. He did not report how many questionnaires he mailed out, but it seems likely that he distributed a total of a thousand, that is, one to each of the "starred scientists" in the first edition of *American Men of Science,* a biographical reference work which he also owned and edited. The questionnaire brought 299 responses, 38 percent of which did not endorse his plan. Two years later, Cattell discussed the responses and elaborated the plan in a book entitled *University Control* (1913).

Cattell's plan for reform rested upon the premise that the control of colleges and universities should be in the hands of the professoriate and not of "kleptocratic" (1913a, p. 439) laymen. Knowing, however, that American law required that the property of chartered institutions be controlled by boards of directors or trustees, he contrived a formula that would satisfy legal necessity and also give faculties preponderant power. Its major provisions for "our larger universities" were these:

1. That the ultimate legal entity be a "large corporation" consisting of three groups of members: the staff of the institution both academic and administrative, dues-paying alumni, and dues-paying members of the general public or—in state universities —all citizens of the state.
2. That each of the groups composing the corporation elect three of the nine members of the board of trustees.
3. That this board act as "trustees and not as directors" and hence that its functions be limited to the care of institutional property, public relations, and the endorsement of the personnel nominations of the faculty senate.
4. That, subject to the approval of the board of trustees, the faculty elect the president for a limited term (desirably, like the rectors of German universities, for a single year) and that "his salary should not be larger, his position more dignified or his powers greater than those of the professor."
5. That the trustees elect "a chancellor and a treasurer who would represent the university in its relations with the community" and that—as in the British universities—the chancellor should be "a man of prominence in the community, who would obtain endowments and represent the university at public functions."
6. That each academic unit of the institution ("school, division, or

department") "have financial as well as educational autonomy" and that it elect its own administrative head subject to the approval of the faculty senate and the board of trustees.

7. That with the assistance of special boards of advisers each academic unit select its own members subject to the approval of the senate and of the board and that elections to full professorships "be for life, except in the case of impeachment after trial."

8. That the senate be made up of full professors representing the academic units and that it "legislate for the university as a whole and be a body coordinate with the trustees."

9. That the executive committees of the board and the senate have joint meetings and that on occasion plenary meetings of the full faculty and board and also of the corporation be held. (Cattell, 1913b, pp. 17–21, 28–30).

Several of Cattell's recommendations (the "large corporation" and the chancellor, in particular) constituted largely public relations devices with little if any effect upon internal operations or power, but the others implemented his desire to put the control of American higher education in the hands of the professoriate by giving it a third of the membership of an emasculated board of trustees, by allocating to faculty groups all educational and associated financial policy decisions, by assigning them the right to select all administrative officers, and by destroying the powers of the presidency.

A second influential medial reconstructionist, Upton Sinclair, offered his own plan in his withering denunciation of American academic government entitled *The Goose-Step* (1923). Therein he alleged that Big Business controlled American colleges and universities and supported them as "an instrument of special privilege." The purpose of American education, he declared, "is not the welfare of mankind, but merely to keep America capitalistic" (Sinclair, 1923, p. 18). Big Business achieved its control, he affirmed by the currently much-discussed device of interlocking directorates, which he described as follows:

> In the office of the Teachers' Union of New York, I inspected a chart, dealing with the interlocking directorates of Columbia University; and except by the label,

you could not tell it from the charts in the three volumes
of the Pujo Reports. It is the same thing, and the men
shown are the same men. They serve J.P. Morgan and
Company as directors in the coal trust, the railroad
trust; they serve also on the boards of schools, colleges,
and universities throughout the United States. You could
not tell a chart of Columbia University from the chart
of the New York Central Railroad, or the Remington
Arms Company. You could not tell a chart of Harvard
University from a chart of Lee, Higginson and Company, the banking house of Boston. You could not tell a
chart of the University of Pennsylvania from a chart of
the United Gas Improvement Company. You could not
tell a chart of the University of Pittsburgh from a chart
of the United States Steel Corporation. You could not
tell a chart of the University of California from one of
the Hydro-Electric Power Trust, one of the Denver University from the Colorado Fuel and Iron Company, one
of the University of Montana from the Anaconda Cop-
per Company, one of the University of Minnesota from
the Ore Trust. These corporations are one, and their
purposes are one [Sinclair, 1923, pp. 27–28].

As a dedicated socialist, Sinclair campaigned for curtailing
the preeminence of men of wealth in American life and hence for
reducing their influence in academic affairs. "The deepest fact of
my nature as I know it," he wrote, "is a fiery, savage hatred of
Wealth, and of all that Wealth stands for. . . . The fact shall be
branded upon my forehead, and upon the lintels of my door"
(1903, p. 1122). In the same article, he proposed that an "American University of Literature" be established, and for it he recommended that a board of trustees be appointed "consisting of the
noblest and truest and most reverent of literary men of the time"
(p. 1125). Thus he did not combat the concept of legal entities
as did Veblen but, rather, their control by men of wealth.

A third noted advocate of the medial position was John E.
Kirkpatrick, who taught political science successively at the University of Michigan, Olivet, and Washburn. During the 1920s, he
wrote several explosive books and numerous articles advocating
"home rule for the college and for academic communities gener-

ally" (1926, p. 302). "Do away with trustees," he argued, or at least "reduce them to the place that theoretically belongs to them, that of mere fiduciaries" (1926, p. 299). Kirkpatrick had wide contemporary influence and, indeed, still has, judging from the continued acceptance by various historians and other writers of his erroneous data. He almost certainly inspired Dean Max McConn of Lehigh University in 1928 to propose that a board of trustees should ideally have twelve members: six from the faculty, three alumni, and three senior students (McConn, 1928, p. 258). He probably also helped animate Professor Savelle of the University of Washington in 1957 to propose that five of the nine members of the legal entities of state universities should come from the faculty (Savelle, 1957, p. 326).

In rebelling against the inadequacies and inequities of American academic government as they experienced them during the late nineteenth and early twentieth centuries, the reconstructionists performed a necessary and valuable service. Like many reformers in other arenas, however, they proposed changes that did not mesh with deeply established American concepts and practices. Although they failed to produce tangible results, they served to prepare the way for the ameliorists, who repudiated their thesis that professors should control academic life and who, instead, successfully campaigned for greater faculty participation in academic government. Thus, although Cattell's major ideas have never been adopted, beyond doubt his questionnaire and the publication of its results in 1913 contributed to the decision that year of eighteen Johns Hopkins professors to set in motion the series of events that led to the formation of the American Association of University Professors (AAUP). Since its founding, the AAUP has consistently sought professorial participation, not monopoly.

Ameliorists

Most American professors have probably never adopted reconstructionist views. The majority might agree with the reviewer of Cattell's *Academic Control* in the *Nation*—most likely Paul Elmer More its editor, a former academic, and a high priest among American humanists:

The mere fact that some thousands of self-respecting gentlemen are teaching in American universities is evidence that presidents are not usually petty tyrants, nor boards of trustees ignorant and arbitrary. Under the fiction of trustee control, many faculties have managed to do very much as they please.

As a matter of fact, appointment or dismissal over the heads of the faculty are so rare in American universities as always [sic] to appear scandalous. Indeed, it is easier to pry a limpet from his rock than an incompetent professor from his chair.

It is the vision of the German university faculty . . . that has led to the suspicion, most tactfully hinted by Professor Cattell, that our university presidents and boards of trustees are superfluous. Such is not the case; they are perfectly logical products of the need of building up institutions masterfully and of maintaining and increasing great endowments.

We are convinced that were there no boards of trustees, the American university, on penalty of bankruptcy, would have to invent them [More, 1913, pp. 472–473].

Many might also endorse the view of Cattell's Columbia colleague, John W. Burgess, who, in the same year, wrote:

The finest thing which civilization has yet produced is a great American university upon a private foundation. A company of gentlemen associate themselves and assume the obligation of providing the means for, and the organization of, an institution for the highest culture, not only without any pecuniary compensation to themselves, but giving freely of their time, effort and substance, and securing, in their aid, the countenance and contributions of their friends and fellow citizens, and a body of scholars, selected by this original association, who, sacrificing at the outset the prospect of worldly gain, devote themselves zealously and enthusiastically to the discovery of truth and its dissemination and to the making of character—such, in brief outline, is this great product of human evolution. No other nation on the earth has brought the like of it forth. It is the peculiar offspring of American conscience and American liberty. To have had an honorable part in the creation of such an institution is a privilege of the highest order [Burgess, 1913, 321].

Some of those who have written about the formative years of the American Association of University Professors (AAUP) appear to believe that it arose primarily to fight for the reformation of academic government, but the facts do not entirely support them. When Professor Arthur O. Lovejoy and his associates at Johns Hopkins early in 1913 petitioned the collaboration of colleagues at nine other institutions to take the initial steps toward the organization of a "national association of university professors," nothing in their letter referred to the then current charges about presidential and trustee tyranny. It stated simply that the writers believed that professors ought to organize "to promote a more general and methodical discussion of the educational problems of the university; to create means for the authoritative expression of the public opinion of the profession; and to make possible collective action, on occasions when such action seems called for" ("A National Association of University Professors," 1914, p. 458).

In response to the Hopkins letter, eighteen delegates from Hopkins, Clark, Columbia, Cornell, Harvard, Princeton, Wisconsin, and Yale met in Baltimore on November 17, 1913, and agreed to create the organization. Its first meeting, held in New York City in January 1915, was attended by some 250 professors from a variety of universities and almost all academic fields. Some raised questions about the purposes of the association before attending. For example, when Lovejoy wrote his fellow philosopher at Cornell, J. E. Creighton, urging him to solicit members among his colleagues there, the latter responded: "One or two of our most prominent men whose names we should especially like to get were anxious to know of what is involved in the proposal. They were impressed by the names of the J.H.U. [Johns Hopkins University] signers; but wanted some assurance that the idea behind the movement was not that of attacking the existing condition of affairs in any destructive or antagonistic spirit" (Creighton, 1955, p. 477).

Lovejoy agreed with Creighton and his Cornell colleagues in opposing a "destructive or antagonistic spirit" in professorial relations with presidents and trustees. He had earlier written, for example, that although he strongly advocated a considerable extension of faculty authority, the "ultimate power of decision" belonged with boards of trustees (Warren, 1914, p. 698). This view was shared by John Dewey, the inaugural president of the association, who himself had written that since "education is primarily a public business," laymen must have a large voice in setting the board policies and ends of educational institutions (Dewey, 1909, p. vi). Dewey also voiced his approval of the academic presidency in a paper he read in August 1915 to the nation's most powerful group of university presidents, namely, the members of the Association of American Universities. Therein he declared that the AAUP "desires relationships of hearty mutual sympathy and cooperation with this body, representing as it does primarily the administrative interests of our higher institutions. Any suggestions or recommendations which this Association as the older and more experienced body may wish to bring to the attention of the new Association will receive, I am sure, the most attentive and respectful consideration" (Dewey, 1915, p. 32). The founding figures of the AAUP, in short, were ameliorists. They knew, in Metzger's words, that "a bellicose attitude toward trustees, a militant stand on academic freedom, any of the usual postures of the trade union, would have alarmed the great majority of American professors" (Hofstadter and Metzger, 1955, p. 478)—not to mention presidents and trustees.

In 1916, the Council of the AAUP appointed its first seventeen committees, beginning with Committee A on Academic Freedom and Tenure and continuing with others on methods of faculty appointment and promotion, causes and remedies for the alleged decline in the intellectual interests of college students, university ethics (chaired by Dewey), distinctions between the several honorary degrees and the basis of conferring them, requirements for the Ph.D. degree, pensions and insurance for university teachers, and conference with other societies on place of annual meetings. Not until the following year, however, did it create Committee T on The Place and Function of Faculties in University Government and Administration—along with others on the encouragement of university research and on summer school organization—and even then not as the result of embroilment with presidents or trustees but instead at the request of the Cincinnati chapter for the appointment of a committee on "cooperation of deans and faculties in preparing budgets" and another on "cooperation of deans and faculties in appointments and dismissals" (American Association of University Professors, 1917, p. 20). The Council assigned both topics to the new committee and appointed Joseph A. Leighton, Ohio State philosopher, as its chairman.

The nineteen members of Committee T decided to start work by conducting a questionnaire study of the status of faculty in 110 leading colleges and universities. After several meetings devoted to collating the replies and to the discussion of "appropriate principles" of academic government, the committee published its landmark report in March 1920. So effectively did this document serve the purposes of the AAUP that three years later, at the suggestion of Leighton, its Council dismissed the committee. None replaced it until 1934. Since then, Committee T has functioned more or less continuously, having more recently been renamed the Committee on College and University Government and taken leadership on what in 1966 came to be the "Statement on Government of Colleges and Universities," of the American Council on Education and the Association of Governing Boards of Universities and Colleges as well as AAUP.

Two passages from the 1920 report illustrate the ameliorative point of view that permeated it. Concerning presidents and other administrators, it had this to say:

> The chief objections urged against . . . thoroughgoing faculty autonomy in university government are as follows: The lack of concentration of authority and responsibility would conduce to inefficiency; there would be a lack of initiative and leadership; personalities and politics would play too large a part in university government and administration; members of the faculty would spend too much of their time in the details of administration and executive work, to the great neglect of their main duties as teachers and investigators. All

these objections seem to me to have some weight. A
university needs *leadership* in its presiding officers
[American Association of University Professors, 1920,
p. 24].

Concerning legal entities, the report included this statement:

Faculties are public servants. They should, like
other public servants, have an effective part in determining the conditions under, and manner in, which their
services are to be rendered; but they must also be held
formally and legally responsible to the body chosen as
custodians of the public interest. . . . . In the matter of
the determination and carrying out of educational policies, the members of the faculty are the experts, and
should usually have the principal voice in the decision.
But it may sometimes happen that a faculty needs to
hear from the trustees on what seem to be urgent needs,
in the way of changes and improvements in educational policies or their execution, that the university's
constituency seeks to have satisfied. It is in this spirit of
joint responsibility and fuller cooperation that the specific recommendations of your committee have been
made [American Association of University Professors,
1920, pp. 24–25].

"Joint responsibility and fuller cooperation"—this phrase epitomizes
the ameliorative doctrine adopted by the AAUP during its early
years. Responsibility for and cooperation in what? The report answered the question with these recommendations:

- *Mechanisms of Cooperation.* The committee suggested several
  plans, but the majority preferred that an elected faculty committee on university policy meet with a counterpart committee
  of the board of trustees (p. 26).
- *Educational Policy.* "There should be a recognized mode of procedure for the joint determination, by trustees and faculty, of
  what is included in the term *educational policies*. . . . Where
  there is a faculty committee, as above recommended, it would

properly serve as the medium of conference between trustees and faculty upon such matters" (p. 27). Presidents, deans, and department deans should be educational leaders and not just "routine executive agents" because "with all due emphasis on the right and duty of faculties to originate and initiate policies, it is doubtful if they will always do so without leadership somewhere in the administrative offices" (p. 32).

- *Selection and Tenure of the President.* "The president should be nominated by a committee of the board of trustees acting jointly with a similar committee selected by the faculty. The nomination of this committee should require confirmation by the board of trustees. The president's term of office should be indefinite" (p. 29).

- *Selection and Tenure of Deans.* "All the members of your committee are agreed that the dean should be chosen by the concurring action, in some form, of faculty, president, and trustees" (p. 30). The committee divided about evenly on the question of whether or not deans should have indefinite tenure.

- *Selection of Department Heads.* "Where departments are weak in personnel and in need of vigorous leadership and upbuilding," department heads should be "appointed by the trustees on the recommendation of the president and deans." In a department administered by a short-term chairman, the nomination of the full professors should be confirmed by the dean and the president and approved by the board. Concerning "the permanent headship" concept of departmental administration, the committee took no position but recommended that a special AAUP committee be appointed on "Departmental Organization and Administration" (pp. 37–38). No such committee being organized, Committee T itself took on the job in 1937 and, while declaring for the democratizing of department government, pointed "with some satisfaction to the fact that a number of universities, especially the larger ones, have ceased to force all departments into a single mold of organization" (American Association of University Professors, 1937, p. 227). In short, it applauded administrative diversity to meet differing circumstances.

- *Budget Making.* "The fundamental principle that your committee subscribes to, with one exception, is that in all cases the faculty should have a recognized voice in the preparation of the annual budget" (p. 32).

- *Selection of Faculty Members.* "The faculty should participate, through appropriate committees, in the selection of full professors and executive officers of departments. . . . All members of the department who are of full professorial rank should have a voice in making a nomination" (p. 35). The committee took no direct position on faculty tenure, possibly because that topic fell within the province of Committee A (Academic Freedom and Tenure), but its report implicitly assumes permanent tenure for full professors.
- *Dismissal of Faculty Members.* A standing judicial committee, its members elected by the general faculty, should investigate and rule on all charges made against a faculty member. "Failure to sustain the charges before the committee should estop dismissal. The judicial committee should report its findings to the president and board of trustees" (p. 35).
- *Voting Degrees.* "All degrees given in courses should be voted by the faculty. Honorary degrees should be voted by the trustees only upon the recommendation of a joint committee of the faculty and trustees" (p. 35).

One might have expected Committee T to endorse faculty membership on boards of trustees, since the three-year experiment at Cornell, begun in 1916, of electing three faculty members to sit with the board and having other elected faculty members meet with three pivotal board committees—general administration, finance, and buildings and grounds—had proven a success and had been made permanent. Despite the merits of the Cornell *modus operandi*, however, Committee T disparaged the idea for the following reasons: (1) "It seems undesirable that faculty representatives should vote on such matters as the appointments, promotions, and salaries of their confreres"; and (2) "Faculty representatives are really in a stronger position to give information and advice if they are not members of the board" (American Association of University Professors, 1920, p. 26).

Not until 1960 did Committee T list board membership for faculty as an approved method for facilitating communication between faculties and legal entities, and even then it did not select it for emphasis. In other words, the committee and through it the AAUP endorsed a multicameral conception of academic government, with faculty and trustee bodies mutually but differentially involved in policy making: the contemporary version of America's original bicameral system of academic government.

Interdependency

In contrast to the ameliorists, the reconstructionists had proposed the reorganization of academic government on the thesis that professors are so high-minded that they should manage colleges and universities with few internal and no external checks. In support of their program, they also claimed that professors were shockingly underprivileged in comparison with lawyers, physicians, and members of other professions. Indeed, averred Richard Hofstadter in 1952, "doctors and lawyers would be appalled at the thought that their professional standards and practices should be exposed to control by laymen" (Hofstadter and Hardy, 1952, p. 129).

This and comparable statements would seem to justify greater professional autonomy for faculty members, but do laymen, namely members of boards of trustees, actually control the "professional standards and practices of professors"? Nothing of the sort! Legal entities control professorial salaries, the physical circumstances under which faculty members work, and the statutes that regulate general institutional procedures, but they do not determine the "standards and procedures" of teaching and research. Nor, indeed, do administrators who, in fact, blanch at the occasionally made suggestion that they should project themselves into such matters. Further, except for those in the lower ranks, academics decide as individuals what courses they will teach, the methods of instruction and examination they will employ, the time of the few office hours a week they will schedule, and the part of the day that their classes will meet. Such facts as these patently belie the criticism under discussion and, instead, sustain the generalization that professors have more individual freedom in deciding upon their procedures and in allocating their time and energies than any other variety of professional people.

A number of other observations need making concerning the professional status of professors. Physicians and lawyers, so a frequently made criticism goes, do not, like professors, have to submit to any important kind of lay controls but, instead, have all but complete freedom of action. On at least three counts, this declaration does not jibe with the facts. In the first place, lawyers, physicians, and most other professionals must pass exacting examinations before being licensed by civil government; but professors are not required to take publicly administered entrance examinations and are not licensed. Second, when physicians practice in hospitals either full time or part time, they work under the direction of lay boards of trustees just as do professors; and, similarly, when lawyers are employed in governmental agencies or in business corporations, they serve under controls much more exacting than those affecting professors. Third, when lawyers and physicians operate as individuals, that is, as private entrepreneurs (and the great majority of both groups are such), they must serve their clients effectively enough to keep their patronage and to stimulate their friends and associates to follow their example. Professors, on the contrary, do not personally have to scurry for students or to keep them by catering to their whims. More than any other professional group, in fact, they are free from the lay controls inherent in the competition to attract and keep clients.

I would emphasize that I do not make these comments about the relative freedom of academics from lay control in a censorious spirit but, rather, to combat a corrosive myth. As a professor I am able to do my work infinitely better because of the freedom available to me and my associates, and as a student of academic government I unequivocally affirm its urgent necessity in the interests not only of colleges and universities but also of society at large. My point is this: Those who compare the academic and other professions to the disadvantage of the former do not have even the shadow of a good case; and worse, their fallacious and cantankerous comparisons obstruct much-needed improvements in both the policy control and operational control of colleges and universities. Most such improvements cannot be initiated, never mind achieved, until professors in general recognize that the most distinctive fact about the academic profession is that its members are *institutional workers* and as such have advantages denied professionals who operate as private entrepreneurs.

No fact about professors seems to me to be more significant than their institutional status or, differently expressed, than that they perform their functions in the cooperative communities called colleges and universities. It has such crucial importance that it needs to be elaborated in relation to the allegation that American colleges and universities are "probably the most undemocratic in the world" (Savelle, 1957, p. 323). Charges of this kind appear in print frequently, and so many faculty people uncritically accept them that no treatise on academic government that seeks to deal with its fundamentals can avoid assessing them.

This assessment can best begin, I suggest, with the question "Why have institutions of higher education been established and by whom?" The answer seems clearly to be, first, that they have been organized to disseminate and to advance socially beneficial knowledge, skills, and attitudes; and second, that civil government has created them for the good of the general community. They have not been founded for the sole or even the primary benefit of professors, administrators, students, trustees, or all of them taken together but, instead, for the benefit of society at large. Hence in all countries, civil government, the most inclusive agency of society, retains the right to create them and, further, to require that the public interest be represented by agencies whose powers it defines.

In the light of these observations, can American colleges and universities be called undemocratic? Those who so assert seem to hold that professors should have final if not exclusive authority in academic government and that the public interest should either be unrepresented on governing boards or be so small as to be impotent. Thorstein Veblen went so far as to propose that lay boards of trustees be wiped from the slate. Scuttling them and turning over the control of colleges and universities to faculties would not, however, be democratic. It would constitute, instead, a species of syndicalism, a political philosophy that rests upon the premise that each group of societal workers should manage its own affairs unchecked by other interest groups and only vaguely, if at all, by society at large (Ford and Foster, 1913; Levine, 1912; Lorwin, 1934). Democracy obtains, however, when all significant interest groups participate in control of a society and of its component units. John Dewey, one of the primary expositors of democracy and, incidentally, the first president of the AAUP, elucidated this definition in a number of statements, including the following two:

> A society which makes provision for participation in its good of all its members on equal terms and which secures flexible readjustments of its institutions through interaction of the different forms of associated life is in so far democratic [Dewey, 1916, p. 115].

> The keynote of democracy as a way of life may be expressed, it seems to me, as the necessity for the participation of every mature human being in formation of the values which regulate the living of men together [Dewey, 1946, p. 58].

In this view—and it seems to me to be incontestable—general societies and individual social institutions are democratic to the extent that all relevant interest groups participate in making their policies. Those who devote their lives to performing the core functions of teaching and research constitute a sine qua non interest group of colleges and universities; but in both the democratic tradition and American law, so also are the representatives of the general public—that is, trustees—and, in turn, so also are presidents and their associates as the agents of both trustees and faculties. True it is that in the past some boards and some presidents have ignored and even trampled upon the views of professors; and some still do. Such institutions are not democratic and deserve the condemnation directed at them. However, institutions controlled by academics would not be democratic either; they would be, as Harold Laski has pointed out, syndicalistic (Laski, 1932).

To give professors the ultimate power in colleges and universities would be comparable to turning over the control of the national defense establishment to military men, organized religion to clergymen, and the general government to civil servants. Fortunately, despite the agitations of reconstructionist professors, deeply established public policy makes such a development inconceivable. So also does the position of the AAUP which, from its earliest years, has opposed syndicalism and championed, instead, the interdependency of all relevant groups in academic government.

References

ADAMS, H. B. *The College of William and Mary.* Washington, D.C.: U.S. Government Printing Office, 1887.

AMERICAN ASSOCIATION OF UNIVERSITY PROFESSORS. Committee on Academic Freedom and Academic Tenure. "General Report." AAUP *Bulletin*, December 1915, *1*, 17–43.

AMERICAN ASSOCIATION OF UNIVERSITY PROFESSORS. "Status of Faculties." AAUP *Bulletin*, February 1917, *2*, 20.

AMERICAN ASSOCIATION OF UNIVERSITY PROFESSORS. Committee T. "Report on Place and Function of Faculties in University Government and Administration." AAUP *Bulletin*, March 1920, *6*, 17–47.

AMERICAN ASSOCIATION OF UNIVERSITY PROFESSORS. Committee T. "The Place and Function of Faculties in University Organization." AAUP *Bulletin*, March 1937, *23*, 220–228.

AMERICAN ASSOCIATION OF UNIVERSITY PROFESSORS. Committee T. "Faculty Participation in College and University Government." AAUP *Bulletin*, Summer 1960, *46*, 203–205.

AMERICAN ASSOCIATION OF UNIVERSITY PROFESSORS. American Council on Education, Association of Governing Boards of Universities and Colleges. "Statement on Government of Colleges and Universities." A.G.B. *Reports,* January 1967. AAUP *Bulletin,* 1966, *52,* 375–379.

ARNOLD, M. *Schools and Universities on the Continent.* London: Macmillan, 1868.

ARNOLD, T. *The Miscellaneous Works of Thomas Arnold.* London: T. Fellows, 1846.

ASSOCIATION OF AMERICAN UNIVERSITIES. *Journal of Proceedings and Addresses.* Chicago: Association of American Universities, 1901.

ASSOCIATION OF AMERICAN UNIVERSITIES. *The Fifteenth Annual Conference.* Chicago: Association of American Universities, 1913.

ASSOCIATION OF AMERICAN UNIVERSITIES. *The Nineteenth Annual Conference.* Chicago: Association of American Universities, 1917.

ASSOCIATION OF AMERICAN UNIVERSITIES. *The Forty-Ninth Annual Conference.* Princeton, N.J.: Princeton University Press, 1948.

BAKER, R. P. *A Chapter in American Education.* New York: Scribner's, 1924.

BALDWIN, S. E. "The Ecclesiastical Constitution of Yale College." *Papers of the New Haven Colony Historical Society.* Vol. 3. New Haven, Conn.: Printed for the Society, 1882.

BARNARD COLLEGE. "Student Self-Determination." *Survey,* May 6, 1922, *48,* 217–218.

BEALE, H. K. *A History of Freedom of Teaching in American Schools.* New York: Scribner's, 1941.

BECKER, C. *Cornell University: Founders and the Founding.* Ithaca, N.Y.: Cornell University Press, 1944.

BELLOC, H. "To the Balliol Men Still in Africa." In H. Belloc, *Complete Verse.* London: Gerald Duckworth, 1970. (Originally published 1910.)

BIRRELL, A. "The Ideal University." In A. Birrell, *The Collected*

Essays and Addresses of the Rt. Hon. Augustine Birrell. London: J. M. Dent, 1922.

BOARD OF TRUSTEES OF THE ILLINOIS INDUSTRIAL UNIVERSITY. *Second Annual Report.* Springfield: State Journal, 1869.

BOARD OF TRUSTEES OF THE UNIVERSITY OF ILLINOIS. *Eighteenth Report.* Springfield: Phillips Brothers, 1896.

BOARDMAN, P. *Patrick Geddes.* Chapel Hill: University of North Carolina Press, 1944.

BOELL, J. Correspondence with W. H. Cowley, 1961. Cowley papers, Stanford University Archives, PN 206.983.

Boston Transcript. Editorial. 1926.

BROWN, E. E. *The Making of Our Middle Schools.* New York: Longmans, 1924. (Originally published 1903.)

BRUCE, P. A. *History of the University of Virginia.* Vol. 2. New York: Macmillan, 1920a.

BRUCE, P. A. *History of the University of Virginia.* Vol. 3. New York: Macmillan, 1920b.

BRUCE, P. A. *History of the University of Virginia.* Vol. 4. New York: Macmillan, 1920c.

BRYAN, W. J. *Speeches of William Jennings Bryan.* Vol. 2. New York: Funk & Wagnalls, 1909.

BUCKLEY, W. F. *God and Man at Yale.* Chicago: Regnery, 1951.

BURGESS, J. W. "Reminiscences of Columbia University in the Last Quarter of the Last Century." *Columbia University Quarterly,* September 1913, *15*, 321–335.

BURROUGHS, W. G. "Oberlin's Part in the Slavery Conflict." *Ohio Archeological and Historical Quarterly,* 1911, *20*, 269–334.

BUSH, G. G. *History of Higher Education in Massachusetts.* Washington, D.C.: U.S. Bureau of Education Circular of Information, No. 6, 1891.

BUTLER, N. M. "To the National Council of Education." In National Education Association, *Journal of Proceedings and Addresses, Session of the Year 1892.* New York: National Education Association, 1893.

BUTLER, N. M. "Reviews." *Educational Review,* February 1894, *7*, 194.

BYRON, G. N. B. "Letter to the Hon. Douglas Kinnaird, February 6,

1822." In R.E. Prothero, *The Works of Lord Byron*. New York: Octagon Books, 1966.

CANBY, H. S. *Alma Mater*. New York: Farrar, Straus & Giroux, 1936.

CAPEN, S. P. "The Principles Which Should Govern Standards and Accrediting Practices." *Educational Record*, April 1931, *12*, 95–96.

CAPEN, S. P. "Comments." In American Council on Education, *Coordination of Accrediting Activities*. Washington, D.C.: American Council on Education, 1939.

CARLSON, A. J. "So This Is the University?" *Bulletin of the American Association of University Professors*, January 1938, pp. 9–18.

CARNEGIE FOUNDATION FOR THE ADVANCEMENT OF TEACHING. *The Financial Status of the Professor in America and in Germany*. New York: Carnegie Foundation for the Advancement of Teaching, 1908.

CARTER, J. F., JR. "These Wild Young People." *Atlantic Monthly*, September 1920, pp. 301–304.

CARTTER, A. M. (Ed.). *American Universities and Colleges*. Washington, D.C.: American Council on Education, 1964.

CATTELL, J. M. "To the Editor of the Nation." *Nation*, May 1913a, *96*, 2496.

CATTELL, J. M. *University Control*. New York: Science Press, 1913b.

CHAMBERLAIN, J. L. *Universities and Their Sons*. Vol. 1. Boston: Herndon, 1898.

CHAPMAN, J. J. *Learning and Other Essays*. New York: Moffat, 1910.

Charter of the President and Fellows of Harvard College. Cambridge, Mass.: Harvard University Press, 1976.

CHASE, H. W. "Making a University Faculty." In Association of American Universities, *Journal of Proceedings and Addresses*. Chicago: University of Chicago Press, 1924.

CHASE, H. W. "Doubts About Liberal Colleges." *American Mercury*, November 1934, *33*, 290–291.

CHEYNEY, E. P. *History of the University of Pennsylvania, 1740–1940*. Philadelphia: University of Pennsylvania Press, 1940.

CLARKE, F. W. "American Colleges Versus American Science." *Popular Science Monthly*, August 1876, *9*, 467–479.

CLEWS, E. W. *Educational Legislation and Administration of the Colonial Governments.* New York: Macmillan, 1899.

COFFMAN, L. D. *The State University.* Minneapolis: University of Minnesota Press, 1934.

"COLLEGE INSTRUCTION AND DISCIPLINE." *American Quarterly Review,* June 1831, *18,* 294–295.

COMMAGER, H. S. *Documents of American History.* New York: Appleton-Century-Crofts, 1949.

COMMAGER, H. S. *The American Mind.* New Haven, Conn.: Yale University Press, 1950.

CONANT, J. B. "Friends and Enemies of Learning." *Yale Review,* Spring 1936, *25,* 462–476.

CONANT, J. B. *Academic Patronage and Superintendence.* Cambridge, Mass.: Harvard University Graduate School of Education, 1938.

CONANT, J. B. *Report of the President of Harvard University to the Board of Overseers, 1937–38.* Cambridge, Mass.: Harvard University, 1939.

CORSON, L. D. "University Problems as Described in the Personal Correspondence Among D. C. Gilman, A. D. White, and C. W. Eliot." Unpublished doctoral dissertation, Stanford University, 1951.

COULTER, E. M. *College Life in the Old South.* Athens: University of Georgia Press, 1928.

COULTON, G. G. "Universities." In P. Monroe (Ed.), *A Cyclopedia of Education.* Vol. 5. New York: Macmillan, 1913.

COULTON, G. G. "Reformation." In W. Benton (Ed.), *Encyclopaedia Britannica,* Vol. 19. Chicago: Encyclopaedia Britannica, 1957.

COWLEY, W. H. "The Disappearing Dean of Men." An address given before the Nineteenth Annual Convention of the National Association of Deans and Advisers of Men, Austin, Texas, April 2, 1937.

COWLEY, W. H. "A Ninety-Year-Old Conflict Erupts Again." *Educational Record,* April 1942, *23,* 192–218.

CREIGHTON, J. E. Quoted in R. Hofstadter and W. Metzger, *The Development of Academic Freedom in the United States.* New York: Columbia University Press, 1955.

CURTI, M., and CARSTENSEN, V. *The University of Wisconsin: A History.* Vol. 1. Madison: University of Wisconsin Press, 1949a.

CURTI, M., and CARSTENSEN, V. *The University of Wisconsin: A History.* Vol. 2. Madison: University of Wisconsin Press, 1949b.

DARTMOUTH COLLEGE SENIOR COMMITTEE. *Report.* Hanover, N.H.: Dartmouth College, 1924.

DAVIS, H. A. *A Narrative of the Embarrassment and Decline of Hamilton College.* Clinton, N.Y.: Hamilton College, 1833.

DEWEY, J. *Moral Principles in Education.* Boston: Houghton Mifflin, 1909.

DEWEY, J. "Faculty Share in University Control." In Association of American Universities, *The Seventeenth Annual Conference.* Chicago: Association of American Universities, 1915.

DEWEY, J. *Democracy and Education.* New York: Macmillan, 1916.

DEWEY, J. *Problems of Men.* New York: Philosophical Library, 1946.

DEXTER, F. B. *Documentary History of Yale University.* New Haven, Conn.: Yale University Press, 1916.

DRAPER, A. S. *Addresses and Papers.* Albany: New York State Education Department, 1907.

DURANT, W. *Caesar and Christ.* New York: Simon & Schuster, 1944.

DURANT, W. *The Reformation.* New York: Simon & Schuster, 1957.

DWIGHT, T. *Memories of Yale Life and Men.* New York: Dodd, Mead, 1903.

EELLS, W. C. "Boards of Control of Universities and Colleges." *Educational Record,* October 1961, *42,* 336–342.

ELIOT, C. W. *President's Report for 1873.* Cambridge, Mass.: Harvard University Press, 1873.

ELIOT, C. W. "Academic Freedom." *Science,* July 1907, *26,* 1–12.

ELIOT, C. W. *University Administration.* Boston: Houghton Mifflin, 1908.

ELIOT, C. W. *A Late Harvest.* Boston: Atlantic Monthly Press, 1924.

ELIOT, C. W. "Inaugural Address as President of Harvard, 1869." In R. Hofstadter and W. Smith (Eds.), *American Higher Education: A Documentary History.* Vol. 2. Chicago: University of Chicago Press, 1961.

ELLIOTT, O. L. *Stanford University: The First Twenty-Five Years.* Stanford, Calif.: Stanford University Press, 1937.

FLEXNER, A. *I Remember.* New York: Simon & Schuster, 1940.

FONER, P. S. *Jack London: American Rebel.* New York: Citadel Press, 1947.

FORD, E. C., and FOSTER, W. Z. *Syndicalism.* Chicago: William Z. Foster, 1913.

FORD, G. S. "The American Scholar Today." In G. S. Ford, *On and Off the Campus.* Minneapolis: University of Minnesota Press, 1938.

FOSDICK, R. B. *Adventure in Giving.* New York: Harper & Row, 1962.

FOSTER, H. D. "Calvinists and Education." In P. Monroe (Ed.), *A Cyclopedia of Education.* Vol. 1. New York: Macmillan, 1911.

FOSTER, W. T. "Faculty Participation in College Government." *School and Society,* April 1916, *3,* 594–599.

FRANKLIN, F. *The Life of Daniel Coit Gilman.* New York: Dodd, Mead, 1910.

FREEDMAN, M. B. "Studies of College Alumni." In N. Sanford (Ed.), *The American College.* New York: Wiley, 1962.

GABRIEL, R. H. *The Course of American Democratic Thought.* New York: Ronald Press, 1940.

GLOVER, T. R. *Life and Letters in the Fourth Century.* New York: G. E. Stechert, 1924. (Originally published 1901.)

GLOVER, T. R. *Cambridge Retrospect.* Cambridge, England: Cambridge University Press, 1943.

GOODSPEED, T. W. *A History of the University of Chicago.* Chicago: University of Chicago Press, 1916.

GOODSPEED, T. W. *William Rainey Harper.* Chicago: University of Chicago Press, 1928.

GRANT, A. *The Story of the University of Edinburgh During Its First Three Hundred Years.* Vol. 1. London: Longmans, 1884.

HALL, G. S. *Life and Confessions of a Psychologist.* New York: Appleton-Century-Crofts, 1923.

HAMILTON, W. "On the Patronage and Superintendence of Universities." *Edinburgh Review,* April 1834.

HAMILTON, W. "Academical Patronage and Regulation in Reference to the University of Edinburgh." In W. Hamilton, *Discussions on Philosophy and Literature, Education, and University Reform.* London: Longmans, 1866.

HANSEN, A. O. *Liberalism and American Education.* New York: Macmillan, 1926.

HARCLEROAD, F. F. "Influence of Organized Student Opinion on American College Curricula: An Historical Survey." Unpublished doctoral dissertation, Stanford University, 1948.

HARPER, W. R. "The College President." *Educational Record,* April 1938, *19,* 178–186.

HASKINS, C. H. *Studies in Medieval Culture.* Oxford, England: Clarendon Press, 1929.

HASKINS, G. L. *Law and Authority in Early Massachusetts.* New York: Macmillan, 1960.

HATCH, L. C. *The History of Bowdoin College.* Portland, Maine: Loring, Short & Harmon, 1927.

HAWKINS, H. *Pioneer: A History of the Johns Hopkins University, 1874–1889.* Ithaca, N.Y.: Cornell University Press, 1960.

HELLER, O. "The Passing of the Professor." *Scientific Monthly,* January 1927, *24,* 35.

HENRY, W. W. *Patrick Henry: Life, Correspondence and Speeches.* New York: Scribner's, 1891.

HERBST, J. "The First Three American Colleges: Schools of the Reformation." In *Perspectives in American History.* Vol. 8. Cambridge, Mass.: Harvard University Press, 1974.

HERBST, J. "The American Revolution and the American University." In *Perspectives in American History.* Vol. 10. Cambridge, Mass.: Harvard University Press, 1976a.

HERBST, J. "From Religion to Politics: Debates and Confrontations over American College Governance in the Mid-Eighteenth Century." *Harvard Educational Review,* August 1976b, *46,* 397–424.

HEWETT, W. T. *Cornell University, A History.* Vol. 1. New York: University Publishing Society, 1905.

HIGGINSON, T. W. "A Plea for Culture." *Atlantic Monthly,* January 1867, *19,* 30–31.

HOFSTADTER, R., and HARDY, C. D. *The Development and Scope of Higher Education in the United States.* New York: Columbia University Press, 1952.

HOFSTADTER, R., and METZGER, W. P. *The Development of Academic Freedom in the United States.* New York: Columbia University Press, 1955.

HOLT, H. *Garrulities of an Octogenarian Editor.* Boston: Houghton Mifflin, 1923.

HOPKINS, L. A. "The University Senate and the Senate Council." In W. Shaw (Ed.), *The University of Michigan: An Encyclopedic Survey.* Vol. 1. Ann Arbor: University of Michigan Press, 1942.

HOWE, M. A. D. *John Jay Chapman and His Letters.* Boston: Houghton Mifflin, 1937.

HUTCHINS, R. M. *No Friendly Voice.* Chicago: University of Chicago Press, 1936.

HUTCHINS, R. M. "The Administrator." *Journal of Higher Education,* 1946, *17,* 395–407.

d'IRSAY, S. "Universities and Colleges." In E. R. A. Seligman (Ed.), *Encyclopedia of the Social Sciences.* Vol. 15. New York: Macmillan, 1934.

JAMES, H. *Charles W. Eliot, President of Harvard University, 1869–1909.* Vol. 1. Boston: Houghton Mifflin, 1930a.

JAMES, H. *Charles W. Eliot, President of Harvard University, 1869–1909.* Vol. 2. Boston: Houghton Mifflin, 1930b.

JASTROW, J. "The Administrative Peril." In J. M. Cattell, *University Control.* New York: Science Press, 1913.

JOHNSON, A. *Pioneer's Progress.* New York: Viking Press, 1952.

JORDAN, D. S. *Report of the Alumni Trustee to the Alumni of Cornell University.* Ithaca, N.Y.: Andrus and Church, 1888.

JORDAN, D. S. *The Days of a Man.* Vol. 1. Yonkers-on-Hudson, N.Y.: World Book, 1922a.

JORDAN, D. S. *The Days of a Man.* Vol. 2. Yonkers-on-Hudson, N.Y.: World Book, 1922b.

JOUGHIN, L. (Ed.). *Academic Freedom and Tenure.* Madison: University of Wisconsin Press, 1969.

KARP, A. "Calvinism and Higher Education in Geneva, 1536–1700." Unpublished manuscript, 1979.

KARP, A., and DURYEA, E. D. "English Antecedents to the Corporate Government of American Colleges and Universities." Paper presented at the annual meeting of the Association for the Study of Higher Education, Washington, D.C., 1979.

KELLY, F. J., and OTHERS. *Collegiate Accreditation by Agencies Within States.* Washington, D.C.: U.S. Office of Education, Bulletin 1940, No. 3.

KIBRE, P. *The Nations in the Mediaeval Universities.* Cambridge, Mass.: Mediaeval Academy of America, 1948.

KINGSLEY, W. L. *Yale College: A Sketch of Its History.* Vol. 1. New York: Holt, Rinehart and Winston, 1879a.

KINGSLEY, W. L. *Yale College: A Sketch of Its History.* Vol. 2. New York: Holt, Rinehart and Winston, 1879b.

KIRKPATRICK, J. E. *The American College and Its Rulers.* New York: New Republic, 1926.

KIRKPATRICK, J. E. *Academic Organization and Control.* Yellow Springs, Ohio: Antioch Press, 1931.

KUEHNEMANN, E. *Charles W. Eliot.* Boston: Houghton Mifflin, 1909.

LA FOLLETTE, R. M. *La Follette's Autobiography: A Personal Narrative of Political Experiences.* Madison, Wis.: Robert M. La Follette, 1913.

LASKI, H. J. "The American College President." *Harper's Monthly Magazine,* 1932, *164,* 319.

LESTER, R. M. *Forty Years of Carnegie Giving.* New York: Scribner's, 1941.

LEVINE, L. "Syndicalism." *North American Review,* July 1912, *196,* 9–19.

LILGE, F. *The Abuse of Learning.* New York: Macmillan, 1948.

LINFORTH, I. M. "Benjamin Ide Wheeler." In D. Malone (Ed.), *Dictionary of American Biography.* New York: Scribner's, 1936.

LORWIN, L. L. "Syndicalism." In E. R. A. Seligman (Ed.), *Encyclopedia of the Social Sciences.* Vol. 14. New York: Macmillan, 1934.

LOWELL, A. L. *Reports of the President and the Treasurer of Harvard College, 1916–1917.* Cambridge, Mass.: Harvard University, 1918.

LOWELL, A. L. *Reports of the President and the Treasurer of Harvard College, 1919–1920.* Cambridge, Mass.: Harvard University, 1921a.

LOWELL, A. L. "The Art of Examination." In J. L. Brumm (Ed.), *Educational Problems in College and University.* Ann Arbor: University of Michigan Press, 1921b.

MC CAUL, R. L. "Dewey and the University of Chicago." *School and Society,* March 1961, *89,* 152–157, 179–183, 202–206.

MC CONN, C. M. *College or Kindergarten?* New York: New Republic, 1928.

MACDONALD, D. *The Ford Foundation.* New York: Reynal, 1956.

MADSEN, D. *The National University: Enduring Dream of the USA.* Detroit, Mich.: Wayne State University Press, 1966.

MALOTT, D. W. Correspondence with W. H. Cowley, 1961. In Cowley papers, Stanford University Archives, PN206.974.

MARROU, H. I. *A History of Education in Antiquity.* New York: Sheed and Ward, 1956.

MARTIN, F. T. *The Passing of the Idle Rich.* New York: Doubleday, 1911.

MARTIN, T. S. "For the Alumni." *Bulletins of the University of Virginia,* Vol. 5, No. 2, 1905.

MARX, G. H. "Some Trends in Higher Education." *Science,* May 1909, *29,* 759–787.

MAXWELL, C. *A History of Trinity College Dublin, 1591–1892.* Dublin: The University Press, 1946.

MAYER, M. *Young Man in a Hurry.* Chicago: University of Chicago Alumni Association, 1941.

MERRIAM, C. E. *Public and Private Government.* New Haven, Conn.: Yale University Press, 1944.

MILLER, P. *Orthodoxy in Massachusetts, 1630–1650.* Cambridge, Mass.: Harvard University Press, 1933.

MILLETT, F. B. *The Rebirth of Liberal Education.* New York: Harcourt Brace Jovanovich, 1945.

MINOT, C. S. "Antrittsvorlesung." *Science,* December 1912, *36,* 771–776.

MONTER, E. W. *Calvin's Geneva.* New York: Wiley, 1967.

MONTGOMERY, T. H. *A History of the University of Pennsylvania, From Its Foundation to A.D. 1770.* Philadelphia: Jacobs, 1900.

MORE, P. E. "Academic Autocracy." *Nation,* May 1913, *96,* 471–473.

MORISON, S. E. *The Founding of Harvard College.* Cambridge, Mass.: Harvard University Press, 1935.

MORISON, S. E. *Harvard College in the Seventeenth Century.* Vol. 1. Cambridge, Mass.: Harvard University Press, 1936a.

MORISON, S. E. *Harvard College in the Seventeenth Century.*

Vol. 2. Cambridge, Mass.: Harvard University Press, 1936b.

MORISON, S. E. *Three Centuries of Harvard.* Cambridge, Mass.: Harvard University Press, 1936c.

MOTLEY, J. L. *The Rise of the Dutch Republic.* Vol. 2. New York: Harper & Row, 1855.

MULLINGER, J. B. *The University of Cambridge.* Vol. 1. Cambridge, England: Cambridge University Press, 1873.

MURDOCK, K. B. *Increase Mather, The Foremost American Puritan.* Cambridge, Mass.: Harvard University Press, 1925.

MURRAY, J. O. *Francis Wayland.* Boston: Houghton Mifflin, 1891.

"A NATIONAL ASSOCIATION OF UNIVERSITY PROFESSORS." *Science,* March 1914, *39,* 458–459.

"NATION'S STUDENTS STRIKE FOR HOUR IN PROTEST ON WAR." *New York Times,* April 14, 1934, p. 1.

NEARING, S. "Who's Who Among College Trustees." *School and Society,* September 8, 1917, *6,* 141.

NEVINS, A. *Illinois.* New York: Oxford University Press, 1917.

NEVINS, A. *John D. Rockefeller: The Heroic Age of American Enterprise.* Vol. 2. New York: Scribner's, 1940.

NEWCOMB, S. "Abstract Science in America, 1776–1876." *North American Review,* January 1876, *122,* 88–123.

NEWMAN, J. H. *University Sketches.* London: Scott, 1902. (Originally published 1856.)

NIELSON, W. A. "The Past Instructs." *American Scholar,* Winter 1941–42, *11,* 3–5.

NORTH, S. N. D. *Old Greek, An Old-Time Professor in an Old-Fashioned-College.* New York: McClure, Phillips, 1905.

NORTON, A. *Remarks on a Report of a Committee of the Overseers of Harvard College.* Cambridge, Mass.: Harvard University Press, 1824.

NYE, R. B. *Fettered Freedom.* East Lansing: Michigan State University Press, 1963. (Originally published 1949.)

ODEGAARD, C. E. "A Description of the Role of the University in Modern Society Together with Encouragement to the Medical School to Turn its Flirtation with the University into a Full Blown Romance." Paper read at the Boerhaave Conference, University of Leyden, December 15–17, 1966.

OSLER, W. "Greek at Oxford." *Nation,* December 1910, *91,* 544–545.

OULLETTE, V. "Daniel Coit Gilman's Administration of the University of California." Unpublished doctoral dissertation, Stanford University, 1951.

"'PA' CORBIN AND GIFFORD PINCHOT STARTED THE FIRST POLITICAL UNION." *Yale Daily News,* May 6, 1937.

PATTISON, M. *Suggestions on Academical Organization, With Especial Reference to Oxford.* Edinburgh: Edmonston and Douglas, 1868.

PAULSEN, F. *The German Universities and University Study.* New York: Scribner's, 1906.

PAULSEN, F. *An Autobiography.* New York: Columbia University Press, 1938.

PEIRCE, B. *A History of Harvard University.* Cambridge, Mass.: Brown, Shattuck, 1833.

PERRY, B. *And Gladly Teach.* Boston: Houghton Mifflin, 1935.

PETERS, W. E. "Legal History of the Ohio University." *Ohio University Bulletin,* Vol. 7, No. 4, 1910.

PHELPS, W. L. *Autobiography with Letters.* New York: Oxford University Press, 1939.

PIERSON, F., and OTHERS. *The Education of American Businessmen.* New York: McGraw-Hill, 1959.

PIERSON, G. W. *Yale College, An Educational History, 1871–1921.* New Haven, Conn.: Yale University Press, 1952.

POLLOCK, F., and MAITLAND, F. W. *The History of English Law Before the Time of Edward I.* Cambridge, England: Cambridge University Press, 1968. (Originally published 1899.)

POOLE, W. F. "Dr. Cutler and the Ordinance of 1787." *North American Review,* April 1876, *122,* 229–265.

POST, G. "Parisian Masters as a Corporation, 1200–46." *Speculum.* Vol. 9. Cambridge, Mass.: Mediaeval Academy of America, 1934.

PRITCHETT, H. S. *Second Annual Report of the President and Treasurer.* New York: Carnegie Foundation for the Advancement of Teaching, 1907.

PRITCHETT, H. S. "Remarks on the Carnegie Foundation." In National Association of State Universities, *Transactions and Proceedings.* Bangor, Maine: National Association of State Universities, 1909.

PRITCHETT, H. S. *Report of the President.* New York: Carnegie Foundation for the Advancement of Teaching, 1913.

QUINCY, J. *The History of Harvard University.* Vol. 1. Cambridge, Mass.: Owen, 1840a.

QUINCY, J. *The History of Harvard University.* Vol. 2. Cambridge, Mass.: Owen, 1840b.

RAINSFORD, G. *Congress and Higher Education in the Nineteenth Century.* Knoxville: University of Tennessee Press, 1972.

RASHDALL, H. "Oxford University." In P. Monroe (Ed.), *A Cyclopedia of Education.* Vol. 4. New York: Macmillan, 1913.

RASHDALL, H. *The Universities of Europe in the Middle Ages.* Vol. 1. Oxford, England: Clarendon Press, 1936a. (Originally published 1895.)

RASHDALL, H. *The Universities of Europe in the Middle Ages.* Vol. 2. Oxford, England: Clarendon Press, 1936b. (Originally published 1895.)

RASHDALL, H. *The Universities of Europe in the Middle Ages.* Vol. 3. Oxford, England: Clarendon Press, 1936c. (Originally published 1895.)

"RATHER THAN BE UNITED. . . ." *Nation,* October 1934, *139,* 422.

RAUSCHENBUSCH, W. *Christianity and the Social Crisis.* New York: Macmillan, 1907.

RAUSCHENBUSCH, W. *Christianizing the Social Order.* New York. Macmillan, 1912.

Register of Stanford University. Stanford, California, 1891–1892.

RICHARDSON, L. B. *History of Dartmouth College.* Vol. 1. Hanover, N.H.: Dartmouth College Publications, 1932a.

RICHARDSON, L. B. *History of Dartmouth College.* Vol. 2. Hanover, N.H.: Dartmouth College Publications, 1932b.

RINGWALT, R. C. "Intercollegiate Debating." *Forum,* January 1897, *22,* 633–634.

ROCKEFELLER, J. D. *Random Reminiscences of Men and Events.* New York: Doubleday 1909.

RUDOLPH, F. *Mark Hopkins and the Log.* New Haven, Conn.: Yale University Press, 1956.

RUDOLPH, F. *The American College and University: A History.* New York: Knopf, 1962.

SANFORD, N. *The American College*. New York: Wiley, 1962.

SAVAGE, H. L. Letter to W. H. Cowley, May 11, 1961.

SAVELLE, M. "Democratic Government of the State University: A Proposal." American Association of University Professors *Bulletin,* June 1957, *43,* 323–328.

SCHACHNER, N. *The Mediaeval Universities*. New York: Barnes, 1938.

SCHMIDT, G. P. *The Old Time College President*. New York: Columbia University Press, 1930.

"SCHOOL AND COLLEGE." *Boston Transcript,* June 6, 1916.

SCHURMAN, J. G. *Eighteenth Annual Report, 1909–10*. Vol. 1, No. 4. Ithaca, N.Y.: Official Publications of Cornell University, 1910.

SCHURMAN, J. G. *Twentieth Annual Report, 1911–12*. Vol. 3, No. 18. Ithaca, N.Y.: Official Publications of Cornell University, 1912.

SELDEN, W. K. *Accreditation: A Struggle Over Standards in Higher Education*. New York: Harper & Row, 1960.

SHAW, W. B. "A New Power in University Affairs." *Scribner's Magazine,* June 1922, *71,* 677–684.

SHEPARD, W. J. "Government: History and Theory." In E. R. A. Seligman (Ed.), *Encyclopaedia of the Social Sciences*. Vol. 7. New York: Macmillan, 1932.

SHIBLEY, G. H. "The University and Social Questions." *Arena,* March 1900, *23,* 293–300.

SHOCKLEY, M. S. "The Sheepskin Myth." *Journal of Higher Education,* December 1954, *25,* 481–487.

SINCLAIR, U. "My Cause." *Independent,* May 1903, *55,* 1122, 1125.

SINCLAIR, U. *The Goose-Step*. Pasadena, Calif.: Published by the Author, 1923.

SLICHTER, C. S. "Polymaths: Technicians, Specialists, and Genius." *Sigma Xi Quarterly,* September 1933, pp. 97–98.

SLOSSON, E. E. *Great American Universities*. New York: Macmillan, 1910.

SMITH, C. H. "The Founding of Yale College." *Papers of the New Haven Colony Historical Society*. Vol. 7. New Haven, Conn.: Printed for the Society, 1908.

SMITH, G. "University Education." *Journal of Social Science,* June 1869, *1,* 30–31.

SMITH, T. V. "On Being Retired." In T. C. Denise and M. H. Williams (Eds.), *Retrospect and Prospect on the Retirement of T. V. Smith.* Syracuse, N.Y.: Syracuse University Press, 1956.

SOLBERG, W. U. *The University of Illinois, 1867–1894.* Urbana: University of Illinois Press, 1968.

SPECIAL TRUSTEE COMMITTEE. *The Role of the Trustees of Columbia University.* New York: New York Times, 1957.

SPRING, L. W. *A History of Williams College.* Boston: Houghton Mifflin, 1917.

STANFORD UNIVERSITY. *Manual of Faculty Organization.* Stanford, Calif.: Stanford University, 1920.

Statutes and Laws of the University in Cambridge, Massachusetts. Cambridge, Mass.: University Press, 1826.

VAN STEENWIJK, J. E. DE VOS. Letter to W. H. Cowley, February 17, 1961. Cowley papers, Stanford University Archives, PN 206.904.

STILES, E. *The Literary Diary of Ezra Stiles.* Vol. 2. New York: Scribner's, 1901. (Originally published 1777.)

SULLIVAN, M. *Our Times: The United States, 1900–1925.* Vol. 2. New York: Scribner's, 1927.

SWIFT, F. H. *European Policies of Financing Public Educational Institutions: IV. Germany.* Berkeley: University of California Press, 1939.

SYMONDS, J. A. *Renaissance in Italy: The Revival of Learning.* New York: Holt, 1877.

TAPPAN, H. P. *University Education.* New York: Putnam, 1851.

THAYER, W. R. "History and Customs of Harvard University." In J. L. Chamberlain (Ed.), *Universities and Their Sons.* Vol. 1. Boston: Herndon, 1898.

THILLY, F. "Preface." In F. Paulsen, *The German Universities and University Study.* (Thilly-Elwang, trans.) New York: Scribner's, 1906.

THWING, C. F. *A History of Higher Education in America.* New York: Appleton-Century-Crofts, 1906.

THWING, C. F. *The American and the German University.* New York: Macmillan, 1928.

TICKNOR, G. *Remarks on Changes Lately Proposed or Adopted in Harvard University*. Boston: Cummings, Hilliard, 1825.

TOLLEMACHE, L. A. *Benjamin Jowett*. New York: Arnold, 1895.

TREVELYAN, G. M. *Trinity College: An Historical Sketch*. Cambridge, England: Cambridge University Press, 1943.

TRUMBULL, B. *A Complete History of Connecticut, Civil and Ecclesiastical*. New Haven, Conn.: Maltby, Goldsmith, and Samuel Wadsworth, 1818.

"TRUSTEES AND FACULTY OF CORNELL UNIVERSITY." *School and Society,* July 1916, *4,* 20–21.

TUCKER, L. L. *Puritan Protagonist: President Clap of Yale College*. Chapel Hill: University of North Carolina Press, 1962.

"TWENTY-ONE STUDENTS. . . ." *Nation,* November 28, 1934, *139,* 604.

TYACK, D. B. *George Ticknor and the Boston Brahmins*. Cambridge, Mass.: Harvard University Press, 1967.

TYLER, L. G. *The College of William and Mary*. Richmond, Va.: Whittet & Shepperson, 1907.

TYLER, W. S. *A History of Amherst College During the Administration of its First Five Presidents from 1821 to 1891*. New York: Hitchcock, 1895.

Union Worthies: Eliphalet Nott. Schenectady, N.Y.: Union College, 1954.

U. S. COMMISSIONER OF EDUCATION. *Report for the Year 1887–88*. Washington, D.C.: U. S. Government Printing Office, 1889.

U. S. PRESIDENT'S COMMISSION ON HIGHER EDUCATION. *Higher Education for American Democracy*. Vol. 3. Washington, D.C.: U. S. Government Printing Office, 1947a.

U. S. PRESIDENT'S COMMISSION ON HIGHER EDUCATION. *Higher Education for American Democracy*. Vol. 6. Washington, D.C.: U. S. Government Printing Office, 1947b.

UNIVERSITY OF ILLINOIS. *Directory for 1929*. Urbana: University of Illinois, 1929.

University of Leyden. Leyden: Van Doesburgh, 1928.

VAN DE GRAAFF, J., and OTHERS. *Academic Power: Patterns of Authority in Seven National Systems of Higher Education*. New York: Praeger, 1978.

"VASSAR GOES TO TOWN." *University of Michigan Daily,* March 9, 1935.

VEBLEN, T. *The Higher Learning in America.* New York: Hill and Wang, 1965. (Originally published 1918.)

WALDEN, J. W. H. *The Universities of Ancient Greece.* New York: Scribner's, 1909.

WARREN, H. G. "Academic Freedom." *Atlantic Monthly,* 1914, *114,* 689–699.

WAYLAND, F. *Report to the Corporation of Brown University on Changes in the System of Collegiate Education, March 28, 1850.* Providence, R.I.: Brown University, 1850.

WECHSLER, J. *Revolt on the Campus.* New York: Covieci-Friede, 1935.

WERT, R. J. "The Impact of Three Nineteenth Century Reorganizations upon Harvard University." Unpublished doctoral dissertation, Stanford University, 1952.

WERTENBAKER, T. J. *Princeton, 1746–1896.* Princeton, N.J.: Princeton University Press, 1946.

WHEELER, B. I. *The Abundant Life.* Berkeley: University of California Press, 1926.

WHITE, A. D. *Autobiography.* Vol. 1. New York: Appleton-Century-Crofts, 1907.

WILL, T. E. "A College for the People." *Arena,* July 1901, *26,* 15–20.

WINSTANLEY, D. A. *Unreformed Cambridge.* Cambridge, England: Cambridge University Press, 1935.

WRISTON, H. M. *The Structure of Brown University.* Providence, R.I.: Brown University, 1946.

WRISTON, H. M. "Fire Bell in the Night." American Association of University Professors *Bulletin,* 1949, *35,* 434–449.

"YOUTH DIVIDES." *New Republic,* August 29, 1934, *80,* 62–63.

"YOUTH IN COLLEGE." *Fortune,* June 1936, *13,* 99–102, 155–157.

ZINSSER, H. *As I Remember Him: The Biography of R.S.* Boston: Little, Brown, 1940.

Index